KILLER ON THE LOOSE

THE TRUE STORY OF SERIAL KILLER
RAYMOND LEE STEWART

DEMCO

KILLER ON THE LOOSE

THE TRUE STORY OF SERIAL KILLER RAYMOND LEE STEWART

by
Greg Kelly

PAPERBOY PRESS
ROCKFORD, ILLINOIS

EDITOR: Barbara Phillips
COVER DESIGN: Pat Curry
—Printed in Rockford, Illinois
—Copyright 1998

ISBN: 0-9668444-0-8

CONTENTS

DEDICATION

This book is dedicated to the memories of
Willie, Albert, Kevin, Kenny, Donald and Richard.

"The fact is Ray Lee Stewart, during his week long
killing spree, happened upon victims who were
deeply loved and are now sorely missed by many
people. Those victims were sons. They were fathers,
husbands, brothers, nephews and friends, whose
deaths not only had a devastating effect on them, but
on the ones close to those they left behind as well."
—Arlene Anderson, Asst. Attorney General

and
to the memory of Bill Phillips.

ACKNOWLEDGMENTS

A very special thanks to my constant pillar of strength, my mother, Barbara Ann.

Additional thanks to:
  The Archdiocese of Chicago, Helen Balasny, Jackie Bange, Ken Baumgarten, Beloit Daily News, Beloit Police Department, Ahnn and Bryan Bennett, Wes Bleed, Cara Bromund, Deborah Brown, Gloria Brown, Muriel Clair, Pat Curry, Karl Farrey, Alex Fredd, Sallie Fredd, Ellen Fiedholtz, Carol Fowler, Dan Gaughan, Che Che and Rich Gambini, Marc Gerke, Tom Gibbons, Jeff Hedburg, Bob Hoffman, Nic Howell, Illinois Attorney General, Illinois Coalition to End the Death Penalty, Illinois Department of Corrections, Illinois Prison Review Board, Yolanda Joe, Patricia Johnson, Jennifer Bishop Jones, Karen Jordan, Robert Jordan, Jim Kelly, Kate Kelly, Mike Kelly, Pat Kelly, Tim Kelly, Eugene Kennedy, Marlene King, Eric Knudson, Joanie Lum, Larry Lyons, Carol Marin, John Mirabelli, Carleen Mosbach, Bill Phillips, Bob Pressman, Steve Ramsey, Rachel Roberts, Rockford Police Department, Rockford Register Star, Rachel Ruiz, Ann Rule, Steve Sanders, Jennifer Schulze, Fred and Joanne Speer, Pat Tanaka, Sharon Taylor, Monica Teague, Monsignor Kenneth Velo, Peter Walker, Lon Weberg, WGN-TV, WGN-Radio, Paul Wheeler, WIFR, Winnebago County Sheriff, Winnebago County State's Attorney, Everett Williams, Maureen Wolf, WREX, WROK, WTVO, and many others.

FORWARD

In WGN's newsroom it's not unusual to see a telephone glued to each of Greg Kelly's ears. In the background, police scanners blare out their calls of crime while news radio and competing television stations complete the stereo sound. In between the noise, Greg assigns reporters and photographers to the day's news stories.

For someone so young, Greg is amazingly reserved at work. I've seen older, more experienced assignment editors crack under all the noise and pressure. Not Greg. He digs through the day with very little emotion. That's why I clearly remember the afternoon of September 1, 1996... the day Greg approached me with the story of Raymond Lee Stewart. His face remained emotionless, but his voice revealed so much. There was an intensity I've never heard before.

It was his day off and he greeted me with a box full of video tapes. He had my story for the day and had done everything BUT written the story. That morning, in Rockford, he'd collected all the file video tape surrounding Stewart's escape. It was everything I'd need for my story. It took me two hours to read all the newspaper articles and view all the tapes. Greg Kelly didn't go home. He waited for me to review all the material.

When I was done with my script, I asked him to review it and hoped it was good enough for him. I knew how much it meant to him. He was a child when the murders occurred in his hometown. To Greg, Raymond Lee Stewart was the boogieman.

I admit I was among those in the office who accused Greg of being obsessed with the murderer. Perhaps he was and still is, but what has emerged from Greg's experience is a stirring well-written book about a midwestern town rocked by a horrible crime. His truthful and often cynical insight into Chicago's television news business only adds to the story.

Everyday when I walk into the newsroom for my afternoon shift, Greg sits at the desk with phones glued to his ears and people crowding around his desk. It's just another day at work. For many of us, hidden beneath the layers of our routine lives is perhaps an experience which has deeply influenced us, conjuring up a memory that may return to us often. The story of Raymond Lee Stewart is that for Greg.

—Jackie Bange
WGN-TV Anchor/Reporter

CHAPTER 1

*"It is better to stir up a question with deciding it,
than to decide it without stirring it up."*

—*Joseph Joubert*

Noon, Thursday, September 12, 1996

The two-year-old Ford Taurus was roaring down Interstate 55 close to 100 miles per hour when I suddenly realized the hand-held cellular phone on the empty passenger seat was ringing. I slowed down a bit to grab the call.

"Hello"

"Kelly, do you want to tell me why I'm stuck working a double today?"

"Gee, I don't know. Maybe because I'm sick."

"Well, yeah . . . but I was looking through the wire-service schedule and I notice your man Ray is having his clemency hearing in Springfield, one o'clock in the Capitol Building. Could this be why I am reaching you in the car on your so-called sick day?"

"Really, I don't know anything about that. I am driving to Rockford to see my family doctor. You know once you find a good. . . ."

"Aw, shut up. You owe me, man. None of these other idiots could figure this out. It is so obvious. Just remember this when I want a three-day weekend."

"Whatever. But I am not bullshitting you. I am going to Rockford" . . . eventually, I thought to myself.

Suddenly the loud and familiar sound of a glaring police scanner rudely interrupted the conversation.

"Got to check something out."

Laughing as I pushed the end button, I threw the phone back on the seat and pushed down on the accelerator. A wake of gravel was flying in the wind and bugs were slamming the glass as I cruised past a bleary sign telling me that Springfield was still thirty miles away.

An hour earlier I had passed the exit for Pontiac. I thought of him. I fantasized about what he was doing today. About what he was like now. About what he was like then. I wanted to know why he did it. Was he on drugs? How did he escape? It was a case many had forgotten. Media attention was minimal lately. Back then it grabbed banner headlines. Somehow, my journalistic instincts knew Ray would make headlines again. I had files full of old clippings. I had seen pictures of those eyes. They were eyes you do not underestimate. My colleagues thought I was nuts when I entered the media lottery to witness the execution. The consensus was that no one in Chicago was going to care about a Rockford serial killer being put to death. My instincts are what I stake my livelihood on. My instincts knew that I had to cover. Raymond Lee Stewart was going out. He was flat-out guilty. His appeals were exhausted. He was one of the most cold-blooded criminals in Illinois history. Although not as infamous, he was right up there with the likes of Richard Speck and John Wayne Gacy. There was no way in hell that Ray Stewart was going to go out quietly.

The Taurus was now speeding through the streets of the state capital. I was fumbling with the map. Tripped up by dead-ends and one-ways, I became more and more frustrated and concerned that I was going to be late for this hearing. Finally, I found a street that led to the Capitol Building. I slid the car into a one hour parking spot and looked up at the massive structure. For a second, I was intimidated. I didn't know exactly what I was doing. I was a TV guy, and this was a newspaper-type assignment. I didn't know where to go. What to write down. Where to sit. I wasn't sure if they were going to search me. I didn't know if I could bring a tape recorder into the courtroom. I worked to combine my excessive materials into one bag when, suddenly, a xerox of an old newspaper caught my eye. I took a deep breath and remembered the first time I saw that edition.

Thursday, January 29, 1981

"THIRD PERSON MURDERED IN CITY WITHIN 24 HOURS." That was the headline on the top paper of a large stack that came flying off the Rockford Register Star delivery truck, landing in the middle of my parents' driveway on that Thursday morning 15 years ago. It was already past six a.m. and the sun was glaring off the snowy streets. I hovered above the newspapers dressed in full winter garb to combat the freezing cold weather. I draped the front end of the newspaper sack over my left shoulder so I could read the entire article. After finishing, I picked up the bundle and ran in the house to tell the news to my mother. Of course, she already knew about it. Unsatisfied, I bolted into my younger brother's room. I woke him up and told him it had happened again. My bleary-eyed brother almost became conscious before my mother was able to eject me from his quarters. The delivery truck had been two hours late with the newspaper drop-off. And, even with the cold weather, my customers would be waiting for their morning paper, with criticism for the carrier.

So, I spread the newspapers out on the living room floor and dumped a pile of rubber bands next to them. I began to fold the papers. My mom helped. The headlines usually dictated our early morning conversation. Mostly, we talked about the hostages in Iran. But in the middle of the final negotiations to bring those 52 prisoners home, we discussed Kevin Kaiser. It was the first time Kaiser got his picture in the paper. There he was, a 17-year-old kid with a thin mustache over a half-cocked smile. His hair was parted down the middle and feathered back, just like my older brother's. It was the hairstyle I had been begging my mother to allow me to adopt. The article said

Kaiser's body was found in the back of the store by a customer who was tired of waiting in the cold for the attendant. When the customer walked into the station, Kaiser was lying in a puddle of blood. He was shot five times at point blank range. The Chief of Police thought it was related to a double homicide at a grocery store earlier in the week. That was the headline I woke up to on Wednesday morning. "GUNMAN KILLS STORE OWNER AND NEPHEW." Willie Fredd, 54, and his nephew, Albert Pearson, 19, had been shot in the middle of the afternoon at Fredd's Grocery on Rockford's west side. No money was missing and police were baffled as to a motive. I didn't think much about all that then. But now, I was scared. What the hell was going on?

The police didn't have much to go on. Someone saw a dark-colored car. Media reports indicated a .357 magnum was used in both shootings. Police weren't saying much. They didn't have much.

I remember some of the faces of my waiting customers as they picked up the late-arriving paper and read the banner headline. A quick squint to confirm the frightening news. Eyes rolled. Heads shook from right to left in disbelief. Some returned my studious glare with a look that narrated the unspoken question: Can you believe this?

Friday, January 30, 1981

Deja vu is a cruel reality when a city is being attacked by a serial killer. "FOURTH MAN SLAIN IN CITY; SPECIAL SQUAD SEEKS CLUES." The news hit my snowy driveway. Shaking from the cold, I read the article before picking up the bundle. The victim was Kenny Foust. The crime was almost identical to the Kaiser killing. Kenny was found by two customers. He was lying in a blood pool in the storage room of the gas station where he worked. Paramedics did what they could, but it was a lost cause. He was pronounced dead at the hospital. Rockford had four murders in three days. Off-duty cops were called into work. Days off were canceled. Police from departments all over the state were being called in to Rockford to help with the case. The police chief thought the murders might be connected. They were all committed within blocks of each other. It was the same style shooting. In the same kind of businesses. Apparently with the same caliber gun. I was ten years old and I knew it was the same guy. Rockford had a serial killer.

Friday night was pizza night for the Kelly family. I was in the living room anxiously awaiting our departure to Villa Capri, when suddenly the audio of my parent's argument grew to a level that my young ears could pick up.

"Jesus, you can't go nuts like everyone else in this town. The restaurant is six blocks away. All of this is happening on the west side. Just relax, and let's go out like we always do."

"Everyone else is using appropriate caution. There is a killer on the loose.

"Honey, these murders, these west side murders, are happening in broad daylight. On the west side! Now, I have been dealing with this b-s at work all day. No one wants to run their routes. I had to do half of the west side pick-ups myself."

"Oh god, honey."

"Well, well, don't worry. Try not to worry. This is probably a drug thing. We can go out six blocks to the Villa Capri. I'm sure it will be fine."

The voices faded and minutes later my parents came parading down the stairs, attempting to put on a brave front. They asked if we were ready for pizza night. We drove down Alpine Road to the local parlor. At first, it was just plain old Rockford. Only figments of my imagination were walking the streets with loaded .357 magnums. Then, you noticed things were different in this midwest town. The gas station at the corner of Alpine and State is closed three hours early. The one across the street is open, but they have a security guard outside the front door. Only a few cars are traveling down the usually bustling streets. You had to look, but the signs of terror were there, even during a short family drive for pizza.

The restaurant was practically empty. Normally, they do good business on Friday night. Not tonight. One couple in the back booth and a single gentlemen at a side table. That was it. We took the restaurant's largest table in the center of the dining area. Our parents asked the routine questions. We, the kids, gave our routine answers. Everyone had murder on their minds, but no one said a word about that.

My dad let us run the money to the front desk to pay the bill. We got the leftovers placed in a doggie bag, which we almost forgot. We all climbed back into the station wagon and began our short trek home. No sign of any boogiemen out to make the Kelly family the next Register Star headline. The questions about school, and meeting girls, and playing football next year had all been asked. So, we traveled in silence. My Dad reached over with his right hand and twisted the knob that turned on the car's AM-only radio. Fred Speer was just starting his news report on WROK.

Four men murdered in three days, a community's worst nightmare. Tonight Mayor Bob McGaw and Police Chief Delbert Petersen meet at City Hall. They are trying to determine if the Mayor should, by executive order, set curfews for service stations and grocery stores. This, despite the fact that all the murders took place during daylight hours. Many business aren't waiting for word from the Mayor. Several closed up shop early tonight. Some business owners say they'll err on the side of caution until this murderer is behind bars. I talked to Mayor McGaw, minutes before his meeting with the Police Chief. He says he wants to be careful to not send the community into panic. But, he also admits that the Rockford Police Department seems to have an out-of-control psychopath on their hands. Fred Speer, W-R-O-K News.

I slid to the floorboard of my family's station wagon. My

younger brother followed suit. My father looked over the seat and down at me. I knew he could read the fear on my face. I felt the warm trail of a tear making a path down my cheek. I was embarrassed. He was embarrassed. He knew he had made a mistake by insisting on maintaining the family Friday night pizza tradition. My mother reached over and gently touched his hand which was wrapped tightly around the steering wheel.

"We're almost home," she said.

The ten o'clock news was way past my bedtime. However, if they didn't want me up late watching television, why the heck did they allow me to have a black and white in my closet? When my parents thought I was sleeping, I would plug the old Magnavox into the socket near the end of my bed, and gently set it out on the dresser, slowly turning the switch from off to on. If I wanted to sit on the bed and watch, I would have to cup my hand over my right ear and concentrate on the announcer's words. This was not good for my young ears. Or sometimes, I would just remain standing in front of the set and watch, while the program was broadcasting literally right in front of my face. This, of course, was not good for my eyes. That night, I was standing. Usually, I turned on the tube to catch some news about the hostages. America Held Hostage was the name of the show. It made Ted Koppel's career. The show eventually became Nightline.

Tonight, I was tuning in for the local news. The killings had grabbed the attention of my young mind. I wanted to know the latest. The newscast opened with a quick recap of the murders. No one else had been killed since Kenny Foust. The police didn't have any new clues. A four-thousand dollar reward was set-up for any information leading to the arrest of the person responsible. The community was in a near panic. One reporter went to a gun shop where people who had never carried firearms before were lining up. They were trying to find a way to buy some security. The news station had learned that the first victim, Willie Fredd, had eight guns in the store. Those guns hadn't done him any good. There was no security with this killer on the loose. They had an interview with a behavioral psychologist. I was young and didn't understand a lot of the jargon she was using, but I got the gist. She said whoever this killer was, he killed because he enjoyed it. I turned the television off. It was a lot to absorb. I didn't think to watch the national news. This killing spree was getting national attention. I hid under the covers. I decided not to bother with Ted Koppel.

Tuesday, February 3, 1981

On the following Tuesday morning, murder was again the talk of the schoolyard. "TWO MEN SLAIN IN BELOIT STORE: LINK TO ROCKFORD MURDERS PROBED." Now, the killing spree had crossed state lines. Richard Boeck and Donald Raines were found murdered at a Radio Shack in nearby Beloit, Wisconsin. The killer shot the two men in the back room of the store. They were execution-style murders. Number five and number six of a midwest killing spree.

I considered every rumor. On the way to school, the word was that the killer was a crazed Vietnam vet who would have a flashback and then go out and kill someone. By lunch time, the report was that the killer had walked into an east side grocery store and killed six more people. On the walk home from school, the killer was held up in a west side shack. He killed the two cops who found him out, and was now surrounded by police and promising they would never take him alive. I got home and turned on the afternoon news. Of course, none of the rumors were true. It is amazing how, years later, I would be obsessed with the facts about this case, when then I was bombarded with tons of misinformation.

When I turned on the five o'clock news, no one else had been killed. However, there was some news about the story that everyone was talking about. The FBI was now in on the case. The news radio station learned that a SWAT team raided a home in Beloit. Three people were taken into custody on John Doe warrants. One of them was charged with obstructing justice. Later that night, two more people were taken into custody.

It all turned out to be nothing. Two days later, they were all released.

Days passed without any leads and without any more murders. A scared clerk at a Rockford Radio Shack saw two black customers that he described as suspicious. He called police and they arrested them both. They drew their guns and slapped on the handcuffs. Their pictures appeared in the newspaper despite the fact that they were both released shortly after the arrests. They were honest customers. They went into the store to buy a needle for a record player. It was obvious the cops were over-anxious. There was hell to pay.

African-American leaders demanded a meeting with cops, and they got it. Religious officials and civil rights leaders claimed life had become unbearable for blacks living in the area. They said white store owners were discriminating against black customers. They described the area as dangerous for blacks because of a mass hysteria. They were absolutely right. Beloit and Rockford police officials both claimed that they were not focusing on blacks. However, they asked local business owners to cool it. Despite the warnings, it is not an understatement to say that for weeks, all black people were considered suspects by many residents. It wasn't right. But, it was true. And even worse, there was nothing the police could do about it. Except, catch the bad guy.

Catching the bad guy proved to be a frustrating affair. At first, the police were under enormous pressure to make an arrest. Every day this killer walked free, more people died. During the week-long spree, many officers felt if they didn't catch the killer today, they would have more crime tape and blood to deal with tomorrow. After the Beloit murders, a couple of weeks passed without any murders. Then, the next phase of frustration hit. What if this maniac gets away with it? Jobs were on the line. Careers hung in the balance.

The unwritten rule about discussing the case in the Kelly household had been abolished. My father was fascinated by the techniques the cops were using to track this killer. Ballistic reports had linked the same gun to three out of four of the Rockford murders. My mother was reluctant to talk about the case. If she could rule the world, none of us would have been exposed to this violent story. My younger brother didn't chime into the dinner talk. He was more interested in coming up with a scheme to avoid eating his green beans. My older brother saw it as an opportunity to torture his two younger, more naive brothers. He thought he was scaring us. He was out of his league. His teasing paled in comparison to the killer's actions. I was asking questions my parents couldn't answer. Why is this happening? Why can't they catch him?

The reward went up to thirty thousand dollars. Apparently, that was enough for Stewart's father. He contacted police, telling them he thought his son was involved. It should have instantly been recognized as the case breaker. Stewart had a checkered history of armed robberies and violent crimes. He had a habit of going on inspired crime sprees. In the 1970s, he served four years in prison for robbing four gas stations in one week. All of them were owned by Clark Oil. Despite this, the name Ray Lee Stewart didn't impress investigators right away. The Rockford Police Department had just opened up a Crime Stoppers unit. It was the first such unit in Illinois and was only two weeks old when the murders went down at Fredd's. Now, it was being tested to the hilt. As many as 80 tips a day were being fielded by over-worked operators. They took down the name, Ray Stewart, and put it in their files. Two days later, police checked out the name. There was a link to Willie Fredd. Fredd had turned evidence against Stewart in 1970. Stewart also had an outstanding warrant for armed robbery. Stewart's name went on the suspects' list. He could be brought in immediately because of the warrant, so police began looking for him. Meanwhile, police were still frustrated. Anonymous tips and promising leads all ended up being dead ends. They were doing what police do when they are stuck; they go back over everything again and interview everybody again. The final break came when detectives were doing a routine check at a hotel near Fredd's Grocery Store. An employee at the hotel turned up a laundry receipt. The name on the ticket was Stewart. The dry cleaners was located in the Beloit Plaza. The three-and-a-half-week nightmare was about to end for exhausted investigators. The case was all but solved. It didn't take long for law enforcement to catch up with their number one suspect.

Investigators from Rockford and Beloit went after the stateline's only serial killer with a renewed passion. They ran the plates on one of Stewart's registered cars and learned he had recently been in Greensboro, North Carolina. Rockford Police Chief Delbert Peterson made a phone call to an old friend. The Chief of Police in Greensboro, William Swing, and Peterson had been classmates in college. Now, Peterson was asking for his help to crack the toughest case of his career. With the help of the FBI, Greensboro police located the car in a matter of hours. Investigators from Rockford and Beloit jumped on a plane.

6 a.m. Saturday, February 21, 1981

Raymond Lee Stewart was taken into custody on a federal warrant for his outstanding armed robbery complaint. Police found a .38 caliber RG 31 revolver and .38 caliber Smith and Wesson. There was still blood and brain matter on his clothes. Two days later he was charged with all six murders. It was three and half weeks after he had walked into Fredd's Grocery Store with nothing but a gun and bad intentions.

The evidence was overwhelming. From the start, it was obvious that the state's case was air-tight. The case was solved. The terror was over. The city could breathe again. Stewart would undoubtedly be sentenced to die in the electric chair.

Monday, January 18, 1982

It took a six-man, six-woman jury a little over two hours to find Raymond Lee Stewart guilty for the murders of Willie Fredd and Albert Pearson.

Life went back to normal in the Kelly household. No more bad dreams. There were basketball games to be played. Scout meeting to attend. Homework to get done. My younger brother was trying out for the winter play. He eventually won the role of The Raddish in Peter Rabbit. My older brother was gearing up for the spring soccer season. He would come home from school dripping with sweat from running up and down flights of stairs. I focused my attention on trying to figure out Reaganomics. After much campaigning, I talked my mom into letting me use my paper route money to buy a subscription to Mad magazine.

Raymond Lee Stewart had disappeared from the headlines. There would be an extradiction hearing for the Wisconsin murders. Eventually, there was going to be some more trials in Illinois. This was boring stuff. With Stewart safely behind bars, I felt secure enough to flip directly to the sports section when the bundles came rolling off the trucks.

The murder spree was no longer the lead story, and many would have preferred that everyone just put the ugly chapter behind them. But, it would never disappear. Even during this period, signs of terror were still evident in Rockford. You could sense that gas station attendants were more cautious. People looked over their shoulders more. For most, the west side was an area where you didn't go at night. It was clear that in one bitter cold week, Raymond Lee Stewart left deep scars and forever changed the pysche of an entire community.

He was behind bars, but he was still breathing, and he wasn't finished.

4:30 p.m. Thursday, April 22, 1982

Stewart was easily convicted in the murders of Willie Fredd and Albert Pearson. He was given the death sentence. Near the end of a second trial, for the murder of Kevin Kaiser, during a routine recess, Ray Lee pulled away from two unarmed baliffs and charged through the complex. He bolted down two flights of stairs before bumping into a plainclothes cop. The officer

*ordered him to halt. Ray stopped for a second. They were about
three feet apart. They stared at each other for a moment, and
then Ray sprinted down the stairs. The cop pulled his gun and
shot twice, the second bullet hitting Stewart in the back just
under his right shoulder. It didn't slow him down. He was now
outside the courthouse, running down Elm Street. Two police
officers spotted him and gave chase. They were inches away
from bringing him down when Stewart was able to accelerate
and outrun them. The officers were losing ground fast as the
chase continued through downtown Rockford. They were a blur
to unsuspecting spectators. By the time the officers turned the
corner from Church Street to West State, Stewart was out of
sight. Raymond Lee Stewart had escaped.*

*It was a convenienent story for the media. All throughout the
trial, the courtroom was packed with reporters. It didn't take
long for word to spread. It didn't take long for panic to spread.
As if in spite, Raymond Lee Stewart was terrorizing Rockford
again.*

*School had just gotten out. I walked home oblivious to the
courthouse developments. When I got home, the phone was
ringing. My mother called first. She wanted to make sure that
we got home okay. I said, "Of course."*

"Well, honey, you remember Ray Stewart?"

"Yeah, yeah of course."

"Well, he escaped."

"What?"

*"He escaped, he's running loose downtown somewhere, it's
all over the radio."*

"Jesus."

"Don't worry, just stay in the house, okay?"

"Okay. How did he escape?"

*"I don't know, but it sounds like there are a lot of cops
downtown. Don't worry, he is not going to come anywhere
near our house. We live a long way from where all this is happening."*

"Jesus!"

"Just stay in the house."

"Okay."

She hung up, and I sprinted outside to find some friends to tell them the news. A council of BMX bikes had gathered at the end of my street. Apparently, I was one of the last to get the word.

Joey Davis heard Stewart killed a guard and stole his gun. Robert Johnson learned Stewart had been spotted in a car heading north to the Beloit area. David Carter reported he was holding hostages in a downtown music store. It was amazing how detailed the rumors were. We all agreed to gang up on him if he dared to come into our neighborhood. I decided to hike back to the house and listen to the radio.

Before I could switch my radio from FM to AM and dial in the news station, my father called.

"Greg, did you hear about the escape?"

"Yeah, what's goin' on?"

"Well, apparently he escaped from the courthouse and they can't find him. Now, I want you to stay in the house. If you see any suspicious people, just call me. I don't think you have any-thing to worry about. You know Stewart is black. If you see anyone that looks like him, just call. You know the number."

"Yes."

"Okay, mom will be home in a little bit."

"Bye."

I was living in a lily white neighborhood. It was rare to see a black man walking down the street. By some strange coinci-dence, that day there was one. I had seen the TV footage of Stewart and pictures of him in the newspaper. This guy looked nothing like Stewart. It didn't matter. I ran up the stairs and into my room. After about ten minutes, I got up enough courage to turn on my radio. It was safe to come out. Stewart had been captured. Once again, the terror was under control.

We watched the news as a family that night. They had video of Stewart being walked out of an alley into a police van. He was bleeding from the gunshot wound. On one side of him was

*an arson investigator, on the other was Officer Friendly. Offi-
cer Friendly was the guy who came to our school and told us
about law enforcement and advised us to stay on the straight
and narrow path. He once handcuffed me to a classmate as a
demonstration. Now, he was walking a bleeding, handcuffed
serial killer back into police custody. The scene was wild. The
news showed police with shotguns running through downtown.
People were panicked and running in every direction. The news
had interview after interview of people describing what they
saw and telling how scared they were.*

Friday, April 23, 1982

*I was up bright and early, anxiously waiting for the news-
paper truck to arrive, not in hopes of insuring tips from early-
rising customers, but to read about the escape.*

*"STEWART SHOT IN ESCAPE, CAUGHT IN DOWNTOWN
ALLEY."*

*I stared down at the top newspaper. The front section of the
paper was loaded with various articles about the courthouse
escape. It had a fantastic photo of Stewart being dragged to the
police van by the two officers. It had a map that detailed his
escape route. It had a feature article on Officer Friendly. He
downplayed the story saying he wasn't a hero, just doing his
job.*

*That year I was doing a tour as a student crossing guard.
Everyone passed by my corner, and everyone was talking
about the escape. One kid was downtown in the middle of all
the action. He saw undercover policemen walking around with
machine guns. Another girl was walking home from school
when two cops picked her up and drove her home to make sure
she was safe. This time, I knew better than to believe all the
stories. Everything from Ray hotwiring a squad car to making
a disguise out of items he found in the trash. One even had
Officer Friendly challenging Ray Lee to a draw and winning. I
was up early and had read the paper. I knew their stories were
all nonsense. I challenged some of the storytellers, but, for the*

most part, my criticism fell on young, deaf ears. Even when the truth is exciting, the temptation to add a little creative pinch was always too tempting for the schoolyard gang.

4 p.m. Thursday, April 29, 1982

Only a week after the escape, Stewart was sentenced to die for the murder of Kevin Kaiser. In Wisconsin, where there is no death penalty, he was given life in prison for murdering Donald Raines and Richard Boeck. Content with twin death sentences in the convictions of the Fredd-Pearson case and the Kaiser case, the State of Illinois didn't prosecute Stewart for the murder of Kenny Foust.

For years, Ray Lee Stewart disappeared from the headlines but never from the minds of the people he terrorized. As I got older and into my teen years, the story would pop into my mind every now and then. One weekday night my father was taking me to a Harlem Globetrotters game at the MetroCentre in downtown Rockford. We were in good spirits. Seeing the Globetrotters was practically an annual event for us. As he navigated through the heavy downtown traffic, we talked about the gags they would pull: Curly showing up in a wig, Geese throwing confetti. Shoot the ball, bang-bang. We parked in a nearby garage and began to hike a couple of blocks towards the arena. Whenever I was downtown, I thought of Ray. It was almost like I expected to see him sprinting down State Street, being chased by the police. I was too old to admit I was scared, but whenever I was down there, I was. That night I asked my dad to show me the alley where they found him. He stopped for a second, and I could sense his mood changing.

"Okay, come on."

It wasn't completely dark yet, or I never could have done it. I had the same feeling in my gut people have when they walk through haunted houses. We turned into the alley and he walked me to the exact spot and pointed. As I carefully studied the spot, my heart was pounding. I thought maybe there would still be bloodstains or some evidence of the frightening inci-

dent. There was nothing. Finally, my dad put his arm around me and said, "Now, let's go watch the Globetrotters."

12:35 p.m. Thursday, September 12, 1996

The glare of the sun flickered off the State Capital Building and into the Ford. Blinded for a second, I finally broke from the gaze. I was running late and couldn't afford to daydream about the case any longer. It was time to start working it. For me, the headlines are hypnotic. I've read all of them hundreds of times. I took a second to reflect on how freakish it was that this curiosity had stayed with me for so many years. Finally, I took a deep breath, opened the door and began walking towards the massive structure in front of me.

As I walked, I thought about other death penalty cases I had covered. There was, of course, John Wayne Gacy. As an intern, I talked to Gacy on the phone, stalling him while another intern feverishly ran through the station looking for the reporter the inmate was asking for. On the night of the execution, I was a desk assistant and had to stay until the late news cut-in was complete. As a joke, some of the employees ordered out the same meal Gacy requested: fried chicken, shrimp, French fries and Coca-Cola. I haven't eaten at Kentucky Fried Chicken since. There were others besides Gacy. I followed the case of Girvies Davis. Despite strong evidence suggesting he was innocent of the specific crime for which he was sentenced, the execution went on without a hitch. The last two went down with little media attention. They were Charles Albanese and George Delvecchio. By this time, I was the overnight assignment editor. I remembered when the story crossed the wires as word of the executions came out of Stateville Prison near Joliet. Executions were becoming more and more routine, and they barely made a mention on the newscasts.

This death penalty case was totally different for me. I had lived with this story for years. I grew up terrified of this man. I wasn't watching the developments from the newsroom; I was breaking the unwritten rules and going out in the field and experiencing it. When the fax had crossed my desk in August, I knew I had to somehow get in the mix. It was a release from the Illinois Supreme Court declaring they had set a date for Raymond Lee Stewart. Anybody else in the newsroom wouldn't have thought twice about it. It was a single sheet of paper, mixed in with several other pages the fax machine had spit out that day. It was only three paragraphs, but those three paragraphs were going to change the top headline of the Register Star morning edition. The fax would change what the Rockford television stations were going to broadcast. In Chicago, the news would be tossed aside as not locally important. Eventually, the Chicago stations would sit up and take notice, but for now those three little paragraphs were headed for the recycling bin. For others involved in the case, both professionally and personally, those three little paragraphs represented the beginning of the end to a fifteen-year journey fraught with emotional burdens, painful memories, and legal twists and turns. I had walked to the cafeteria, fax in hand, and stared at it while I read it over and over again:

> CHICAGO—The Illinois Supreme Court has set an execution date of Sept. 18 for convicted multiple murderer Raymond Lee Stewart.
>
> "All of Stewart's federal and state appeals have been exhausted and no further obstacle exists to prevent his lawful execution," said Attorney General Jim Ryan, whose Criminal Appeals Bureau is representing the state in Stewart's appeals. Last month, the Bureau filed a motion asking the Supreme Court to set a final execution date.
>
> Stewart, now 44, has been incarcerated on Death Row at Pontiac Correctional Center

*since 1982. He would become the eigth
inmate executed by lethal injection since Illinois reinstated the death penalty in 1977.*

With fax in hand, I had slipped into my news director's
office. I explained my relationship to the case and asked if I
could enter a request to witness the execution. She didn't think
the story was going to be any big deal, so she said yes. I
drafted a letter and got the phone call a couple of days before
the clemency hearing. I was going to be there if they killed Ray
Lee.

First, I was going to go to the hearing. The clemency hearing is a last ditch stand for condemned people. In reality, it usually ends up being a mere formality. For someone like me,
fascinated and obsessed with the case, the Ray Stewart hearing
was a goldmine of macabre nostalgia.

Like a true amateur, I charged up the front steps to the
entrance of the Capitol Building, swung open the large door, as
if I were re-creating a scene from "Mr. Smith Goes to Washington," and headed for the second floor room where the
clemency hearing was about to begin.

CHAPTER 2

"We are what we repeatedly do. Excellence, then, is not an act, but a habit."

—*Aristotle*

1:45 p.m. Thursday, September 12, 1996

After taking a few wrong turns and climbing up what seemed like a million steps, I finally found the doors to the room where the clemency hearing was going to take place. I took a deep breath, grabbed the handle and swung open the heavy door. I looked around. About forty people were sitting in the room, all waiting for the hearing to begin. Things weren't really rolling yet. I walked to the front and staked out a seat in the first row. I wanted to make sure I could hear everything. I reached into my briefcase and retrieved my tape recorder and the reporter's notebook I stole from the supply cabinet at work. It looked like I had a few minutes, so I pried open the battery cover and pulled out the batteries. I shoved my hand back into the briefcase and fumbled around until I found an unopened package of fresh batteries. I put them into the machine and gave it a quick check. Ready to record the event, I took a minute and looked around the room again. There were about a dozen reporters, mostly newspaper writers and wire service people. I was mildly surprised to see camera people setting up; mostly Rockford stations, but one was from Chicago. I quickly realized this hearing was wide open to the media. I wished for a second I would have talked my station into covering this. There were a couple of officers dressed in uniform. One guy had on a Rockford police uniform; the other looked like some sort of Winnebago County officer. In the back of the room, I noticed Paul Logli, the current State's Attorney for Winnebago County. I knew he was not in office when the murders went down, and I wondered why he was there. Glancing to the right, I saw the familiar face of Alex Fredd. Alex gave a nod and waved me over. I got up and carefully walked over to other side of the room. Alex is the son of Willie Fredd, Stewart's first victim. A couple of weeks earlier, I was able to persuade the powers that be at the station to let me take a crew to Rockford and shoot a story. Alex was one of the people I interviewed for the piece. Alex is a large man, in his thirties. It is not an understatement to say his life was destroyed by the actions of Ray Lee. As I approached, Alex extended his hand and we shook.

"Did you get the tape?," I asked.

I was referring to the three-minute piece that aired. The plan was to send my parents a dub, who would in turn give it to Alex.

"Yes," said Fredd.

"What did you think?" I asked.

"It was good. It was a lot longer than the Carol Marin piece."

Carol Marin is a legend in the Chicago television market. For the last few years, she had owned the anchor chair at WMAQ television. She was one of the people who always got a heads up phone call when a big story was about to break. When the feds came down on the Gangster Disciples, she was out with the coppers shooting stand-ups, while they broke down doors. Our station learned about the raids when we saw her reporting it on the air. She had apparently caught wind of the Ray Stewart story and was boning up to cover it. About a week before I put together a Rockford story, she went up there and did a piece. Like me, she was also able to get on the list of media witnesses to see the execution, assuming there was going to be an execution.

"Yeah, well, believe me I had to fight for every second," I said.

Alex continued, "I really liked the stuff Tom Gibbons had to say and Fred Speer was just great."

"Well, that Freddy Speer is something else."

Fred Speer is the local newshound for WROK radio in Rockford. He is truly one of a kind. A lot of his competitors dubbed him "Spread Fear," because he had a reputation for injecting excitement into his broadcast copy, regardless of whether or not the story warranted it. One thing the critics could never take away from him was that he knew how to break a story. Speer was always the first newsman at a big Rockford crime scene and sometimes he would show up at the same time the cops did. He had covered all the Stewart murders. He covered the escape. He was the first guy I called when I got the green light to do a piece.

2 p.m. Sunday, September 1, 1996

We pulled up to his driveway on the east side of Rockford. It was an ordinary ranch house with a small patch of grass as a front yard. This was a last minute thing, and I felt a little insecure because I was wearing blue jeans and hadn't shaved in a couple of days. As I got out of the car, Fred walked up to the screen door to see who had pulled in his drive. He gave a wave. I waved back, and we started gathering the camera equipment for the interview. I walked ahead of my photographer, Marc Gerke, and as I approached the door, I shifted the gear I was carrying to my left side so I could extend my hand to shake Speer's.

He greeted us and introduced his wife. Fred could have easily passed for the local reporter on the Andy Griffin show. He has sort of a golly-gee attitude about everything that would fit nicely in the Mayberry community. At the same time, he is a crack reporter. After talking to him for awhile, you begin to see just how intelligent he is. He is certainly bright enough to pull off a gig in a big market. Rockford is home, and when it comes to Rockford crime history, he is the guy to talk to.

We talked about where we wanted to set up. After some debate, we decided to do the interview on his back porch. It was a sunny day, and he had a nice porch that could provide all the light we needed. While Marc was setting up, we talked a little bit about the case. He told me that as far as interesting stories he had covered went, Ray Stewart's saga was right near the top. His wife, who almost seemed more interested in the whole thing than Fred, interrupted through the back screen door and mentioned the Simon Peter Nelson case. Simon Peter Nelson was really the only other mass murderer in Rockford's history. In 1978, he butchered his six children with a hunting knife. Fred nodded in agreement with his wife and said how horrible that story was. Then he pointed out that the difference was that the Nelson case had a clear suspect from the beginning. With Stewart, no one knew who the murderer was or when the killing spree was going to end.

Marc was all set up, and he gave me the nod to go ahead and start asking my questions. I started off by asking him about the first murders, but before I could finish, we were interrupted by Mrs. Speer. Her curiosity got the best of her, and she said she had to come outside and watch the interview. We took a minute while she set up a lawn chair, and then I began again.

"Take us back in time to the week of January 27th, when the first murders happened at Fredd's Grocery Store," I asked.

My strategy was to try and get Speer to tell as much of the story as possible. I was doing the legwork for a piece that would be handed off to one of our reporters. The reporter probably wasn't going to shoot a stand-up, so I figured it could be effective to get him to tell some of the story, and maybe we would be able to run some file footage over his voice.

Speer gave a perspective answer.

"Back at the time, a lot of violence was very unfamiliar in Rockford. The gangs, and a lot of the drug activity, and the drive-bys, that hadn't happened here yet. And, when the first murders went down at Fredd's, I don't think people thought a whole lot about it. But, then when the second one occurred and the third one occurred, for the first time in my career, I saw people in Rockford not only concerned, but scared. Maybe

people who had never locked their doors before, were locking their doors. It was certainly a bizarre situation."

It was good bite, and a nice way to start off the interview. He delivered the answer with emotion, punching key words and intertwining meaningful pauses. I knew that looking him up for this piece was a good move. I wanted to try to engage him in a conversation and avoid making it sound like a Q and A session, so, in that spirit, I talked into the next question.

"You are a person, like me, who monitors scanners constantly?"

"Right."

"And, when you hear about a story, you usually know about it before everyone else. Fredd's happened first and then there was the gas station murder," I said.

Speer was nodding his head like he wanted to comment, so I paused and let him answer.

"The one on Kilburn Avenue, right?" he asked.

"Yep. Now, what were you thinking when you heard this? You heard about the one on Kilburn. You heard about the one the next morning, the E-Z Go station. By the time the E-Z Go one happened, you had to have known."

Speer interrupted, "It was obvious at that time there was definitely a pattern and that is when I think people in the city here became very concerned and frightened that this wasn't a situation, like a domestic situation where you have a homicide, and it is pretty cut and dry, and most people know it is not going to go beyond this. It became quite obvious we had a killer on the loose."

A killer on the loose. For a second, I went back in time. I remember being a young child and hearing the reports on the radio and listening to all the talk around town. It was such an extraordinary time; I wanted to know what the crime scenes were like; what was being said when the microphones weren't around. Sitting six feet away from me was a man who knew, and I tried to extract it from him.

"What was the morale of the police department? You must

know a lot of these guys, and they are now investigating four murders in three days. Maybe, they were in a little over their heads at this point. What was their thinking at this point in the investigation, and how did they handle it?" I asked.

Speer took a second to think. You could see he was focusing on the crime scenes. It had to have been a crazy time to be a reporter. Every day, breaking the bad news to listeners; it has happened again; maybe it is time to be terrified.

He swatted away a pesky fly and answered the question.

"At that particular time the police department pooled all their resources. I think they even made contact with the FBI and some other area law enforcement agencies, because they knew they had a serious problem on their hands. They knew there was certainly an indication that possibly the killings were not going to stop," he explained.

The pressure the police must have been under had to be enormous. Four murders in three days with no apparent end in sight. I can't imagine the sense of urgency the department was faced with at that time. Police were desperate, and they were taking help from anyone who could possibly give it. They sent all the slugs to the Illinois Crime Lab to confirm what they already knew: the same person did all of these horrible crimes. They told residents to call the cops if they saw anyone suspicious. They called in the FBI and rushed the case file to the agency's Serial Crime Unit. They were doing everything they could, but the simple fact of the matter was, at that stage of the investigation, they didn't have any idea what they were dealing with. They were so desperate, they even circulated a photo of a Maurice Powell who was wanted on suspicion of armed robbery in the Chicago area. They had no solid information Powell was linked, and it was a clear indication they were ready to do almost anything, including bend a few rules, to solve this case and insure they wouldn't have another dead body on their hands the next morning.

Speer continued, "They put various businesses on high alert. Especially your gas stations and convenience stores, you know, the all-night operations. For the first time, these types of businesses were beginning to tighten up and take precautionary measures. Since that time, and as a ripple effect of the Ray Lee Stewart escapade, in town here, that is the reason you see employees at a lot of these all-night operations behind bulletproof glass and in enclosed, confined areas."

When he said that, I thought of Ray Lee's fourth victim Kenny Foust. There wasn't a lot of information on Foust. Most of Ray Lee's victims had family members who were very active throughout the trial and pending execution procedures. However, nobody was ever around for Foust. Kenny was 35 years old when he died at the hands of Stewart. The only reaction from anyone who knew him came from his roommate a couple of days after the murder. His roommate was Dave Meier and he told a Rockford Register Star reporter that Kenny was very much aware there was a killer out there. In fact, the night before, Foust confessed to Meier that he was nervous about going in and working his shift. He said he didn't want to work alone and expressed interest in obtaining a gun. He had a baseball bat in the store, but there was no way a bat would have been any match for Ray Lee who walked into the E-Z Go station with a .38 caliber just before seven a.m. and shot Foust in the head and in the neck. I wonder if Foust even had time to realize that the bad guy the whole town was talking about was about to make him victim number four.

At this point in the interview, I was stumped. I couldn't think of a question. It could have been I was getting so wrapped up in the story that I was losing focus. I am not a reporter and rarely am I put in a position where I conduct interviews. Speer gave me a look that indicated he was ready for the next question. It took me a minute before I finally gave up and blurted out a question I was really trying to save for the end of   the interview.

"How significant a story was this? How much of an impact did it have? How does it rate with all the other stories you've

covered in Rockford?" I asked.

Speer immediately answered, "Very close to the top. No question about it, Greg. No question about it."

He stopped for a second and looked at a plane that was passing over. He squinted a little bit, and then he continued, but now he had shifted to an intentionally slow and emotional tone.

"It was a rampage of ruthless, cold-blooded killing. The victims, with no resistance, handed over the money, and he shot them, for the simple reason that he didn't want to leave any witnesses."

Shaking his head, he finished, "It was crazy."

That was the peak of the interview. It was clearly a bite that had to be put in the piece. I felt a little more comfortable, knowing I had already secured some good sound. It was obvious Speer had a complete understanding of the emotional aspects of the murder spree, and, luckily, I was able to capture a little of that on tape.

We continued by talking a little bit about the logistics of the criminal investigation and how they finally caught up to the alleged killer in Greensboro, North Carolina. Of course, when they caught up to Ray Lee, Speer got a phone call at home tipping him off to the news that they nabbed the bad guy. He mentioned that when police finally figured out the link between Stewart and Willie Fredd, it became obvious they were looking for Ray. The one thing that really slammed the door on the case was the fact that when they caught Stewart, he still had both guns on him. It was one more bizarre twist that made the case so unbelievable.

"I can't understand that. That is the number one question I want to ask him if I ever get him on the phone. Why didn't he ditch the guns because that clearly incriminated him? He drove cross country with the evidence on him," I said.

Speer added, "Without the evidence, who knows? He may have been a free man today."

It was a scary thought, but it was true. Stewart did the pros-

ecutors a huge favor by holding on to his guns. Whatever the reason, whether he was paranoid or careless or didn't care or maybe he wasn't done using them, he handed the state's attorney a gift. The case was a lock from day one. He was the guy, and no way was he getting away with it. The death penalty was designed for guys like him. Normally, Fred Speer's involvement in the story would end right about here. There would be a trial, a sentence and a punishment. Nothing too exciting. However, it didn't happen that way. What was probably the most exciting day in Speer's career happened on April 22, 1982, the day Stewart escaped. Speer had probably narrated the story thousands of times to thousands of different people. I asked him to do it one more time.

Speer told the story, "Ray Lee Stewart was making a routine court appearance. I'll never forget, he had on a powder blue suit. While making that appearance, he made a break for freedom and, for a very short time, was successful, running through the Winnebago County Courthouse. Sheriff's Officer Jim Kraut was coming up a courthouse staircase and they collided. Kraut said Stewart probably thought he had had it, and retreated to a corner in the hallway of the courthouse and covered his throat, because he thought Jim was going to shoot him. When Stewart realized he wasn't going to shoot him, he got up and took off again."

Speer was really getting into telling the story. He was using hand gestures and raising his voice. His intensity was high. I listened to every word and stared at every facial expression while he continued telling the remarkable story.

"You have to keep in mind, there was a lot of activity in the courthouse. People, even children, were everywhere. Officer Kraut had to be careful, if and when he shot. He shot once, and hit the door. As the door was closing on Stewart, he shot again and he saw red up on his shoulder, and he knew he got him that time. Kraut was on light duty, coming off back surgery, and he chased him out of the courthouse and saw Ray Lee Stewart getting into an automobile. Kraut called out to Stewart and said,

'I am going to shoot you again if you don't get out of that car.'
At that time, Stewart got out of the car and then, unbelievably,
took off running into the downtown area. Kraut said he could-
n't pursue him because his back was killing him. So, Ray Lee
Stewart disappeared into the immediate downtown area. They
knew he was down there, but where was the question. After
that, there was just a massive barrage of police officers in
downtown Rockford."

It wasn't hard for me to picture the images he was talking
about. Just a few days before, I did a thorough, station-wide
archive search for Ray Stewart tape. We didn't have much, but
we did have video of the escape. When I popped it into the
machine and pushed play, it brought it all back for me. There
was Ray being pulled out of the alley, with his bloody shirt, and
police officers on both sides of him. As you listened to the
noise, in the background you could hear Speer's out-of-breath
voice reporting the story live for WROK.

> *"They got him. I am on the portable, here. He is on*
> *North Main Street; he is surrounded by police offi-*
> *cers. The escape of Ray Lee Stewart has been short-*
> *lived. He is being placed, right now, in a Rockford*
> *Police emergency white car. He is surrounded by*
> *police officers. He will be taken to Swedish Ameri-*
> *can or Rockford Memorial for emergency treatment.*
> *The white car is pulling out of the mall on State*
> *Street. He didn't get very far."*

I perceived that Speer was only half-done telling the story,
so I pressed on.
"When they captured him, you were right there?" I asked.
Speer continued, "I've never seen anything like it. He was
wounded, and they knew he had to be downtown somewhere. It
was Officer Reffet and Officer Gibbons who checked out an
alley near the South Main and State Street intersection, behind
the old dry goods store. When they went down the alley, they

could see the top of Stewart's head sticking out of a 55 gallon drum barrel. At the time, I was at the edge of the alley by North Main Street, and Officer Gibbons walked up to the drum and screwed the barrel of his gun into Ray Lee Stewart's ear and ordered him out of the barrel, and no trouble. As he came out, I could see that he had been wounded. The shoulder area of his suit was all bloodstained. They led him down the alley to an ambulance, and he was taken to the hospital."

Speer was finished telling the story. He pushed himself back from the edge of his chair and relaxed.

Finally, I needed to get Speer's opinion on the execution. I didn't really care, but I had to ask to make the piece timely. The peg of the story was that next month the state was going to kill this man, and in order to sell the piece as "news," I had to ask everyone I interviewed what their reaction to the upcoming execution was.

So, I asked, "How do you feel about the execution? I remember when he was sentenced to die, there was a report that he jokingly told one of the guards it was going to take the state seven or eight years to kill him."

Speer interrupted, "It took them twice as long."

"It took them twice as long. It does say something about the speed of capital punishment. Does the story end on the 18th?"

It was a two-part question, and Fred took a few seconds to collect his thoughts. He answered the second part first.

"You know, Greg, conversation about Ray Lee Stewart has never stopped. It seems to always generate some talk from time to time. The story has never really died, and I suppose it is going to take some time now."

He paused and began to think of his answer for the other part of the question. I never felt comfortable asking people what they thought about controversial issues. This was a man who I sought out because he knew the facts of the case, not because he had some important opinion to offer our viewers. While Fred finished gathering his thoughts, I was wishing I didn't have to ask it.

Speer finally gave his answer, "How do I feel about the death penalty? I am in favor of the death penalty, only if the evidence is overwhelming. If there is no doubt. Speck. Gacy. Overwhelming. Because we have put some people to death who, you know, it later turned out were innocent. In Stewart's case, it is overwhelming. No doubt about it. He did it. It sends a message. It sends a message to Ray. His crimes were deadly, calculated, cold-blooded. His victims complied, and he still cut them down."

"Fred, I wish I had more time," I said, indicating to him and to Marc that the interview was over.

We took some cutaway shots of Fred sitting in his lawn chair talking to me. Mostly we talked about my parents; Fred had worked with my stepfather, Bill Phillips, for years at WROK radio. We dropped a few names about various people we both knew in the news business, and when Marc was finished, we went inside the house.

I had a VHS copy of the capture video from 1982, and I wanted to get some shots of Speer watching the tape. It was kind of a cheap TV effect, but one that ended up working pretty well. I could tell it brought back a lot of memories for Fred, and I watched intently as he relived the pandemonium of that April afternoon.

After watching the tape four times, I asked Marc to pack up the gear, and I popped the tape out of the machine. Then, Fred surprised me with one last observation.

"For a newsman, any newsman, to cover an event like that, especially in the Rockford market, it was a once-in-a-lifetime opportunity," he said.

As Marc carefully loaded the gear into the trunk, I asked Fred if he had any suggestions for doing the story. He said the guy to talk to was Jim Kraut, the man who shot Ray during the escape attempt. I explained that Kraut wasn't home when I called, and I only had one day to shoot in Rockford. Then, I revealed our next stop was to talk to Tom Gibbons. He nodded and assured me Gibbons' story would give me a great per-

spective.

His wife shouted, "Don't forget to say hello to your folks for us," as we drove out of the driveway and towards our next interview.

CHAPTER 3

"In the future, everybody will have fifteen minutes of fame."

—*Andy Warhol*

This unscheduled working visit to my hometown proved to be quite a feat. This was a real last minute thing, and I spent the entire trip to Rockford on the cell phone trying to get everything set up before we arrived. I was able to reach Speer before we left the station, so I knew we had him. My stepfather knew him, so there was a connection there and as soon as I told him who I was, he immediately agreed to do it. Traveling down I-90 at 85 miles per hour, I called all the Rockford TV stations in an attempt to beef up our small arsenal of Ray Stewart file tape. WREX agreed to make a dub, and I told them I would drop by the station to pick it up. I called WIFR and Karen Jordan answered the phone.

Karen is the daughter of one of our veteran reporters, Bob Jordan. After exchanging a few stories about her old man, I told her what I wanted and she promised to check it out for me and give me a call back in the car. After about twenty minutes, I called the station back to check up on the progress. This time, I got transferred to the news director. She explained that the station's resources were swamped with Rockford's annual "On The Waterfront" festival in full swing. They were broadcasting live from downtown. I understood and thanked her anyway. That would have been the end of it, but about ten minutes later I got a call from Karen who said she worked it out and we could swing by to pick up a tape. I don't know *for sure what went on at the station, but after a few years in the business, I had a pretty good idea. When it came to working the Ray Stewart story, it seemed like I had a lot people going to bat for me.*

I called Alex Fredd whom my stepfather knew through Alcoholics Anonymous. Bill had mentioned to him I might be interested in doing a piece sometime down the road, and fortunately for me, Bill got his home phone number. Alex agreed to an interview.

Then I called Tom Gibbons. I was happily surprised when his home number was listed in the phone book. His wife seemed excited about the story I was working on. I explained that I remembered the days when Gibbons used to play Officer Friendly and she laughed, pointing out he gets that a lot from folks. She told me Tom was in charge of the police for On The Waterfront and was working the afternoon shift. She said I could probably go down there and catch him at the temporary police headquarters they had set up for the event. I almost dropped the cell phone when she told me where it was. For the weekend, the police had taken over a storefront off State by the old Soda Bar Restaurant. Ironically, it was less than a block away from where Stewart was captured.

The story was locked up by the time we hit the Marengo Toll Plaza which is 36 miles away from Rockford. I finally shoved the cellular phone back into the holder and looked at Marc and started laughing. He asked why, and I explained how I was able to get everything lined up. There was some sort of six degrees of separation at work that afternoon. I was fibbing a little when I guaranteed the producers I would have a solid story for them when I returned to Chicago. The truth is, I didn't know what I was going to get in Rockford when we left. A lot of it was connections, but, more than that, a lot of it was luck. Gibbons dated my mom's best friend in high school. Speer worked with my stepfather at WROK. Karen Jordan answered the phone when I called WIFR. My parents had just recently met Alex Fredd. Rockford is a small town, but it isn't that small.

I let Marc in on the game plan, and for a second he was able to break my high. He pointed out there was no way we could make all those stops and still get back for the newscast. Assignment editors aren't always practical when it comes to logistics. However, they certainly are resourceful. After thinking about it, I agreed, and picked up the phone which was still hot from rubbing off my ear for the last thirty minutes and called my most reliable contact, dear old mom. Without any questions, she agreed to run by both TV stations and pick up the tapes for us. I put the phone down for the last time and looked over at Marc, who was shaking his head in disbelief.

It took about a half-hour to get wrapped up with the Speers. Afterwards, we headed downtown to try and catch Gibbons before his shift ended. On the Waterfront is the biggest event of the year for Rockford. Every Labor Day weekend, they rope off most of downtown and set up a three-day party. Blues bands, live jazz, rock and roll; the festival had it all. Not to mention ethnic food, carnival rides and beer gardens. I saw one of the best shows of my life when local heroes Cheap Trick played there a few years ago. Everyone in the city seems to come out for this festival. It is the kind of event where you run into people you haven't seen in months.

I hadn't seen Tom Gibbon in years. I was in fourth grade the last time he paid a visit to our class as Officer Friendly. I remember him showing us a mini-movie about a kid who fell to peer pressure and started committing petty crimes like shoplifting and vandalism. Eventually the character in the movie graduated to burglary and finally got caught when an older woman he had robbed recognized him. It is bizarre how I remember, in detail, his visits to the classroom, but, at the same time, I can't remember half the state capitals. After he showed that movie, one of my classmates told me he had tried shoplifting a few times, but the film had scared him and he vowed to never do it again. I remember when he showed the class a bunch of narcotics glued to a posterboard. The one thing that stuck with me about his drug talks was when he explained how filthy the con-

ditions were at the illegal labs they raided. Legal pharmacies were nice and neat, but these places were just a hair better than a sewer, he explained. I am not sure if they still do the Officer Friendly bit in Rockford, but it is safe to say that during my elementary years the program had a positive and lasting impact.

It took awhile to find a spot in the packed downtown area. We finally parked illegally about a block and a half away from where we needed to be. We gathered up the gear and started walking towards the festival's entrance gate. The familiar smell of pork chop sandwiches was heavy in the air. The pork chop sandwich booth is one of the festival's biggest draws. We arrived at the entrance gate and flashed our media badges. The lady at the counter was ecstatic to see a station from Chicago covering the Waterfront. I didn't have the time or the heart to explain to her what our real purpose was.

We approached the cop shop and through the large glass windows I could see about forty officers walking around, taking care of police business. I was looking hard for Gibbons, but couldn't pick him out. We entered the building, and about half the officers stopped what they were doing and looked at us. They started whispering amongst themselves. The reception desk was an old card table with a uniformed officer behind it. I walked up and told him I was there to see Tom Gibbons. He didn't bother getting up, just turned his head to the side and shouted for Tom. Gibbons was about twenty feet away with his back to us. He turned around and held up one finger indicating we would have to wait for a couple of minutes.

Officer Friendly had aged gracefully, but he had definitely aged. He was carrying a few more pounds and his head was full of white hair. He had replaced his heavy plastic glasses with a modern wire rim pair. The mustache was gone. He was wearing a white police shirt which meant he had probably moved up some ranks in the last few years. He finished whatever he was doing and walked over to the front of the room where we were waiting.

We introduced ourselves, and he explained he didn't have a lot of time. I told him we would only be asking a couple of questions, and I promised to make it as quick as possible. I looked over at Marc and told him not to bother with the lavalier microphone system, and he handed me a stick mic. While Marc was getting everything ready, we talked about his years as Officer Friendly. He told me I was probably one of thousands of Rockford grown-ups who remember him from his tour as the city's cop mentor. Marc gave me the go-ahead nod, and I started the interview by getting right to the point.

"In April of 1982, where were you when you heard the news that Raymond Lee Stewart had escaped?" I asked.

Gibbons was really busy, and didn't have a lot of time to chat with us, so I didn't want to take up anymore of his time than I had to. There were a lot of questions I could have asked him, but only a couple I really needed to ask him, and I thought it was best if we cut to the chase and got right to the day Stewart escaped.

Gibbons answered, "I was leaving the Public Safety Building where the Rockford Police Department operates. It was the end of my tour of duty, and I was getting ready to go home when we heard that Raymond Lee Stewart had escaped from the Winnebago County Jail."

Gibbons was one of those cops who talked in police lingo when he was doing interviews. Police officers are trained to give out just the barebone facts when they are talking to the press. They try to avoid incorporating any emotion or excitement into their speech. Often, they overstress times and locations when they talk about things. I made a mental note to try and break him out of that mode at some point in the interview and try to draw out some personal observations. However, for now, I had to get him on tape talking about the events that happened on that April afternoon, 14 years ago.

I continued, " You were involved in the search in the immediate downtown area, and that is pretty much where police officers thought he was. In fact, he never did get out of downtown.

What sort of assignments were you doing? How were you try-ing to catch Stewart?"

There was quite an audience of people watching us conduct the interview. Several of the police officers were staring at us with puzzled looks on their faces. A local news crew was there interviewing another officer about On the Waterfront, but all eyes were on us because we were the out-of-town guys. At one point, the local reporter looked over with a confused look and then continued with his own interview. I don't know if Gibbons even noticed the onlookers because he didn't miss a beat as he answered my questions.

"At the beginning, it was chaotic. Every police officer in the immediate downtown area flooded the streets, and we started to complete a grid search in the business section, actually just a few businesses from where we are right now."

As he talked, I made a mental note to go to the alley and shoot that before we left.

He continued, "We had checked and had no success in locating him. I, along with two officers, had gone down a base-ment stairwell; it was dark and we didn't have our flashlights with us. Keep in mind, we were on our way home from work. The area had been checked several times. Approximately an hour later, I located an officer with a flashlight and asked him if he would care to go back down there with me and check it again. We did, and that is where we found him in a 55 gallon drum that was tipped on its side."

He had told me how it unfolded; now I wanted to fish for some juicy stuff about the capture. Maybe stuff that was never out there before. I took a minute to think, and I finally figured out what it was that I wanted to know.

I asked him, "What was the exchange between you and Stewart? Obviously, he was a dangerous fugitive, and you had to treat him very seriously. What happened?"

"I issued certain orders and he complied. We removed him from the barrel and he was taken into custody. During the escape, Winnebago County Sheriff's Officer Jim Kraut had shot at him and did hit him, and he was wounded. So, when we removed him from the barrel, we noticed the injury, and we put him in a white car, which was an ambulance-type vehicle. I administered first aid to him en route to the hospital. Once we got to the hospital, he was turned over to medical personnel there, and eventually to the detective bureau here in Rockford," he said.

He was still very much in cop lingo mode, but that was okay. These were good sound bites, and they were going to work nicely with the video we had of the capture. I still wanted some personal touch, and I struggled to come up with a question that would do the trick. I cracked a smile and dropped my tone to a more friendly level.

I asked him, "Now, how many times have you been asked to tell this story? Is this something where, for the rest of your life, people are going to ask Tom Gibbons about Ray Stewart?"

The question seemed to do the trick. He smiled and chuckled while he nodded his head confirming what I had thought; he knew this story by heart and had told it a million times.

"Well, you have to understand, this case is probably the most horrendous case that Winnebago County or Rockford has ever experienced. The Ray Lee Stewart saga, with the number of homicides that he committed, is probably the worst. And, yes, it is asked a lot of times, not only of me but of other detectives like Detective Don Ericson, Detective Reffett and Sgt. Tom Nimmo, who originated the case. We all have been asked many, many times to recount the incidents concerning Raymond Lee Stewart," he said, while grinning and shaking his head.

Once again, I came to the point where I had to try to make my interview current. I needed to ask what he thought about the upcoming execution even though I didn't think his stance on capital punishment was necessarily relevant to the story. I figured he had lived with this case and had been talking about it on and off for the last 14 years, so when I asked him what his thoughts were now that it was all coming to an end, I was surprised at his somewhat emotional reaction.

"Let me think about this for a second; I want to collect myself for this one," he told me.

He looked away for a moment. He was thinking about what he wanted to say. I was surprised that suddenly he had really gotten into the interview. I could see him working on phrasing his words just right.

Finally he said, " I don't think anyone is ever going to be able to conclude what Raymond Lee Stewart has done. What he has done will affect many, many people for generations to come, perhaps. But, at least we can say that the incident, or Raymond Lee Stewart, will be concluded on September 18th, and perhaps we can put this matter to rest. Justice will be served."

At that point, I knew it would be foolish to ask another question. It was a great bite. He had pretty much said everything he could say about his involvement in the case, and there was really no reason to waste anymore time. I thanked him and told Marc to pack it up.

While I was shaking hands with Gibbons, I asked him if he could point me in the right direction of the alleyway where he found Stewart. I was expecting him just to tell me, but I was pleasantly surprised when he volunteered to walk out there with us. I suspect he was getting into this whole thing again, because just five minutes earlier he had asked us to be brief, and now he was taking a break to show us around. We waited a minute while he signed out and grabbed his hat. While we were waiting, one of the officers who had been watching was pushed towards us. He was apparently the elected spokesperson for a group of curious cops. He asked what we were doing, and I explained we were working on a story about Ray Stewart. He asked when it was going to be on, and I told him at nine o'clock. He returned to his group of colleagues.

It didn't take us long to reach the infamous alley. Marc was getting shots of him walking as Gibbons was verbally painting a clear picture of the afternoon escape. We quickly made our way though the festival towards the site. At one point he stopped. Pointing down Main Street, he said, "This was the area where hundreds of police officers were. I mean, everyone that was available was down here."

We continued to the alley. This was fantastic video for the piece. Shots of the decorated officer returning to the scene of his most heroic encounter. As we walked, he was talking about how the buildings in the area had all changed and how it looked completely different today. Gibbons was about 100 feet down the alleyway when he stopped and pointed to the spot where he had found Stewart. He said he saw the hair on his head sticking out of the barrel, and he knew right away he had located the fugitive. The images of him bringing the killer out of this alley were broadcast on the local TV stations. Gibbon's picture was on the front page of the newspaper the next morning. As a child, I remember shouting that morning, "Mom, mom, look! It's Officer Friendly!" I was totally in awe.

As we walked away and the camera was off, we talked about the murders. I asked him why he thought Stewart did it. He stopped and explained his theory to me. He shaped his right hand in the form of a handgun and told me he thought the main thing with Stewart was that he learned to never, ever leave witnesses. While he was on the rampage, if you saw his face, he made sure you weren't going to be able to testify against him.

Gibbons also pointed out a very interesting fact while we were making our way back towards the police station. He said the gunshot was centimeters away from killing Ray Stewart. He didn't know which vital organ the bullet was close to hitting, but he said the doctors told him if it had been a fraction closer, the matter would have been concluded right then and there, instead of having to wait for September 18th, fourteen years later.

We came out of the alley, and I was a little embarrassed when a couple of old friends came up to me to say hello. These were people whom I hadn't seen in years. The last thing I wanted was to see friends when I wasn't shaven and had been working non-stop for hours. I thanked Sergeant Gibbons for everything. We shook hands, and he headed back to work.

While I played catch-up with my old buddies, Marc got some generic shots of the festival. About five minutes later, Marc returned and told me he had enough tape. I said good-bye to my friends, and we started to make our way back to the crew car. It was the first time in years that I left On the Waterfront without getting a pork chop sandwich, but I didn't mind. Amazingly, I had gotten everything I came to Rockford to get that afternoon.

Renew items at: www.
rockfordpubliclibrary.org

Item ID: 31112016290641
Title: Killer on the loose :
the true story of serial ki
Date due: 2/1/2021,23:59

Total checkouts for session:
1
Total checkouts:3

Do you know that by
borrowing from RPL today
you just saved: $9.95

CHAPTER 4

"Perhaps some of us have to go through the dark and devious days before we can find the river of peace or the highroad to the soul's destination."
—*Fredrick Pierce*

12:55 p.m. Thursday, September 12, 1996

The empty seats in the large room at the State Capital Building were starting to fill up. There were a few more reporters setting up in the front section, and I thought it was probably the appropriate time to reclaim my position. I said good-bye to Alex, and returned to my seat.

Covering these kinds of stories can be tricky business for journalists. The room was packed with witnesses who had passionate convictions about the pending execution of Ray Stewart. It was a peculiar environment, where you were constantly bumping into people from both sides of the issue. The crowded bathroom during recess breaks was a telling sight. There were family members of victims next to family members of Ray next to police officers next to defense attorneys. It was an unnatural mix. For a journalist interested in effecting a balanced coverage of the story, it was important to keep a mental note of to whom you were talking and for how long, and who was watching when you did it. I didn't want to misrepresent myself, but at the same time I didn't want to alienate anyone either. The entire afternoon was a balancing act.

The front of the room, where the Review Board was set up, had a large horseshoe-shaped table equipped with a microphone for

43

each of the eleven seats. There were name plates in front of each chair. The middle of the table was where the Chairman of the Board presided. The board members had assumed their respective positions and were laying out their notepads and files. They were settling in for a long day. Many placed large cups of coffee or cans of soda on the desktop. It was an odd contrast because the room was in the Capital Building and looked very official, but the atmosphere was relaxed and seemed almost informal. In the middle of the horseshoe was a small wooden table with two chairs and a microphone that could be twisted to accommodate the person who was speaking. There were no tables designated for the lawyers who would be presenting each side of the issue.

On my left side, the opponents of the clemency petition were set up in the front row. There was a woman who looked like she was in her thirties, who was there to represent the Attorney General of Illinois. Her name was Arlene Anderson. She had a manicured, organized look about her as she neatly stacked her files and notes.

On my other side, for the proponents, was a older gentleman sporting a bow tie as the finishing touch to his liberal-looking costume. He was set up on the far right side of room about three rows back, very close to where his witnesses were seated. His name was Joshua Sachs. He looked familiar; I had seen him on TV a few times, but I couldn't remember the cases. He was wearing an older suit, and his hair looked like it had been combed over for the first time in a couple of weeks. He had a look that was full of character. At first glance, you instantly realized this fellow was a true believer and was there because of his convictions against capital punishment. Anyone could have walked into the room and correctly guessed which side was representing which cause.

Sitting at the helm of the board table was Chairman Jim Williams. He was probably the oldest· member of the board. He was wearing a white shirt with a striped tie. His jacket was slung over the back of his chair. He gave a quick microphone check and started the proceeding. He explained that the Illinois Prison Review Board was not a court of law and that they operated formally and informally at the same time. He asked the attorneys to make sure that everyone who came before the board took an oath of truthfulness. He revealed he was not going to limit the amount of time anyone could speak, but encouraged all participants to be brief. At the conclusion of the hearing, the board was going to take up the issue behind closed doors and probably give the Governor their recommendation the next morning. The board members introduced themselves. They were from different cities throughout the State of Illinois. Finally, he asked Sachs to start his presentation.

Sachs slowly made his way to the center table. He started his address by showcasing his respect for the board. He thanked the chairman for giving him the floor. He asked the members of the board to inform him if they wanted him to speak up. He asked the chairman if he had a preference for whether he conducted his presentation while sitting or standing. After the formalities, he took a seat and began by introducing himself.

He stated his name and told the board he had represented Stewart since 1988. He said he was here to ask the Governor to commute Ray's sentence to life in prison without parole. He had five witnesses who were going to speak. He wanted to make three points about the Stewart case. The first one was not going to require any testimony; it was the issue of Ray's death sentence being handed out under conditions that were misleading and would be illegal in today's court system. (What Sachs was talking about was the issue of the instructions to the jury. In the sentencing phase of the trials, the juries were told if they didn't sentence Stewart to death, there was a chance he could get out one day. In 1982, that was a legal argument. However, that was changed by both the Illinois Supreme Court and eventually the U.S. Supreme Court. Today, the jury would have to be clearly instructed by the judge that life without parole was a possible sentence).

Sachs didn't elaborate and started addressing his second point, about Ray's abusive childhood.

"We want to put on witnesses to testify about Mr. Stewart's early family life: vicious, ugly, ongoing physical abuse. We are absolutely aware that no abuse and no mistreatment is an excuse for murder. What happened to Mr. Stewart is a factor the Governor should consider in determining whether the ultimate penalty of death should, in fact, be carried out in this case," said Sachs.

Before he could finish, Williams interrupted him and asked him to return to the legal issue that he briefly touched on. He stated he had read through court documents and thought the courts had finished ruling on this whole issue. He wanted Sachs to outline what he thought the reasoning was behind their decision.

I got a sense that Sachs was reluctant to dive into this matter again. This was the strongest legal appeal his client had. However, he was not in a court of law and his strategy was probably to highlight some of the ethical and more emotional arguments as to why the state should spare Stewart's life. Sachs knew he had some good witnesses, and, it seemed to me, he was racing to get them in front of the microphone.

Sachs quickly summarized the complicated legal history behind the jury instructions issue. Basically, what it came down to was that Stewart had "missed the bus." He said if the law had started to change when Ray's automatic appeal was still open, he might have had a shot at a new sentencing hearing and then, who knows? He pointed out that a death sentence from a jury has to be unanimous.

"Keep in mind, as you know, in Illinois, a death sentence has to be unanimous. There is no such thing as a hung jury in a capital case. If one juror out of twelve has reservations, there is no death penalty. If one juror out of twelve had said, 'He is never getting out, ever again; I am satisified if we are protected; we don't have to execute him.' If one juror had felt that way, Mr. Stewart would not have been sentenced to death," said Sachs.

The bow-tied attorney quickly finished summarizing the legal points, and Chairman Williams acknowledged he was finally content with the presentation and nodded at Sachs to continue with his opening statements.

Before leaving the issue behind for good, Sachs quickly added, "The Governor can cut through this knot in due fairness. That is what I am saying."

Sachs continued by introducing his third point. He said people who have been around Stewart in the last few years say he is a changed man. They say he readily admits his guilt and wishes he could undo the past. He characterized the condemned man as a passionate person, much different than the troubled Raymond Lee Stewart who went on a killing rampage in 1981. Sachs was careful not to belittle the horrible crimes his client was convicted of.

Sachs stated, "There is no sense in turning away from what is obvious. Many people died. Mr. Stewart is a murderer. He has been convicted and he has admitted the crimes. We are not saying that he should ever, ever again be out of prison. We are asking only, for the reasons we set forward, that the ultimate penalty of death not be carried out."

This was probably a difficult afternoon for Sachs. He had to have known he was sitting only a few feet away from family members whose lives his client had destroyed. Sachs had a very mellow style. His delivery was slow and precise. He was skilled at quickly organizing his arguments in an intelligent order. He seemed to be a very compassionate man and that shone through when he was presenting his case. Several times he went out of his way to make sure he didn't offend the memory of the victims. During the entire proceeding, he never became confrontational, and he always extended the board the upmost respect.

Before he introduced his first speaker, he took a second to "tease" his star witness. Her name is Constance Mitchell. She is the mother of Albert Pearson, Stewart's second victim. As soon as he revealed Mitchell was going to testify, I knew this was going to make news. The mother of a victim, fighting for the killer's life. It makes good copy. This was the strongest clemency argument they had. Sachs told the board she was deeply hurt by the actions of Ray Lee; however, she was here to ask them to commute the sentence. At that point, I knew it was going to be an interesting afternoon.

Sachs took a moment to prepare the board members for the inevitable onslaught of grieving family members the Attorney General was surely going to call to testify.

He stated, "He has put a lot of people through hell, and you will hear from different people who walked through the fire because of Mr. Stewart, and they will come out with different conclusions."

Then, he introduced his first witness. Sachs said she was not directly touched by Ray's actions but knew firsthand the pain that came with losing a loved one to violence. She had lost a sister to a killer and, afterwards, through a bizarre chain of events, came to know Ray and was prepared to tell the board her impressions.

He said, "I would like, with the board's permission, to call Jennifer Bishop Jones."

CHAPTER 5

"As we are liberated from our own fears, our presence automatically liberates others!"
—Nelson Mandela

April, 1990

I was a freshman at Rock Valley College when the Langert murder case went down. It found its way to the lead story slot several times during 1990 and 1991. Richard and Nancy Langert were shot in the basement of their posh suburban home off the north shore of Lake Michigan. Richard was handcuffed and shot execution-style in the back of the neck with a .357 magnum. Nancy was shot twice, in the back and in the stomach. She was pregnant. It took months before the Winnetka Police Department made an arrest. The police and the press took a dramatic wrong turn when they started circulating elaborate and bizarre theories about possible motives, the most famous being a possible family link to the Irish Republican Army. None of them were true. In the end, a 17-year-old neighbor boy named David Biro was convicted of the brutal murders.

The Langert case still incites passionate debates in the newsroom from time to time. The motive for the murders remains unclear. Biro was a rich kid and apparently didn't even know the Langerts. There is the theory that he wanted to get away with the perfect crime. Police had very little physical evidence to go on. There were no witnesses. They never would have caught Biro, expect for the fact that he couldn't keep a secret. He told his high school friend, Phu Hoang, the gritty details of the crime. Three months later, Hoang *finally came forward and told the Winnetka Police. When they arrested Biro, they found the gun under his pillow. The case was closed. David Biro was eventually sentenced to life in prison without parole.*

It is not unusual for heinous acts of violence to be committed in nice neighborhoods by teenagers. In fact, Rockford had its own case when 15-year-old Paul Bouchard killed Kimberly Shattuck in 1987. He stabbed her 55 times with a Navy survival knife. I remember the buzz around Rockford East High School when word came out that the police were questioning a fellow student. I can still remember the shock when I saw Bouchard's mug shot on the front page of the Register Star. This guy's locker was two down from mine. I once interviewed him for an expose I did for the high school newspaper. The piece was on unhealthy techniques the wrestling coaches were encouraging their athletes to use in order to make their weight division. He was very approachable and gave me a decent interview. There are elaborate theories about why Bouchard snapped and killed Shattuck, the most plausible being he was attracted to a classmate who was dating a guy who owned the same kind of car Shattuck owned. He killed Kimberly because he wanted to get the car. Neither of these murders makes logical sense to the sane mind.

These teenage murder types are a mystery to investigators. However, there is a clear pattern to their crimes. They aren't dumb, so they do a decent job of covering their tracks. They almost always live nearby. They usually pick victims they can easily overpower. When the newsroom gets a report that an elderly woman in a rich neighborhood was found murdered, some of the more cynical journalists start taking bets that the perpetrator is going to end up being a teenage neighbor.

Jennifer Bishop Jones had collected some psychological baggage through the years. The media reports were checkered with misinformation during the coverage of her baby sister's murder. Her family was linked to the Irish Republican Army simply because one family member had a thin connection to a human rights organization that took on some of the issues in Ireland. The execution-style manner in which Biro shot Richard Langert caused the media to spread reports about possible South American drug dealers being involved. There were also inaccurate reports about gambling debts. It is safe to say that beyond the pain of losing loved ones, Jennifer and her family had further suffered through the scrutiny of being connected to a high profile murder case, where everyone was looking to break the big story.

There were no visible signs of the hardships she must have suffered, as she approached the table to present her testimony to the board. She walked up under a breeze of confidence. I could tell she had some emotional attachment to this case, but she didn't appear nervous at all. When she took her place in front of the board, I wondered what had brought this woman to the Ray Stewart story.

She had a sweet, but intelligent look about her. She was modestly dressed for the occasion, wearing a colorful sweater and tan pants. It would not have been hard to guess that she is a history teacher. I think she is the kind of teacher I would have enjoyed having; someone who probably is in touch with her students, but makes sure they learn something in her class. This was the kind of person who could have an impact on the board: someone who had firsthand experience, spoke well, and was prominent in the community. There was a sincere and emotional tone to her testimony.

Jennifer introduced herself and told the board she was from Kankakee, Illinois. Joshua Sachs only asked her one question: how she came to be involved in this matter. From there, Jennifer launched into her story. She began by telling the board about how her life was devastated when David Biro killed her sister and brother-in-law. For Jennifer, this crime was more than just losing loved ones; it was a springboard that triggered some deep thinking about crime and punishment.

"That tragedy, which propelled us into all sorts of news media and trials and trauma, brought me to a place where I had to decide how I was going to deal with grief and with loss and with violence. It is absolutely clear to me that killing is wrong, and I came from that position to understand that capital punishment was just one more form of violence," she stated.

There were considerable differences between David Biro and Ray Stewart. Stewart had been on death row for years and had ample time to think about the crimes he had committed. Biro had only spent a few years at the prison in Menard, Illinois. But, like Biro, during the early years of his incarceration, Stewart was not only unresponsive to the families of the victims, he was outright vicious. He was famous for taunting them during the trials. Stewart never showed any compassion until the last few years of his life. David Biro has never publicly admitted to the crime; he has never offered any explanation for his actions; he has never shown any remorse. Stewart was a career criminal when he crossed the line and added murder to his long list of crimes. Stewart clearly came from a home that was plagued with abuse and neglect. From all appearances, Biro grew up under privileged conditions.

Despite the differences, Jennifer linked her involvement in the two different stories for the board. She explained she was at a time in her life when she was struggling to come up with non-violent solutions to crime when she spotted a letter in a newspaper by Constance Mitchell. Mitchell is the mother of Stewart's second victim, Albert Pearson. In the letter, Mitchell said she had forgiven Ray for killing her son. She was intrigued and decided to contact Constance. The relationship sparked a roller coaster ride for Jennifer.

She explained, "I found her story so compelling and her relationship with the killer so compelling, that I became quite interested in the case. I would start by saying having met Ray now, and knowing him quite well as I do, I would give anything if the man who killed my sister, David Biro, were like Ray Stewart. Accepting full responsibility for what he has done. Being very, very contrite and, of course, coming out of a tragic, tragic childhood. I have found the contrast between Ray Stewart and David Biro to be the defining point of my life."

This had to be a heart-wrenching endeavor for Jennifer. She knew the audience was packed with family members of Ray's victims. She knew firsthand the pain that comes with losing family at the hands of violence. However, she was going to bat for a man who didn't harm her personally. Jennifer ran the risk of being viewed as audacious by family members who didn't share the same forgiving view she had. The last thing she wanted to do was agitate wounds she was all too familiar with. However, her story was a unique one, and she belonged at the hearing. It is possible that she knew Raymond Lee Stewart better than anyone. She gave her testimony without interruption from the audience or the board. Although many in the room had to disagree with her, I doubt anybody questioned her sincerity and passion.

The board members were all looking up at her as she continued to tell them about how she befriended Raymond Lee Stewart. They started sending letters to each other and, eventually, she began visiting him at the prison. She told the board she found Ray to be a "good and gentle man." When she said that, I almost fell off the bench I was sitting on. Who the hell was she talking about? This was the first time I ever heard anything positive being said about Raymond Lee Stewart. This guy was the monster of my childhood, and now this lady was saying he was a great guy! My ears perked up, as she explained her first impressions of Ray.

"I was amazed at the way he was able to find little ways to be generous and considerate to me and to a friend of mine. The one thing you could always hear him say over and over again in every single conversation we had, was the standard by which he judged all of his actions: would it help to make up for the wrong he has done? We talked about different things I would try to get him to do, and he would say, 'no, I don't think that would help the families.' Or 'yes, I think that would help the families.' This is the only thing he has lived for in recent years," she said.

Jennifer was definitely outlining a fresh perception of Ray Stewart. In a way, this testimony was the most interesting of the day because of her impressions about the killer. This stuff was all new. The things that were going to be said later would probably be repeats of things that had been said before. This was a new perspective, from a new player.

Jennifer continued by explaining how Ray interacted with other people. She said Ray was liked by folks at the prison. There were many times Jennifer saw Ray joking around with the guards and his fellow prisoners. She said he had a reputation for being considerate and generous.

During her testimony I had been scanning the room, trying to find a way to get my microphone closer to the speaker's table. Everything was working great with my trusty recorder, but I was worried that the amplified audio in the room wasn't loud enough for a clear recording. I knew the better the quality of sound was on my tape, the easier my job would be later. When Jennifer started talking about her interactions with Ray, I quit worrying about the recorder and began to listen intently to her words.

I was astonished at her closeness to the killer. This was a woman who had unbelievable access to Raymond Lee Stewart. She could probably speak for hours on this man's state of mind. The subject was one I was fascinated with. In a way, I was envious of her. I didn't want to make friends with Ray Stewart, but he was someone who had a dramatic impact on my life, and I was hungry for information about what made him tick. Despite the fact they were slanted and opinionated, the descriptions and the stories Jennifer was telling were the closest things to answers I had ever come across up to that point. I knew I had to try and talk to her before I left Springfield. I had to ask her my own questions. I had to see if she would be able to get me in touch with Stewart.

Jennifer continued by telling the board Ray didn't like to talk about his childhood because he didn't want to sound like he was making excuses for his actions. Jennifer knew Ray was deeply hurt about things that happened when he was a kid.

She explained, "I find he is clearly a man who had a very, very traumatic life to the point where I can't even begin to fathom how he is standing. It is obvious from the stories I have heard from his family and from him about his childhood, that he had a life that, to me, speaks volumes about the way violence begets more violence. He has told me about the way his alcoholic father abused his mother and sisters and brothers. Sexually abused them, beat him constantly and threw him out of the house for trying to defend his mother and sisters from his (father's) violent and drunken rages."

This was nothing the clemency board hadn't heard before. It is common for people who are fighting for a convicted man's life to whip up stories about neglect and abuse. I could read the disdain on some of the board members' faces when she brought up the abuse in Stewart's family life. However, she was a compelling speaker and she did a decent job of selling the story. In a way, she was able to make the old song and dance about the killer coming from a broken home sound new. I could tell most of the members hadn't tuned her out, and some were even struggling to mask their disgusted reactions to the conditions under which Ray Stewart was raised.

Jennifer went on pointing out how the abuse had affected Ray's life. She revealed Ray was thrown out of the house when he was fourteen years old. While living on the streets, Ray gave into despair and concluded his life was hopeless. He admits he brutally murdered six people, but since then he has changed. He realized the cycle of violence had come full circle, and he had embodied the very thing he despised. He was now a Christian. He was now rehabilitated.

"He is the very kind of person that we say, if we can send somebody through the prison system, we would want them to turn out like this. Accepting responsibility. Being a good and gentle person. I think, therefore, it would be a tragic mistake to use the highest form of penalty for this man who has had this horrible, horrible childhood. Who is not well in many ways and is very, very sorry for what he has done. I think this would be a real bad message to send. I hope you will consider recommending commuting his sentence to life without parole," she said, to finish her testimony.

Jim Williams was writing notes on a legal pad when he suddenly realized Jennifer was done speaking. He looked up and nodded at her to confirm she was through. She nodded back, and he set his pen down and spoke into his microphone.

"Thank you. Any questions from the panel? Thank you Mrs. Jones," said Chairman Williams.

Jennifer scooted the chair back and got up while Joshua Sachs prepared to call his next witness. As Jennifer returned to her seat, she looked around the room. It appeared she was taking an inventory of who was there. She finally sat down alone in the fourth row, just in front of the Stewart family.

Later in the afternoon, I was standing in the hallway during a recess, stretching out, trying to get some circulation into my tired body, when Jennifer approached me. She introduced herself and asked who I was with. She acted surprised when I told her I worked for WGN. We began talking about the hearing, and I asked her about some of the terrible things Ray said to the families during the trials. She never got angry at any of my questions as she explained that she knew Ray was an absolute pyscho back then. She told me he had such a tempestuous life that his value system was completely out of whack. Jennifer was easy to talk to. She was a nice person, who never appeared threatened or intimidated. This was the first of many conversations we were going to have in the next couple of weeks. I revealed I had written to Ray Stewart and was desperately trying to secure an interview. She promised to talk to Ray about it, and she took my business card which I had already prepared by writing in my home phone number. We were discussing the broad issue of capital punishment when she spotted the sister of Kevin Kaiser. Minutes earlier Kelly had completed an emotional testimony, and her face was still soaked with tears. I witnessed Jennifer's facial expression change to sadness. She excused herself and went to try and talk to the young lady. I didn't think much of the conversation at the time, but ultimately it ended up being the most important moment of the afternoon for me.

Jennifer Bishop Jones didn't have to throw herself back into the public eye by aligning herself with Ray Stewart. She had a lot to lose. The media limelight was probably the last place she wanted to return to. I have no doubts she is a true believer. Ray Stewart had become her close friend. It was going to be painful for her when he died. Jennifer was smart enough to know the odds were against Stewart, and that the whole clemency business was more of a formality than anything. She was a good and brave friend to Ray.

CHAPTER 6

"Dissect a mother's heart and see the properties it doth contain—pearls of love, gems of hope—a mother's heart beats not in vain."

—Caleb Dunn

1:09 p.m. Tuesday, January 27, 1981

Rockford firefighter Ron Hill was called over to Fredd's Grocery by a store patron who had just made a gruesome discovery. Hill was working out of Fire Station Number Six, which was right across the street from the store. He made the short trek to the crime scene and started to administer first aid on Albert Pearson. The nineteen-year-old was lying on his stomach in a pool of blood. It didn't take long for the firefighter to realize there was nothing he could do.

Pearson was shot three times in the back. Police figured he was running for the door when the first bullet hit him. The next two shots were fired at close range. He was only a few feet away from the door when he was gunned down. He almost made it out.

From all appearances, Ray Stewart walked into the grocery store to settle a score with Willie Fredd. The first hard prison time Ray ever served was in 1970 when he pleaded guilty to armed robbery for holding up Johnny-on-the-Spot Cleaners in Rockford. Fredd had turned Stewart in, and he served fifteen months in prison. That afternoon Stewart got his revenge on Fredd. Stewart didn't have a beef with Albert; he just got in the way. He killed a man who did absolutely nothing to him. He made the mistake of leaving witnesses in the past; he wasn't going to do it again. He made sure Albert

58

wasn't going to be able to talk. He made sure that he was dead, very dead, before he left the store.

Constance Mitchell lost her beloved son at the hands of Raymond Lee Stewart. She was now a 63-year-old woman with a grandmotherly look . You would expect her to have a purse full of pictures of her children and grandchildren. She was dressed up for the occasion wearing a white dress suit with a turquoise blouse. Her hair was short and she wore large glasses that were slightly tinted. She had bracelets hanging down from each wrist and a long gold necklace around her neck.

She looked fragile as she walked up to the speaker's table. It was difficult to get a feel for this woman from where I was sitting. Constance took her time and settled in before she indicated to Joshua Sachs that she was ready to begin. In contrast to the other people in the room, she had a very simple appearance. There was nothing elaborate or fancy about her. She was someone people could easily underestimate. It wouldn't take long for her to dispel any beliefs that she was a simpleton. Everyone in the room would soon learn this was a woman with some thought-provoking and spiritually-rich convictions.

It was evident this was one of the few times Constance had ever spoken in public in her life. She wasn't ineffective, but she was clearly nervous. There was a shaky tone to her voice, and it was obvious she felt a little awkward . The attorneys and the board members had been through stuff like this thousands of times. There was a definite contrast between their delivery and Constance's testimony. Despite that, she never hesitated as she told her story to the board.

Constance introduced herself and told the board she still lived in Rockford. Joshua Sachs asked her if she was the mother of Albert Pearson, who was killed by Raymond Lee Stewart. She immediately corrected him.

"I am still the mother of Albert Pearson," she stated.

"Of course, of course," acknowledged Sachs.

For a second, Joshua Sachs appeared to be embarrassed by the slip-up, but the exchange definitely was an attention-getter.

People who were slumped down in their chairs straightened up, and all eyes and ears were on Constance Mitchell. Sachs proceeded and asked her to make her statement to the board.

Constance began telling her story in a polite style. She was careful to always address the board with the appropriate courtesy. She explained she was a very religious woman who believed Albert's spirit was always with her. What Ray Stewart did to her was terrible, but, despite that, she thought it was only the place of God to take a human being's life.

"The reason I am here is that I do not believe in the death penalty. I believe only God has the right to take somebody's life. I am not here to say this man didn't do a horrible thing, because he did. He hurt a lot of people. He hurt me. But, I forgave him and I believe with all my heart that my son is in heaven. My son's spirit is all around me. I carry him in my heart," she said.

I was stunned by her comments. The murder of Albert Pearson was a brutal and senseless crime. This was a kid whose existence was violently cut short at the prime of his life. Ray Stewart took a child from this mother, and now she was begging the board to spare the killer's life. This was unusual for a clemency hearing. It clearly wandered from the traditional script. I was on the edge of my seat as she continued to tell the board how she came to this position and why they should save Raymond Lee Stewart.

It took a few minutes for Constance to get warmed up, but she was starting to establish a nice rhythm. I think after the first couple of sentences, she had shaken her nerves and was gaining confidence. The apprehension in her voice was fading. Her words were getting louder and clearer.

Constance began to talk about grieving. She told the board she decided she was not going to waste the rest of her life grieving over her dead son. That is not what God wanted. Grieving was important to her, but it had its time and its place. Living also had to have its time and place.

She explained, "Your child is a part of you, and if someone

takes that part from you, you grieve and then you search within yourself to find the part that was missing so you can go on with your life. After my grieving period, I had to dig down, way down in my soul, to find the peace that was missing."

This woman was the best witness that Ray Stewart had on his side. Her credibility was indisputable. She was a sweet, aging lady who had lost her son. Her sincerity was evident from the beginning of her statement. She was devasted by the murder, but she didn't let that destroy her. She was still alive. Constance had thought a lot about this issue, and she was going to make others in that room think about it, too. Suddenly, this wasn't cut and dry.

The room quickly reacted to Constance's words. This was the story of the day. Photographers were sent to the front of the room to get photos of her talking. Ink pens were flying across reporter's notepads. Tape recorders that had been off, were quickly turned on. The board members listened carefully as Mitchell continued to deliver her statement.

Apparently, overwhelming curiosity about Ray's mother had created this scenario. For years, Constance had wondered what she was like and how she was coping. She knew it had to be hard being the mother of the most hated man in Rockford.

Friday, November 6, 1993

The Raymond Lee Stewart story found its way back into the headlines. The Rockford Salvation Army was sponsoring an event that showcased artwork by Illinois prisoners. The exhibit included two paintings by Stewart. The community outrage was enormous. The Salvation Army got hundreds of calls. It was the hot topic of the week for the local talk radio station. Protesters promised to picket the exhibit. The organizers ended up pulling the paintings. During that time, Constance had heard Ray's mother, Willa Mae Stewart, was being harassed and that upset her. She decided to draft a letter to the Rockford Register Star. The letter was a declaration of love for mother-hood.

"I knew I had to forgive him because no one had ever mentioned his mother, and I had sympathy. I am in love with all mothers. I had heard she was a good person. So, I wrote the newspaper a letter wondering why no one had mentioned his mother because I knew she had to be in as much pain as I was in, or more. She had to be suffering. But for the grace of God, go I. It could have been one of my sons, and I would want someone to have mercy on him. I thought if I forgave him, a little bit of that hurt would go away. Not a lot of it, but just a little," she said.

It was at this moment I realized what a remarkable woman Constance Mitchell is. I couldn't help but think of my own mother. How would she cope with the grief if I were murdered? How would she cope with the guilt if I were a murderer? It takes a powerful speaker to get an audience thinking about their own lives. This world is a self-centered place. The genius of Constance is that she knows she isn't the only person on this earth. She has a rare talent for truly being able to see the souls of other people without discrimination. For most, losing a loved one to a killer would never trigger thoughts about what the mother of the murderer was going through. Not to mention, sympathy. This was truly a woman of love. When I ditched work to go this clemency hearing, I didn't know what I was going to get out of it. It was beyond being interesting; it was enlightening.

The newspaper letter ended up being more than just a statement. It was a gateway to the killer. Ray Stewart saw the article and decided to contact Mitchell. The prison phone system is computerized, and it takes two weeks for an Illinois prisoner to get a phone number into the system. Stewart submitted Mitchell's name, and, two weeks later, he called her at home. It was a phone call to say thanks.

"Someone showed him that clipping. A mother of a man who was in prison took it. He called me. He said he was pleased with what I had said about his mother, and no one had forgiven him. I told him, I forgave him. He never denied what he had done. He told me he had done it, and he was sorry about it. He said, 'Mrs. Mitchell, I do not want to hurt you. I didn't mean to hurt Albert, and I am very sorry.' I told him his apology was accepted."

This was the first of many phone calls. Ray told Constance it felt good to talk to her, and she extended him the option of calling her whenever he felt like he needed to talk. She promised Ray she would always accept the collect call charges. For years, they wrote each other and talked on the phone. They never met face to face, and when you talk to Constance, she makes it clear she was not friends with this man. She did this because it helped Raymond Lee Stewart, who, to her, was a fellow human being who just happened to have murdered her son. More than that, she did it to ease some of the pain of Ray's mother.

Forgiving Ray Stewart is a difficult concept to grasp. Albert Pearson did not deserve to die. None of the victims deserved to die. This was either a remarkable feat of a great woman or a huge mistake by a bleeding heart. Regardless of one's perception, it would have been hard to take on Constance Mitchell. It would be like picking a fight with the Pope. The board members never interrupted her or asked her any questions while she talked. This spiritual woman doesn't think in the same terms as most of society. Her thought processes are different. She has a different value system. God is the only judge in her eyes. The question is, is she right when she says everyone has a soul and deserves forgiveness, or are there some crimes and sins that cross a threshold of humanity that mortals simply cannot be expected to tolerate?

Constance continued by telling the board her impressions of the Ray Stewart she came to know. This was a changed man, she said. He wasn't like the old Ray Stewart who gunned down six people in one week. He wasn't like the old Ray Stewart who used to taunt family members during his trials.

She explained, "I didn't go to any of the trials because I didn't want to see any of my son's bloody clothes. I would see it on television and see how Ray was acting out, but now it seems he has mellowed and he has softened. When he talks to me, he talks with respect. He respects me. When he writes me, if you didn't know this man had done all these things, you wouldn't believe it. I just believe God didn't put us here to judge anybody. I think He is the one that is supposed to take our life away, and I just never believed in the death penalty, and I would like to see this man get the rest of his life in prison without parole."

This was the second good guy speech of the day about this killer. It was strange hearing words like decent and good in the same sentence as Raymond Lee Stewart. The anti-death penalty people were doing a good job presenting their case. I never would have guessed they would have such compelling witnesses. It would have been impossible for them to convince me that Ray Stewart was a great guy, but they certainly put a human face on the man whose date with death was less than a week away.

Constance Mitchell didn't come to this hearing to explain why this man did what he did, but she did say the reason the Ray Stewarts of this world exist is because of a lack of role models in our society. She explained there are two roads in life: the wide, crooked road and the straight and narrow road. Ray Stewart got on the wide, crooked road and, judging from his family life, Constance believed there weren't any role models to push him back onto the straight and narrow. She speculated that if there had been a good role model in his life, he might not have ended up where he did.

The last point Constance tried to get across was that taking life belonged to God and no one else. This was something she firmly believed in her heart before her life was touched by the cold hand of violence. The fact that she buried her murdered son didn't change her convictions. There was an intense exchange of eye contact between Constance and the board as she made her final statements.

"I am just asking you to really give it some thought about

this man. I don't believe in anybody getting the death penalty. I think someone, one of these days, is going to have to answer for it because all of us are going to be judged and all of us have done things we shouldn't have done, and we have wanted God to forgive us. I think we need to be about forgiving, instead of condemning people," she concluded.

Constance thanked the board for listening to her, stood up and started making her way towards her seat. When she sat down, Jennifer Bishop Jones came over to embrace her and congratulate her on doing a good job. I didn't run into Constance that afternoon, but Jennifer told me they were planning some rallies in Chicago over the weekend and that Constance was going to be speaking at them. This was something I could easily get a crew for, so I scribbled a reminder in my notebook and asked Jennifer to call me with the details.

Raymond Lee Stewart and Constance Mitchell were an unlikely pair. It is hard to imagine their phone conversations. Regardless of whether you agreed with what Constance believed and said, it was impossible to write her off. Her picture was the one that appeared in all the newspapers the next day. She has a remarkable story, but more than that, she is a remarkable person. It is rare to find people who can force you to really think about man's place in God's world. Those subjects seem to be unfashionable in today's culture. Constance is a rare disciple.

CHAPTER 7

"Children have never been good at listening to their elders, but they never fail to imitate them."
                                    —*James Baldwin*

Wednesday, January 20, 1982

Raymond Lee Stewart was facing sentencing for the murders of Willie Fredd and Albert Pearson. The State's Attorney of Winnebago County was seeking the death penalty, so there had to be a sentence hearing, where the jury would listen to arguments on both sides and make a sentence recommendation to the judge. Earlier in the week, it took the same jury a couple of hours to find Stewart guilty of the double homicide. Now, they had to decide if he should die for the crime.

Tina Stewart was on the stand, testifying on behalf of her older brother. Throughout the trial, Ray Stewart made a nasty reputation for himself by acting out and being a smart ass. Now, he was no longer joking. He was in tears. His sister was outlining the abuse that Raymond suffered at the hands of their father, Raymond Lee Miller. She said her father was the one who should be on trial. Miller was sitting in the front row and reportedly showed no emotion. Tina was one of many family members who begged the jury to spare Ray Stewart's life. It took those jurors close to six hours to decide otherwise.

The reports of a traumatic upbringing didn't completely come out of left field, but the exact details of Raymond Lee Stewart's family life were really a mystery until this clemency hearing. During the sentencing phase of Stewart's court proceedings, some family members did testify about rampant abuse in the household. However, Stewart's early attorneys never attempted to hit hard on the dysfunctional family concept. When Joshua Sachs took over Ray's case in 1988, he immediately started preparing arguments that focused on abusive childhood conditions. In several appeals, Sachs argued that Stewart's juries did not have enough information about the horrible abuse that took place while his client was growing up. Until that point, very little was said about Stewart's childhood.

There were a lot of unanswered questions. What kind of abuse did Ray suffer? Could it have been bad enough to turn him into a psychopathic killer? What happened to other family members who suffered this alleged abuse? Did people around Ray know that something at home was affecting his behavior? Not all of these questions would be answered by the end of the day, but there would certainly be a clearer picture after Faith Crocker finished her testimony.

Faith is an attractive woman; tall, thin, smooth-skinned. Though 36, she looked younger. She was wearing a tight dress that fit her persona well. It was just a little bit longer than a mini-skirt, and it was black with what looked like some sort of animal print as a trim. The persona and the dress might have been a little too wild for the hallowed halls of the State Capital Building. She was wearing a considerable amount of make-up. Her hair was straight and came down just below her shoulders.

There was a lengthy whispering exchange going on between Crocker and Sachs, and finally Chairman Williams intervened to break it up. Sachs explained to the board that Faith had a diary she wanted to refer to and asked the chairman if that would be okay. Williams explained that witnesses were allowed to refer to anything they wished.

Sachs handled this witness differently than the first two. He was asking her questions and coaching her along. He began by introducing Faith to the board. He asked her name, age, relationship to the inmate, city of residence and so on. At one point, the proceeding was interrupted and Crocker was asked to speak more directly into the microphone. Sachs continued to quiz Faith on basic information. He asked if she had the same father as Ray Lee Stewart. She did. It was revealed that Raymond Lee Miller was alive and living in a nursing home in Rockford. He explained to her that the board was not going to set a time limit for her, but they were asking all of the speakers to try and be precise. He told her to take as much time as she needed. Finally, he asked her to tell the board what she thought they needed to know.

Faith started by going back to the last day that she remembered Ray in her childhood. It was an historically sad day for the country. She said it was a day like many others in the Miller-Stewart household; a day that was filled with violence.

"The last I remember of Ray was the day Martin Luther King died and daddy said nobody leaves the house. And, Ray left the house. In my childhood, Ray called me tattletell Faith. I told that Ray left the house. When he got back to the house, daddy was waiting on him. Ray came through the door and they got to fighting in the kitchen and daddy picked him up and threw him off into the trash can. He busted Ray's lip and his nose. There was blood all over Ray. He picked him up out of the trash can, threw him against the wall and pushed him out the door. At the same time, he told him never to come back," she said.

The tone of Faith's voice was somber as she relived the event for the board members. It appeared she had told this story before, and was comfortable talking about it. Still, the details were sad. The image of a father continuing to beat his blood-soaked son and finally throwing him out of the family home forever is a terrifying one.

Sachs asked Crocker how old Ray was when this episode occurred. She said fourteen. It was probably an honest mistake by Faith. Ray was born on January 21, 1952. Martin Luther King was assassinated on April 4, 1968. Ray would have been sixteen years old. This would be brought up later in the hearing, but it didn't really have an impact on the content of Faith's testimony.

Faith continued by explaining how her father singled Ray out. Ray was always trying to break up fights between his dad and his mom, and often ended up becoming the victim as a result. Ray suffered years of abuse, and he suffered as he had to watch the ones he loved get abused.

She explained, "Daddy just hated Ray. Out of all twelve of us, he hated Ray the most, because he would always stop him from jumping on mommy all the time. Ray always protected mommy, period. Another incident I remember, daddy was jumping on mommy, he was knocking her down the stairs and whipping her. I heard her hit the floor, then she was yelling, 'Ray, Ray come take me to the hospital. I think my arms and my legs are broke.' She was just laying down on the floor, whining like a puppy and yelling out all kinds of yells. Ray ran and got help."

This was another good guy speech about Raymond Lee Stewart, the third of the day. It was peculiar to picture this notorious serial killer frantically running to get help for his injured mother. I had been listening to Ray Stewart supporters now for close to an hour, and it was still awkward to hear nice things being said about this man. If anything, this speaks to how frightening the image of Ray Lee is to people who grew up around these crimes.

Faith was still under control, but she was beginning to become unraveled. Her voice was getting more than a little shaky. The speed of her speech was slowly increasing. This was emotional stuff. Regardless of how many times abuse victims confront demons like these, it still hurts to talk about them. This was a public setting and her brother's life was on the line; she was starting to cave under the pressure.

Joshua Sachs appeared concerned as his witness continued to testify. Faith said she was always nervous when her father was around. She described Raymond Lee Miller as a complete tyrant, causing everyone in the house to always be on edge. She began talking about a beating she suffered which left her scarred emotionally and physically.

"Daddy was just terrible, He had our household scared of him. I lived in fear, constantly, on a daily basis. You mentioned daddy, uh-uh. I had tears in my eyes every single day. We would always be scared half to death of him, because, you know, he was shell-shocked, schizo and just drunk every single day. He used to always take and beat us with extension cords all the time. I couldn't have been more than five at the time, and he was whipping me real hard with extension cords one day, and I have the mark that is showing in a horseshoe shape right here on my arm," she said, while rolling up her dress sleeve to show the mark.

Faith held up her arm to show the board members the scar that her father caused. Only about half of the board members looked like they were straining to see it. It was a tactic that demonstrated how out of place Faith was in this setting. She was desperately trying to offer the board some tangible evidence of her father's brutality, which she says may have been to blame for her brother's behavior.

She continued, "When he got done whipping me that day, it was red, blue, green and had all kinds of puss coming out of it. I went running into mommy's room, and mommy was laying down on the bed, and I said, 'Mommy, mommy look what daddy did.' I remember showing it to her, and she jumped up, and they tore the whole house up fighting. Daddy is the one who should be in that electric chair, period. That is the bottom line. I know he wasn't the one who physically pulled the trigger or anything like that, but it was him totally."

This was starting to get ugly. Faith was focusing on the abuse she suffered, and it appeared she was about to have a breakdown in front of the audience and the board members. The people in the room were difficult to read. There were people who were obviously compelled by the testimony, and there were people who were obviously not impressed or interested in anything Faith had to say. It looked like some of the folks were having a hard time following the story. Faith was quickly jumping from one incident to another and her emotions were all over the place; one second she would be crying and the next she would be laughing. Photographers were not as interested in her as they were in Constance Mitchell, but occasionally the room was lit up by the glow of a flashbulb.

Stories of sexual abuse by parents against their children is more common these days, but they are never easy to hear. Faith continued by explaining to the board that her father was always trying to get away with some sort of perversion against her and her sisters. He used to take them off to cheap hotels and fondle them and sometimes rape them, according to Faith. She said she knows at least two of her sisters were raped. She never was. However, she made it clear her father did a lot of things that dads aren't suppose to do to their little girls.

"He was awful nasty and dirty. He always messed with each and every one of us girls in the house. He was just always after me sexually, in every type of way. He was climbing in each and every one of our beds at night. Every day mommy was in there trying to whip him out of our rooms. I remember one day, he got in my bed and he took his thing out. He said, 'Let it lay on you, let it lay on you.' The next thing you know, he ejaculated. I was a kid and I didn't know what was going on, but he ejaculated all in between my thighs and when he got up, he took a rag and washed it off."

Faith was crying. This was sickening stuff. Everyone was now listening and looking at Faith. It would have been impossible for her to make this up. The details were too vivid and too revolting.

Sachs intervened and attempted to steer Faith back to stories about Ray Stewart. He asked her to tell the board more about her father's relationship with her brother. Sachs was handling Faith with kid gloves and appeared nervous about her shaky demeanor.

Faith was able to regain some composure and started talking

about what life was like after her brother was kicked out of the house. She said Ray would frequently visit the house, behind their dad's back, and check on the family. He was always asking about his mother, according to Faith. He wanted to know if their father was still beating her. Faith said she loved Ray because he always looked out for her. She said that out of all her brothers and sisters, Ray was her favorite.

It was not unusual to see squad cars with flashing lights parked outside the home. Police made frequent visits to the house, according to Faith. After Ray was gone, the anger in the house remained. Faith said her father kept throwing violent tantrums and continued to abuse the children. It especially angered her when her dad would beat up her younger brothers. It further angered her when the cops would show up, diffuse the situation, and then drive away.

She explained, "I got a brother that he (Faith's dad) just used to smack so hard in the face as a kid. He just kept beating him, and I just cried. He really made me so mad as a little girl looking at him in my childhood; just smacking my brother around like that. The police were called to the house three times and Pee-Wee, his name is William but we called him Pee-Wee, was totally knocked out and bloody each time the police came to the house. I was always wondering why nobody would stop him regardless of any and everything."

Why wasn't anything done? It was a good question. Cops always say the calls they hate the most are the domestic disputes. They always say they feel powerless. It is not realistic to think a police officer can arrive at a household and always make accurate judgment calls as to how bad the abuse in the house really is. However, there comes a time when someone in the system has to stand up and demand that something be done. Of course, in retrospect everything is clearer. It is unfair to suggest that such action might have changed the course of the Raymond Lee Stewart story; however, it is obvious just by listening to this damaged woman speak, that something should have been done.

Faith finally came unglued. She started babbling about how her drunk dad used to drive like a maniac all over town. In the beginning, she was choosing her words carefully. Now, she was flying through her sentences, and it seemed like she was in a different world. It was obvious she had lost control. Finally, Chairman Williams interrupted her and told her that in his opinion they had a fair idea of what the family life was like. Sachs nodded in agreement. They both thanked Faith for speaking, and she got up and returned to her seat next to her mother.

It was the right move to cut her off. It was important to keep things moving, but more than that, the hearing was on the verge of becoming a circus. She talked for fourteen minutes. I got a sense that in a couple more minutes, she might have completely snapped. Sachs seemed relieved after the chairman stopped her testimony. She had successfully demonstrated to the board what they needed to know, and it was time to move on.

Despite being cut short, I think Crocker was effective at painting a clear picture of what growing up was like for Ray Stewart. When I talked to her later, she regretted she wasn't allowed the time to make one crucial point that never came up in the rest of the hearing. It seems that when Ray was very young, he suffered some sort of head injury in a car accident. Faith noticed Ray's behavior was different after this accident. According to her, this is when Ray began to act "strange." Faith couldn't say for sure that the accident had anything to do with the downward turn Ray's life took as adult, but she did note to me, "He was never the same after that accident."

There were still a lot unanswered questions. Later in the afternoon, it would be revealed that none of Ray's other siblings had serious problems with the law. If the conditions were so abusive and so terrible in that household that it forced Ray Stewart into a life of violent crime, how did his brothers and sisters escape the same fate? The question about Ray's own family was never addressed. Throughout the day there was no mention of Tina Brooks. She is the mother of Ray's daughter. Apparently, Ray wanted to settle down and raise a family with this woman. Days before the shooting spree, Brooks had the child without telling Ray and indicated she didn't want anything to do with him. There was also no evidence of abuse and neglect from sources outside the family. No counselors testified about any encounters they might have had with Ray Stewart. No teachers were there to describe his behavior during his school years.

Faith's testimony did shed some light on the story. Obviously, her story was slanted and opinionated. She had a clear agenda: to try and help save her brother's life. For Raymond Lee Stewart, the mitigating circumstances defense might have come too late to do him any good. If this information would have come out earlier, he might have had a decent appeal for mercy. It looks like there were some troubling conditions under which this man grew up. It didn't excuse the crimes, but it is conceivable that it might have had some bearing on how society dealt with the criminal. In the end, Stewart probably played this card a little too late. It looked too much like a last ditch effort by a man trying to avoid his punishment. If anything, Faith Crocker allowed us to peek into some of the seeds that yielded this killer. The stories she told were disgusting, but much more than her words, her frenzied demeanor and her trembling voice were indisputable evidence that some crazy and unjust things did occur in that household.

CHAPTER 8

"In the eye of its mother, every beetle is a gazelle."
—*Moroccan Proverb*

Willa Mae Stewart is the mother of the murdering monster that brought all of these people together. This is the mother of the son who took Albert's human life from Constance. She was quietly sitting in the fourth row. Joshua Sachs asked the board if he could have a moment to check on his next witness. He got up and walked over to the row where Willa Mae was sitting, knelt down to her and started whispering. I couldn't hear what they were saying, but it appeared as if Sachs was trying to figure out if she was up to the task of talking to the board. After about a minute, she slowly got up and Sachs helped her walk over to the speaker's table. Finally, he leaned over and announced his witness.

The room was filled with talking after Sachs stated that Willa Mae would be testifying. Through the years, reporters were never able to get access to this woman. Once again, the pens were poised and reporters went on alert, waiting to hear what she had to say.

Willa Mae is an older woman. You could tell she had been through a lot. She had a tired, worn-out look about her. She was wearing a new dress that didn't look natural on her. It was obvious she was uncomfortable as she shifted around in the small wooden chair next to the attorney.

Sachs started by asking her to state her name. She did, but it was too hard to hear, and Chairman Williams asked her to speak louder and more directly into the microphone. Sachs asked her if she was the mother of Raymond Lee Stewart. She said, "Yes," this time into the microphone and everyone in the room could hear her. Willa Mae had a soft, but firm voice. Her nervousness came through in her words. Talking to the board in front of this audience was definitely not going to be a high point in her life, but I imagine she felt an obligation to say something on behalf of her condemned son.

Sachs asked, "Is there anything about your son that you could tell the board? Anything that you think the board should know?"

Willa Mae took a deep breath. It looked like she was thinking hard and struggling to find the words she wanted to say. What could she say? Her son had killed six innocent people. Those families were in the audience. Her daughter had just finished testifying about graphic abuse in the household. She needed to show the board that even though Ray Lee did horrible things, he was still loved. That is all she could do.

"Well, um, Ray Lee was a good boy. I never had no trouble out of Ray in no kind of way. Anywhere I needed to go, he would take me. His daddy did, I remember, whip him two times. But, he ran away. So, after then, he would still come back and visit me and see if there was anything he could do," she said, and then she suddenly stopped and looked as if she had lost her place.

There was a newspaper photographer boldly set-up on the floor in front of the Review Board. He was snapping several pictures of the witness. The chairman looked confused as to why Willa Mae had suddenly stopped. He asked her if the cameras were bothering her. She shook her head and said, "No." The photographer continued to take photos as she finished her statement.

"He never laid a hand on me or harmed me in no kind of way. I love him," she said.

She stopped suddenly again. Joshua Sachs turned his head to look at her. He was straining to pick up on her non-verbal communication. This went on for a few seconds. Finally, he realized she was done. That was all she was going to say. In a somber tone, he thanked her for speaking.

Willa Mae was standing up and starting to return to her seat when to everyone's surprise, a board member asked her a question.

"Did Ray ever have any trouble in school? Was he kicked out of school?" asked board member Barbara Hubbard.

This seemed a little strange. No one had asked the first two witnesses any questions, so this was the first question of the day. Here was a woman who had obviously said what she came to the hearing to say: she loved her son. The witness was unmistakably uncomfortable and eager to return to her seat. Furthermore, the case was a slam dunk. It was unlikely they were going to spend too much time debating their recommendation to the Governor. Now, the board wanted to pry into the petitioner's scholastic records? I sensed a couple of the board members concurred with my assessment as they rolled their eyes after Hubbard asked the question. Willa Mae sat back down and took a second to think, before answering.

"Not as I know of," she replied.

The truth is that Ray wasn't much of a student during his childhood, according to the clemency petition that Sachs had filed. He went to school in Chester, Pennsylvania, until his family moved to the South Beloit area in 1967. He apparently was not fond of traditional schooling and enrolled in an apprentice program for students who wanted to learn how to cook and become chefs. When that fell through, he started going to South Beloit High School. In the middle of his freshman year, he dropped out. He tried to return to school later that month, but after one week, he ended up quitting for good.

There were no other questions from the board, so Willa Mae got up again and returned to her seat. People in the room seemed restless. It was getting close to the point where a break was needed. After Willa Mae was finished, several wire service reporters got up and left the room. I could imagine being back in the newsroom and seeing the stories cross the wires. I was glad I came to the hearing and was taking in the action as it was happening, instead of reading about it on my office computer.

The only real issue to come out of this testimony was Willa Mae's contention that the household was not plagued with abuse. Maybe she hadn't come to grips with what had happened. It is not unusual for abuse victims to forget the past. Bad memories can be a painful thing. Bad memories can lead to bad memories. Maybe Faith Crocker was exaggerating the truth in an effort to help her brother's cause. The real truth behind Ray's childhood will probably never be known. Regardless, nothing was going to erase the fact that something snapped in this young man's mind, and he killed six people.

It is an understatement to say that Willa Mae's testimony was short. It lasted only a couple of minutes. There were only eight sentences; that is all she had to say about her son at the hearing to decide his fate. There probably were some heavy guilt issues she had to deal with through the years, and maybe justifiably so. There wasn't much more she could have said. It could be perceived as being short and sweet. It could also be perceived as explicative.

Every killer is still some mother's son. The bond between mother and son is a strong one. No matter what, Willa Mae did love Ray. After talking to Ray, I can safely say he loved her back.

CHAPTER 9

"Hear thou in Heaven thy dwelling place and when thou hearest, forgive."

—*Moroccan Proverb*

There was a little black ball that barely covered the microphone at the speaker's table. Throughout the course of the day, the pesky ball kept hopping off the mike. Several times the action in the room came to a screeching halt, and participants were asked to look for the tiny missing piece of equipment. As Pastor Shelly Sullivan took his place, he accidentally knocked the ball off, and it went flying onto the floor of the room. The chairman quickly mentioned it and the search began. Finally, Sachs spotted it on the floor. He walked over, picked it up and secured it back onto the microphone. It seemed like such a trivial, ordinary thing to be happening at a hearing to decide life and death; like people eating and chatting after a funeral.

Sullivan was one of two religious leaders Sachs was going to call. He was from the Christian Faith Center in Wilmington, Illinois. The other man of the cloth would be a priest representing the Roman Catholic Archdiocese. These were the last two witnesses that Sachs was going to present.

Shelly Sullivan is an average size man. He was wearing a modest suit with a wide tie. His hair was short and in a neat, feathered style. He was wearing glasses. It wasn't hard to tell that he was a pastor. He had a serene sort of look to him. I imagine many people in the room typecast him in their minds the same way I did; this was prob-

79

ably some liberal Christian-type who was morally opposed to capital punishment. However, that impression was incorrect. Sullivan quickly established himself as a complicated man, who understood, and had compassion for, the many aspects surrounding the issue before this board. It was a series of odd events that brought him to this hearing. He had insights into the Stewart case that are interesting and significant.

The pastor had known Ray Stewart for three months. In that time, they had several lengthy conversations about spirituality and peace. Sullivan says he contacted Ray Stewart because the sister of one of the Beloit victims asked him to make sure the killer was at peace with God and with himself. He refused to identify the family member who contacted him. He did say he really didn't know the person. She had contacted him because she had heard good things about his ministry, which is geographically close to the prison in Pontiac. Sullivan informed Stewart he wanted to visit him. As soon as Stewart learned he was doing this on behalf of a victim's family member, he readily agreed. After several conversations with Stewart, the pastor did decide Stewart's life was worth saving. However, he wanted to make it clear to everyone in the room that it wasn't an automatic conclusion.

"I find him to very much have peace with God. I also found something that was quite surprising to me; the amount of peace he has with himself. I do an extensive amount of counseling. I look for certain things and one of the things you have to do in order to have peace within yourself is to take full responsibility for actions or deeds. I found that to be very, very present in Raymond. I am challenged today because I have been a supporter of capital punishment, so I am challenged in my own belief system. But, this man really impressed me personally," said Sullivan.

This witness was more interesting than I thought he was going to be. The fact that he was a man of God who was for capital punishment, but thought Ray Stewart deserved clemency, made his case a little more credible. This wasn't some Jesus freak who was preaching love and passivity in all cases. It was someone who had done a lot of thinking about the specific issue at hand: whether the state should execute Ray Stewart for his crimes. In the end, he was persuaded by the words of Ray Stewart.

Shelly Sullivan had rare insights into the case. He came to know Ray Stewart, the way he was in 1996. He started to tell stories about how Ray refused to blame the murder spree on his childhood. The pastor noted that during his time in prison, Ray had thoroughly thought about his actions and the impact they had. It was obvious the Ray Lee Stewart whom Shelley Sullivan was describing was not a stupid man. Rather, this Ray Lee Stewart was a man who had an almost panoramic perspective about his crimes.

Sullivan explained, "One of the things he said has really stuck in my mind, and I've even transferred it to my congregation. He stated it is impossible for a person to perform an act or a deed and to just be isolated to that one incident. He has just simply been overwhelmed and amazed that the acts he performed have affected hundreds and even more hundreds of lives, and the ripple effect just continues to grow. He definitely feels very sorrowful for that. I would surmise he is very repentant for his actions. He regrets the pain deeply."

This was a prelude to the remainder of the afternoon. Ray Stewart's actions had touched many lives. There truly is a "ripple effect" in this case. Many of the family members of the victims would testify that when Ray killed their loved ones, he basically killed them too. There are siblings of the victims who will not have children because they vividly remember what their parents went through when Ray murdered their child, and they want to insure that such a morbid misfortune never happens to them. Several people say the community of Rockford was forever changed after the Ray Lee Stewart savagery. People became more cautious and less trusting. Ray was right on the money when he explained this domino effect to Sullivan. His murderous rampage affected thousands of lives.

It seemed like the board members were anxious to take some shots at Sullivan. There might be some unwritten rule that you can't go after family members, but there was no such rule about religious leaders. Maybe the board members were taking advantage of an opportunity to get their name in the transcript. Maybe they felt like they should justify their existence. They really put Sullivan through the ringer. He spent about ten minutes answering questions from the board. They asked him if he knew anything about his bad conduct in prison. Sullivan knew very little. They wanted to know if Stewart had asked him to talk to the board. The pastor said no. They asked several questions he had already answered during his original testimony. It was almost like they didn't listen to him until the question and answer session came around. Finally, one of the board members nailed the question I wanted to ask Sullivan.

"Pastor, maybe you should enlighten me. You say that in your conversations, he indicates he has no excuse for his actions, that he has taken full responsibilities for his deeds, and he is remorseful for hurting so many people. Yet, you testify he is at peace with himself. That seems to be a conflict in my way of thinking. Can you explain that to me?" asked board member Jim Donohue.

Sullivan paused for a second and then replied, "Well, it would be in my way (of thinking) as well. In his words, he said, 'I have done all I can do to correct what I have done, but I can't erase it. I have accepted full responsibility. I am accountable for everything.' I think peace with himself is a way of saying, 'I can't undo anything, but I am regretful and sorry for what I have done and in that sense I am at peace because, if there is something I can do and am unwilling to do it, I would not be at peace with myself.' "

"Does he seem to be in agony?" replied Donohue.

"Oh yes, yes. He is in much agony in that sense. My opinion is that it bothers him every day what he has done. When he mentions peace, now, he says, 'There is nothing I can do about it.' In his words now, 'If I can ease their pain in anyway, even up to the very last day, I would be grateful for the opportunity to do that,' " answered Sullivan.

This was a sentiment that Jennifer Bishop Jones touched on earlier. According to both witnesses, Stewart was obsessed with judging his actions now by the impact they would have on the families of the victims. From all indications, he embraced all the family members who approached him during his last few years of incarceration. Ultimately, the only thing most of the family members wanted was for him to die. He caused these people a great deal of agony and now he was asking for an opportunity to ease their pain? The only thing they wanted was for his execution to come sooner and be more painful. It is hard to blame them. It seems like a natural sentiment. This man gunned down their innocent loved ones for no real reason, laughed at them during the trials, used every known appeal to get out of his sentence, and even insinuated threats to them from prison.

Sullivan's testimony did humanize this killer. It was an interesting revelation that Ray Stewart understood he did terrible things, regretted them and wanted to erase them, but knew he couldn't. This was as close as Stewart came to testifying at the hearing. Several times during his testimony, Sullivan referred to Stewart's own words. He had inadvertently taken on the role of Stewart's spokesperson at this hearing. I don't think anybody planned it that way, but that is the way it came out. Stewart could have issued a written or videotaped statement to the board, but he chose not to.

On the night of the execution, Shelly Sullivan drove up to the guard's gate at Statesville Prison in Joliet and asked to see Ray Stewart so he could minister to him. He was turned away. Prisoners about to be executed were only allowed to have Department of Corrections approved ministers. After the execution and in light of the incident, the D.O.C. changed the rule so that condemned inmates could have their chosen religious leader at the prison on execution night.

The last witness was a priest from the Archdiocese of

Chicago who didn't have a personal connection to the case. He was sent by the church to represent their long-standing opposition to the death penalty in general. He was a taller man, dressed in a regular suit. His name was Reverend George Brooks. His testimony was brief, and it sounded like he was merely reading from a prepared statement.

"First of all, on behalf of the Illinois Bishops and Cardinal Bernardin, I express deep heartfelt sympathy for the families of the victims. We pray there will be healing and peace for these families. They, however, do believe that healing and peace will not come through the execution of Mr. Stewart," he said.

Joseph Cardinal Bernardin was the most beloved man in Chicago at this time. He was fighting pancreatic cancer, and the entire city was dreading his inevitable death. In November of 1996, he died. Bernardin never shied away from controversy. He made a name for himself by coming out in strong opposition to nuclear weapons. On his death bed, he wrote to the U.S. Supreme Court, encouraging them to make physician-assisted suicide illegal. He was the kind of leader who could make you think twice about the issues of the day. Before it was all over, he would find his way even further into the Ray Stewart story.

At the time of the hearing, Bernardin was receiving the Presidential Medal of Freedom in Washington D.C. This is one of the highest honors that an American can receive. Brooks explained that the D.C. trip caused a little bit of confusion in the Chicago Archdiocese office. He said Bernardin wanted to present the board with a letter asking them to spare Stewart's life. There was a mix-up, and the letter wasn't quite ready.

"There is a letter on his desk, that he has approved, but hasn't signed. He will be back in Chicago on Friday, and will sign the letter and will be faxing it to the Governor's office. In that letter, on his behalf and on behalf of all the Illinois bishops, I respectfully request there be clemency and that Mr.

Stewart have life in prison, and the death penalty not be imposed."

I didn't get any sort of sense of what Rev. Brooks was all about. He seemed to simply be running errands on behalf of his employer. He looked uncomfortable; he was just going through the motions. Chairman Williams asked him to fax the letter to the board, in addition to the Governor. He promised to do so and got up and took his seat. Joshua Sachs stood up in dramatic courtroom-type fashion and stated that the presentation on behalf of the petitioner was complete.

The religious leaders who testified at the hearing didn't impress me all that much in the grand scheme of that hearing. It was an expected move by the anti-death penalty folks. In the hallway, Jennifer Bishop Jones told me that she believed Cardinal Bernardin was going to be taking a more active role in this proceeding. I didn't think much of the tip at the time. I should have taken her more seriously. It turned out to be some legitimate foreshadowing. In the end, it was the religious leaders that made the Ray Stewart execution the lead story on newscasts across the nation.

CHAPTER 10

"No fewer than three of the Justices with whom I have served have maintained that the death penalty is unconstitutional, even though its use is explicitly contemplated in the Constitution. The Due Process Clause of the Fifth and Fourteenth Amendments says that no person shall be deprived of life without due process of law."
— *U.S. Sup. Court Justice Antonin Scalia*

The office of the Attorney General is responsible for handling the appeals of condemned inmates at the state and federal level. The office is also responsible for representing the state at the clemency hearing. Jim Ryan is the Attorney General of Illinois. He is a controversial man. Before he was elected to the office of Attorney General, he was the State's Attorney for DuPage County. He was in charge when an 11-year-old girl named Jeanne Nicarico was kidnapped, raped and murdered in the Chicago suburb of Naperville in 1983. His office got indictments against Rolando Cruz, Alejandro Hernandez and Stephen Buckley in 1984. In 1987, charges were dropped against Buckley and he was freed. After years of court battles, Cruz and Hernandez were eventually freed in 1995. At the time of this clemency hearing, a special grand jury was deliberating to decide if anyone involved in the Cruz prosecution should be charged with a crime. In December of 1996, the grand jury returned a 47-count indictment against three prosecutors and four sheriff's officers. They were charged with hiding evidence that was favorable to the defendant and manufacturing evidence against him. William Kunkle, a famous Chicago lawyer, was named special prosecutor. The indictments were truly a rarity, as prosecutors almost never face criminal charges for misconduct. Jim Ryan was not indicted.

The Rolando Cruz case is cited by both pro and anti-death penalty activists. Pro-death penalty people say this is an example of how today's appeal system can catch any mistakes made during the initial prosecution. The anti-death penalty advocates point out the death penalty is a punishment that cannot be reversed. They say the Rolando Cruz case is an example of how a person can be sent to death row for a crime he may not have committed. They claim that only by some extraordinary luck was Cruz able to get off death row. In the Ray Stewart case, there was never any question about his guilt. The two cases are completely different. During my interview with Ray Stewart, he criticized Ryan for the way the Attorney General's office handled the clemency hearing. He was upset over some reports that linked him to a prison gang and blamed Ryan, saying he was up to the same tricks he used during the Nicarico case. It was a cheap shot by Stewart who was obviously trying to take advantage of the intense criticism Ryan was under for the Rolando Cruz case. I doubt Ryan spent too much time going over Ray's clemency petition at all. For the most part, Ray Stewart's case was open and shut.

2:20 p.m.

The person who was responsible for handling Ray's clemency petition on behalf of the state was Arlene Anderson. In contrast to Joshua Sachs, Anderson had a very professional look to her. You could tell by the way she carried herself that she was prepared for anything and was highly organized. She fit the bill of the traditional attorney. She had the right hair, the right make-up and was probably wearing the most expensive suit in the room.

The people who were going to testify against Ray Stewart

were asked to stand and take an oath. It was quite a commotion, as a number of people stood up and raised their right hands. There was a significantly higher number of people testifying against Ray, versus the small number of people who testified for him.

After the oath, Arlene began to address the board. She was obviously very confident and knew exactly what she was going to say and what was going to happen. Weeks of fact-finding research went into this presentation. Her tone was precise and she wasted no time getting to the facts of the case. The most difficult thing had to be tracking down all these witnesses so many years after the murders were committed. She stated that once she found them, she had no problem getting them to help her. There were a lot of people who wanted to make sure Ray Stewart got the punishment they thought he deserved.

"There is a rule they teach students in law school, in court class to be exact. You take your victims as you find them. During the past week, that old rule has run through my mind again and again, as I have talked to people who have expressed amazement at the number of witnesses who would be here today, as well as the number of letters we have gotten at the Attorney General's office opposing clemency in this case," she stated.

The board was about to be bombarded with some emotional testimony. Stories of pain and suffering and loss were now on the docket. With six victims, the number of people Ray hurt was high. The victims in this case were usually just mentioned by name and age. Now, they were going to be given faces and personalities by the people who knew them best.

Anderson explained, "The fact is Ray Lee Stewart, during his week long killing spree, happened upon victims who were deeply loved and are now sorely missed by many people. Those victims were sons. They were fathers, husbands, brothers, nephews and friends, whose deaths not only had a devastating effect on them, but on the ones close to those they left behind as well. Many of the people robbed of their loved ones by Ray Stewart are here today and would like the board and Governor Edgar to hear their stories."

The confident attorney outlined her plan of attack for the board. She said Paul Logli, the current State's Attorney for Winnebago County was going to speak first. Ray DuBlanc, the State's Attorney for Rock County, Wisconsin, at the time of the murders, was going to speak last. Inbetween, we were going to hear firsthand accounts of the brutality of these murders by the police officers who investigated them. We were also going to hear heart-wrenching testimony from the family members of Ray's victims. It was going to be an emotional afternoon.

Before continuing, she took a minute to thank someone who helped her out. Gigi Swing is the Victim Assistance Coordinator for the Rockford Police Department. Arlene said that Gigi helped a lot of people make it through the Ray Stewart saga. Arlene explained that during the trials, she not only provided services for the families of the Rockford victims, but also took members of the Wisconsin victims' families under her wing as well. Gigi wasn't at the hearing, but she had helped Arlene track down several of the witnesses who were there and who were going to testify.

Arlene Anderson did a good job representing the state. For the most part, she stayed out of the proceedings and let the witnesses tell their stories. Her opening and closing remarks were very brief. She knew she didn't have to whip up any great metaphors to convince the board members; what her witnesses were going to say would be more than enough. Her opening remarks were less than five minutes long. Afterwards, she quickly called her first witness and the presentation for the people opposed to granting clemency for Raymond Lee Stewart was underway.

CHAPTER 11

"Murder is the most terrible crime there is. Anything less than the death penalty is an insult to the victim and society. It says . . . that we don't value the victim's life enough to punish the killer fully."
—*Mike Royko*

The first witness for Arlene Anderson was Paul Logli. She didn't spend much time setting him up. He is the State's Attorney for Winnebago County. I imagine most people in the room already knew who he was. If they didn't, the fact that he was the elected state's attorney was probably introduction enough. The members of the board knew the office had a lot of power and that this guy had to be a pillar in the community to be the criminal investigation boss for the largest Illinois county outside of the Chicago area. He was wearing a standard business suit, and he quickly took his place at the speaker's table. There were a few grey hairs, but for the most part he was sporting a headful of black, short hair. His expensive wire rim glasses rested on his rather large nose. If I didn't know who he was, I could have easily figured out that he was someone important. He had that politician-type look to him. In a regular courthouse setting, he might have blended in better, but at this hearing he stuck out right away.

Paul Logli is a big player in the Rockford area. There were several times he was rumored to be the Republican's choice to seek office in the local congressional district. He never ran. At first it was rather surprising to see him at the hearing; his involvement in the case was minimal. In 1981, he was in a private practice. Later that year he became an associate judge for Winnebago County. However, he had no direct involvement with the Stewart case. In 1986, he was elected State's Attorney of Winnebago County. By that time, a number of appeals had already been rejected by the State and U.S. Supreme Courts. Stewart did return to the Rockford Public Safety Building in 1987 when the Illinois Supreme Court ordered a hearing to determine if one of Stewart's public defenders, Gary Pumilia, followed proper procedure in conferring with Stewart. The judge ruled that Pumilia did, and Stewart was immediately sent back to death row. Besides that, Logli's role was merely reduced to giving reporters some legal expertise after one of Stewart's Supreme Court appeals was denied. He was often asked to make predictions about when the execution would take place. In the end, it took longer than even he thought.

Logli is in a highly visible position and is often interviewed on the news in Rockford. There were times when he made some controversial moves as the State's Attorney. In 1990, he charged a mother with murder after the woman's baby was born addicted to cocaine and eventually died. The story made national news and even earned Logli a live interview spot on Today.

I took a special interest in what this man had to say. Logli had close to celebrity status in my mind. I don't know him personally, but my parents are friends with him. When I was named one of the Rockford Register Star's Paper Carriers of the Year, Logli was the speaker at the banquet. It must have been a good speech, because I can still remember some of the details. He was really able to relate to the audience of paperboys and girls. Logli said he was an early morning jogger and shared the same perspective we had of watching the world wake up from the night. He also said he enjoyed talking to a group of good kids. Everyday he was handed files about kids who made the wrong choices. He told us it was refreshing to see some youngsters who were making some right choices. He knew his audience, and he handled himself well.

Logli looked comfortable sitting at the chair in front of the microphone. He was the first skilled speaker to address the board. Anderson was smart to lead off with him, as he set a nice tone for her presentation. He was obviously used to the pressure of talking in public and knew exactly what his role was at the hearing.

In typical political fashion, Logli began by dishing out some compliments. He explained he was confident Arlene Anderson and the Attorney General's office were going to do a capable job of representing the people at this hearing. He said the families of the loved ones would be able to represent the tragedy that came with this case and the law enforcement officers would be able to paint an accurate picture of what this man was really like. In a way, he was complimenting all the people who were going to testify and was, at the same time, outlining what was going to happen in the next couple of hours.

The one thing Logli had to clear up was why his office didn't seek another conviction against Stewart for the murder of Kenny Foust. After the first three Illinois convictions, charges against Stewart for the Foust murder were dropped. Logli explained it wasn't because of lack of evidence; it was simply because they had already achieved their goal in the first three cases: two death sentences. He didn't want the board to forget about the Foust murder, though. Logli stated that ballistic evidence demonstrated Stewart was responsible for that victim, too. (During my interview with him, Stewart conceded that he did kill Foust.)

With the formalities out of the way, it was time for Logli to switch gears and turn on some of the emotional afterburners. You could hear his voice shift up a notch as he began to explain how Ray Stewart terrified his community.

"This man, in one week in our community, not only terrorized the families who will appear before you today, but terrorized the entire community. I don't think it is an overstatement to say he terrorized a generation of people in our community. I was speaking this week to a person who was in his twenties who remembers that when this occurred, he was eleven or twelve years old, and he was terrified to leave the house and move about the city," he said.

This was the second time at this hearing that we heard about the sweeping impact of Ray's actions. It is hard to explain to people who didn't live in the area at the time, but this man really made his mark on the psyche of the Rockford-area community. I had a hard time selling this story to the newsroom big shots. They didn't understand the "ripple effect" was already incredibly far-reaching, and it would continue to grow as the execution got closer. Somehow, some way, I knew the execution was going to be a big deal. In the end, I put the station in the perfect position to cover what turned out to be the story of the week.

It was unnerving listening to Logli talk about this man in his twenties and his memories of the killing spree. It could just as easily have been me he was talking about. When I got the fax that said Ray's execution date was in September, it brought everything back to me: the killing spree, the dramatic escape; it all seemed like yesterday. I was only ten years old, but the memories and the fear are very vivid. I can't believe any of the kids in my schoolyard have forgotten about Ray Stewart. For Rockford, his crimes are a legacy.

The real story behind the killing spree is the panic he sent the stateline community into. Logli said it was an unbelievable time in the Rockford area. He explained that even though he was not directly involved at the time of murders, he did feel the impact firsthand.

He said, "I can recall my own experience of altering my route, to come back into Rockford after having been out of town for an evening, not to go through the part of town where these shootings occurred. This man terrorized our community, a generation of people, and that terror did not end until a month later when he was apprehended in another state."

It was a crazy time. Everyone I talk to has similar stories about what they did to stay clear of this unknown murderer's path. There was story after story published in the Rockford Register Star about people acquiring guns, business owners hiring security officers, gas stations closing early and people staying home at night. Police departments from all over the area were bombarded with reports of suspicious people. People were panicking at the drop of a hat. During that time, the community was completely on edge.

Paul was really putting on a show for the board members. He was creating personal, compelling stories. His speech was extremely effective; he was stressing the right words and had a great pace. He had captured everyone's attention. He is a slick guy, able to charm with down-to-earth images, like the one of him driving the long way home during the murders. He was clearly a pro at this. He looked like he was in his natural setting.

"It is hard not to be emotional about this case. I will leave the emotion up to the families. I just want to say, that for fifteen years the defendant's legal arguments and appeals have been uniformly denied. The people of this state overwhelmingly support the death penalty. They have indicated that over and over again by the laws that have been passed by the General Assembly. It might be convenient to consider life without parole in this case, but it would be a very bad indication to the people of this state if that were to be the result here," he said.

It was an ironic statement as Logli passionately declared he was not going to get emotional about this case. The truth is that his entire speech was pretty emotional. He couldn't be effective without being emotional. From the outset, he was punching key words and relating personal stories to this case.

Logli did bring up some general legal issues and thoughts about the capital punishment debate. This was really his role here: to speak on behalf of the residents of Rockford about what they felt was the appropriate punishment for this man. He is the man the city elected to fight criminals in the courtroom. He is the legal representative on behalf of the law-abiding citizens of Winnebago County. Logli needed to spell out where he stood on the death penalty issue, and he needed to put this case into perspective as it related to the state's capital punishment policy.

Logli explained, "This case just begs that questions be asked. If we don't impose the death penalty in this case, then in what case do we impose the death penalty? If we don't do it now, then when? The answer is, I believe, that this case, this defendant, truly deserves the death penalty. After fifteen years of trials, appeals, post-conviction proceedings, and tedious and fair due process, the time is now to put finality and closure to this terrible chapter in our state's history."

This was truly the question at hand, the thing that was really working against Ray Stewart: if not in this case, then in which case? The State of Illinois had already executed men for far less. Would it be fair to let Stewart slide because of some family problems? For Stewart supporters, it was hard to get around the fact that the only way to defend not killing Ray Stewart, was to attack the capital punishment issue altogether. His crimes were too heinous. There were too many victims. He was too guilty. It was too easy for the people who wanted to see this man die by lethal injection to say this case was a textbook example of when the state should implement the death sentence.

Logli thanked the board for listening to him. As he got up, he tugged on the bottom of his suitcoat to straighten it out, and then he connected the buttons in front. He pushed the chair back into the speaker's table, turned around and reclaimed his seat which was two rows behind me. His entire testimony lasted only five minutes. It was short, but effective. It really set up the rest of the afternoon for the all people that were there in opposition to Ray Stewart's clemency petition.

Paul Logli was undoubtedly the best speaker of the day in terms of style and technique. More importantly, he seemed to truly believe what he was saying. There had to be some political factors at stake in the whole Stewart execution proceedings.

If something would have gone wrong, and Stewart's sentence was somehow commuted, there would have been an incredible backlash. It would not have been Logli's fault, but that has never stopped voters from ruining a politician's career. Politics aside, he was able to really come across as a genuine citizen concerned about the conclusion of this case.

Logli was able to intelligently bring out two very important points. The first was that these murders were not just crimes against the victims and their families; they were crimes against a whole community. I can say with absolute certainty that Ray Stewart did terrorize a whole generation. The other point is that if society is going to endorse the death penalty, there probably has never been a stronger candidate than Raymond Lee Stewart. Logli was an important speaker because of where he was placed as well. He came on the heels of several compelling witnesses who testified on Ray's behalf. Logli was able to grab the baton from those people and totally divert the attention of everyone in the room back to the fact that this man was a cold-blooded, vicious killer. Paul Logli's skillful testimony was the beginning of the end for Ray Stewart's fight to stay alive.

CHAPTER 12

"Man is the only animal who laughs and weeps for he is the only animal who knows the difference between what things are and what they ought to be."
—William Hazlitt

He is a large man and was wearing a Rockford Police Department uniform. As he walked up to the microphone, he had an intimidating presence. His uniform was spotless and had obviously been neatly pressed for the hearing. He was wearing one of those police utility-type belts around his waist. His stomach slumped slightly over his pants, but he did look like he was in decent physical shape. His hair and mustache were a black and gray mix. The uniform gave him and his presentation some leverage in the legitimacy department. I wouldn't doubt it if the Attorney General's office had asked him to wear it. Even if this man had been in street clothes, it wouldn't have taken long to mark him as a cop.

His name is Tom Nimmo. He is a thirty-one year veteran of the Rockford Police Department, a sergeant, only a few years away from retirement. Throughout his long tenure, he has investigated hundreds of violent crimes. However, it was right in the middle of his career that he got his biggest case. He is the detective of record for the Stewart murders investigation.

Nimmo is the one name you hear over and over again when you talk to reporters and police officers who were around during the Stewart murders. This was the guy everybody told me to talk to. I smiled when I heard his name and thought to myself how astounding it was that all the players in this story, except one, were right here in this room at the same time; that is, the ones still alive.

Arlene Anderson took a minute to introduce her second witness. She said the sergeant had come to talk about the investigation of Stewart's four Rockford victims. She named all four victims in the introduction. It was a tactic that wasn't accidental, and she continued to repeat their names whenever she would introduce someone to the board. Chairman Williams thanked Nimmo for coming and asked him to proceed.

Nimmo jumped right into his testimony. He only took a minute to explain he was a long-time Rockford police officer and he had investigated these murders fifteen years ago. This was another one of those guys who talked in cop lingo. He referred to every incident by month, day and year. At first, it was like he was reading off a police report. However, police reports don't usually capture the emotions that surround crimes. Before his testimony was over, Nimmo would.

The most famous murder investigation Tom Nimmo would ever handle started on January 27, 1981. That afternoon he was called to Fredd's Grocery to investigate a double homicide. Shootings were rare in Rockford back then, but they did happen from time to time. At the crime scene, law enforcement officials could not have possibly perceived what was going to occur in the next few days. They had no idea what they had on their hands. However, Nimmo pointed out that just by looking at the first crime scene, they knew they were looking for a vicious criminal.

"These murders, ladies and gentlemen, were the result of multiple gunshot wounds. These murders were of innocent individuals, who would have given up whatever contraband this individual wished to take. In Mr. Pearson's case, he was fleeing for his life from the basement of this grocery store. He nearly made it to the front door when he was shot in the back."

This was an atrocious image. When Nimmo described it, you could almost picture the innocent nineteen-year-old running for his life. You could hear the gunshots. You could see Albert Pearson falling to the floor of the store in a spray of blood. This was something the Ray supporters couldn't hide from. For them, it was a very damaging image. Even though this kid's mother had testified on Stewart's behalf, it is hard to expect people to muster up compassion for a man who did this to an innocent teenager.

Nimmo looked nervous and intimidating at the same time. He looked like the macho quarterback delivering the team prayer. This was definitely not his natural setting. However, he knew the case backwards and forwards and that showed. This was a guy who faced thousands of bad guys, and it seemed unlikely he was going to be intimidated by a few Prison Review Board members. It also seemed he sincerely wanted this man to get the death sentence the jury had given to him. There might have been some question in the back of some people's minds, but there wasn't in Nimmo's mind. He had absolutely nothing but disgust for Raymond Lee Stewart.

The gritty details of crime scenes are something police officers rarely discuss outside law enforcement circles. It is an unwritten rule of decorum that police officers don't talk about the specifics of a murder scene. The Stewart murders were repulsive. The crime scenes were gruesome. These victims were shot multiple times at close range. Nimmo was on a mission to make it clear that these were horrendous crimes.

Nimmo explained, "Mr. Kaiser, if you can imagine, was shot so many times that my senior partner at the time, when I commented that the wounds did not bleed, said you will not see that often because he was executed in a manner and was continually shot after he was already dead. He was forced to kneel to this offender and he was shot. Additionally, he had defense wounds in his hands, where he put his hands up, to prevent this type of incident."

This is the worst image in the entire Raymond Lee Stewart story. It is legendary in police circles. This scene has been explained in a number of crime books throughout the years.

The victim was on his knees and the first bullet went through the hand. It was a futile attempt to stop the inevitable from happening. He was shot five times with a .38 caliber handgun. The last two bullet wounds weren't bleeding. The victim's heart had stopped pumping blood. It was as if the gunman wanted to do more than just kill him. He pulled the trigger two more times after Kaiser had to have been visibly dead. This was a seventeen-year-old kid who had absolutely no connection to Ray Stewart. The killer took a small amount of money before leaving the scene, but, even at this stage in the investigation, police were fairly confident they were dealing with a psychotic and not a robber.

The reaction to Nimmo's presentation was mixed. Several audience members were turned off by the violent descriptions he was offering. Some people might have tuned him out simply because he was wearing a police uniform. They could have incorrectly assumed his testimony was going to be purely factual but completely slanted. There were others who were listening intently as he talked. I noticed that some people were squirming a little as he described the gory crime scenes. The media was paying close attention. It was unlikely that too many writers were going to quote Nimmo, but he was laying down a descriptive account of the crimes.

It wouldn't take long for Nimmo to earn the attention of the entire room. He seemed desperate to make it clear to everyone that these were terrible, terrible crimes. I suspect that Nimmo was riding up in his seat while the anti-death penalty people cited reasons to keep this man alive. I doubt he had much compassion for their arguments. Nimmo started to raise his voice as he continued to stress to the board that Raymond Lee Stewart was a ferocious murderer, regardless of what anybody said.

"I have read in the newspaper lately that these were not extremely brutal murders. Yes, they were. Extremely brutal murders. Execution-style murders by an individual who later on was determined to have two weapons. If you enter an establishment with no disguise and with two loaded weapons, your intent is to murder. My chief has said it publicly, and I agree with him, he killed because he enjoyed it. He killed because he enjoyed it," he repeated.

Nimmo was really letting it all hang out at this point. He was practically screaming some of his words. Everyone was listening now. He had picked up the pace dramatically and was starting to let his emotions about this case be seen.

His words were a wake-up call to the reality of how vicious these crimes were. The fact that Ray walked into these places without a disguise and took very little from the employees he murdered spoke volumes to the psyche of this killer. It was an interesting observation. This life-long policeman had some fascinating insights. Ordinary people don't always think like cops do, and Nimmo was making some intriguing points. Ultimately, he was telling us these six murders were even more brutal than we thought.

His theory about the reason Ray Lee Stewart pulled the trigger was rather simple: he killed because he enjoyed it. It was clearly more complicated than that. It is possible Nimmo excused all of the psychological theories out there as mere intellectual rubbish. There were a number of mitigating factors that led the killer down this bloody path, but Nimmo wasn't going to go there. The stories of abuse had already been told to the board. Ray's girlfriend had given birth to their baby, but the girlfriend didn't want anything to do with Ray. Additionally, there was a dispute between Stewart and a landlady over a security deposit. Ray thought he was getting screwed on the deal, and he threatened the lady, who then called the police. In Ray's mind, nothing was working out for him. In Nimmo's mind, the end result of these stories was that this man evolved into a creature who simply killed for enjoyment.

There had to have been times during the investigation when Nimmo felt like they weren't going to catch this guy. It took them four-and-a-half weeks to figure it out and track down Ray Stewart. The police department was undoubtedly under a tremendous amount of pressure. It must have been quite a thrill when they finally caught him. The investigators had to have known they got their man, along with some incredibly damaging evidence. They found him with both guns. His clothes still had blood on them. The only thing left to do was to interview him and start the long paperwork process. Tom Nimmo got to go to North Carolina and come face to face with the killer he had been tracking for weeks. Stewart didn't leave Nimmo with a good first impression.

Nimmo explained, "I spent quite a bit of time with Raymond Lee Stewart. We attempted to interview Mr. Stewart. I found Mr. Stewart to be a cold, calculated criminal who cared nothing for himself or others. He was afforded his rights. He tore up the rights waiver. He would talk to us about certain things, and when he got tired he would put his head on the table. When we finally had to leave the room, ladies and gentlemen, to use the facility, he attempted an escape from that room down there by removing the panels from the ceiling. When I came back I said, 'Ray, what is going on?' He said, 'It was worth a try.' It was worth a try."

This was the first time I ever heard about Ray's first escape attempt. It was a significant story. Ray Stewart took every opportunity to try and escape justice. In light of what happened later, it would be foolish to say there was no chance of escape for this man. Nimmo was describing Ray as an uncooperative man without remorse. Throughout Stewart's questioning, he was thumbing his nose at law enforcement, according to Nimmo. To Stewart, this was all just a big drag.

It was a frenzied time for the media in Rockford. Police departments will often tip the media off as to exactly what time a prisoner is going to be transported, so they can be in place to take pictures of the bad guy. The television stations in Greensboro had picked up on the story, and they were all there when Stewart was paraded into Federal Court. The affiliates in Rockford and in Greensboro were trading footage with each other. It was the first time Rockford-area residents were able to see what the killer looked like. He looked young and was a short man. He was wearing a sweater vest over a plaid shirt that didn't match. When Stewart escaped from the courthouse 14 months later, he looked a lot older. Jail can really age a person. There were several erroneous reports that Stewart was found with a .38 and a .357. It is safe to say that a lot of times the "police sources" are wrong. Both guns were .38 caliber handguns. The news of the arrest appeared in banner headlines in the Rockford Register Star. There were side-bar stories and several follow-up stories detailing how police cracked the case. The media wanted everyone to know it was now time to breathe a sigh of relief.

Nimmo might have been afraid of what Ray Stewart represented. Ray was one of those members of our society who no longer saw the lines of decency and morality. These people are rare and incredibly dangerous. Stewart definitely had nothing to lose. Nimmo truly believed this man had ice-cold blood pumping through his veins. He was the kind of guy who had absolutely no respect for the angel of death. Nimmo said he learned this firsthand during the flight back to Rockford.

"Picture, if you will, a light aircraft over the wooded and mountainous area of North Carolina. A light aircraft heavily loaded with individuals and evidence. A light aircraft experiencing engine trouble. Everyone aboard this aircraft who was reading or was rather nonchalant, became concerned. I will never forget this. Thirty-one years I have been in law enforcement now. I will never forget looking in this man's face. He had absolutely no concern whatsoever. I thought, you don't care about anybody else and you don't care about yourself. This is the type of individual that we are dealing with, ladies and gentlemen," said Nimmo.

This was also a brand new story. I knew the plane had problems and was forced to make an emergency landing in Bristol, Tennessee. I remember reading in the Register Star about Stewart snacking on a candy bar in the airport while the repairs were being made. However, this observation about Ray's reaction to the event was completely new. The scene of a calm Ray

Stewart, letting fate takes its course while a jet plane struggled to fly through the sky is a revealing episode in this story. Nimmo was successfully painting Stewart as a man who had no regard for human life. This could have been a ploy by Nimmo. It might be easier to execute a man who was in some ways subhuman and didn't have any sort of appreciation for life. However, it was probably true. The attitude fit the description of a man who could kill six people.

Nimmo turned out to be one of the most interesting witnesses of the day. It was amazing the amount of access this guy had to the case. He stood over the bloody bodies. He looked the killer in the eye and tried to interrogate him. He would follow the case from beginning to end. At the execution, he would be sitting in the third row of the viewing room next to Paul Logli and right in front of me.

It wasn't any mystery where Tom Nimmo stood on the capital punishment issue. It was clear he thought death was the only appropriate punishment for Raymond Lee Stewart. He explained to the board this was the kind of criminal the death penalty was designed for. Nimmo went a step further and said Ray Stewart was a man who wouldn't think twice about killing again if he were given the opportunity.

Nimmo explained, "This is the type of individual whose record indicates to me that the death penalty is appropriate. I have investigated a number of violent murder cases. And, I have agreed that sometimes it is not appropriate. In this case, this penalty is appropriate. This man, if he walked into this room, in my opinion, would have no problem, whatsoever, executing anyone he chose. I ask you to deny clemency to this individual, to recommend to Governor Edgar that the death penalty be administered to this individual."

At the time, I thought this statement was just an attempt at a dramatic appeal. I looked around the room at the people sitting on the benches. For a second, I let my mind create an imaginary scene where Stewart came bolting into the room and attacked everybody. It might have been too many horror movies as a kid, or maybe it was that this man had invaded my nightmares when I was a youngster. Of course, nothing like that was going to happen. I thought about what it would really be like if Ray was allowed to attend this hearing. I think he probably would have been disruptive. It would have doubled the work for the journalists, as they would have to listen to the speakers and at the same time monitor the facial reaction of Stewart. When Nimmo said Stewart would have no problem killing anyone, he was trying to describe the mindset of this man. Nimmo saw Stewart as a selfish man. It is hard to argue with the sergeant. He spent an awful lot of time with the killer. If it would benefit him to kill again, Nimmo firmly believed Stewart wouldn't have thought twice about it.

Nimmo's testimony was very compelling. Arlene Anderson had two great speakers right off the bat. They had totally taken away momentum from the people who were there to try and save Ray's life. They were down-to-earth, likable people who came forward and told the board things they truly believed. It was obvious it was no accident this man ended up on death row. He did terrible things, and they made sure the board wasn't going to lose sight of that.

Nimmo was not the kind of guy I would like to run into in the field. I imagine he didn't make life easy for journalists who were trying to cover breaking crime news. He was an intimidating, serious man. I don't think he spent too much time joking around on the job. Sometimes, you need cops that are just as tough as the bad guys. Nimmo was a tough guy, and made a strong case against Raymond Lee Stewart.

CHAPTER 13

"Do not pollute the land where you are. Bloodshed pollutes the land, and atonement cannot be made for the land on which blood has been shed, except by the blood of the one who shed it."
—*Numbers 35:33*

  Beloit is one of those border towns where, when you drive into it, you see the shacks of several entrepreneurs who are hoping to make a fortune peddling fireworks to out-of-staters. Illinois has strict anti-fireworks laws and Wisconsin does not. So, if Illinois folks want to get their hands on some bottle rockets, they have to trek across the stateline to buy them. These shacks really pack them in during 4th of July week. While I was growing up, Beloit had the reputation of being a party town. Back in the old days, teenagers from Rockford used to drive the short trip to Beloit on Friday and Saturday nights and partake in some adolescent experimenting at the various taverns. In those days, the legal drinking age for Wisconsin was 18. In Illinois, it was 21. It was a rite of passage I never experienced. By the time I was 18, Wisconsin caved into federal pressure and raised their age to 21. The days of going on "beer runs" to Beloit were gone forever. There are different laws in the two states. They also have different ways of handling their criminals. Wisconsin did get to prosecute Ray Stewart for two counts of first degree murder; however, they weren't able to sentence him to death. Wisconsin doesn't have the death penalty. Like the Jeffrey Dahmer case, the death penalty wasn't an option, and Ray Stewart was sentenced to *life in prison. After the sentence, he was extradited back to death row in Illinois.*

The presentation to convince the board to execute Raymond Lee Stewart was going smoothly and quickly for Arlene Anderson. She wasn't wasting a lot of time introducing her witnesses. She was simply telling the board their names and their relationship to the case. The witnesses were gliding through their testimony with minimal coaching. The pace was considerably faster than Joshua Sachs' presentation. Arlene stood up and told the board that Bob Hurley was the man who investigated the Radio Shack murders for the Beloit Police Department.

Robert Hurley had short hair, almost crew-cut length. He was wearing square eye glasses that it looked like he had owned for many years. He didn't seem to be the kind of guy who would trade in his old specs simply because they were out of fashion. His outfit was fairly basic. He was wearing a plain white shirt and striped tie. His appearance didn't stand out as the typical cop look. Hurley looked like a regular midwestern guy.

Monday, February 2, 1981

The Beloit murders went down around 3:30 in the afternoon. It was daylight outside. The Beloit Mall was open for business and had an average flow of customers when Ray Stewart walked into the Radio Shack store and gunned down the store manager along with a customer. Before fleeing the scene, he took a police scanner. It was the most daring crime Ray Lee ever committed. They were the last two people he ever killed. Richard Boeck and Donald Raines were shot multiple times in the head and chest. Their bodies were found by another customer. The murder spree had crossed state lines, and the FBI became fully committed to solving the case. These murders made the hunt for the killer a national task with police departments from two states involved, along with the feds.

In a way, these are often the forgotten murders in the Ray

Lee Stewart story. Beloit is about 15 miles or so away from the Rockford city limits. It is very much a part of the Rockford urban area. Several residents live there and commute across the stateline and vice versa. The Rockford murders were close in proximity to each other and dragged on through the course of three days. It completely paralyzed the entire west side. Everyone was scared they were going to become the next Register Star headline. This kind of terror was present in the Beloit community immediately after the double homicide; however, there weren't any more murders, and the fear did not blossom to the same colossal level it did in Rockford. There is considerably more media located in Rockford. In fact, the Rockford crime scenes are only a short drive away from where all of the city's television stations are located. Beloit doesn't have any local television news. For the most part, their residents tune into the Rockford stations. With less media and fewer crime scenes, Ray Lee Stewart is much more widely known as the murderer from Rockford. However, the murders in Wisconsin were hardly forgettable.

Robert Hurley told the board he was a retired police sergeant from Beloit. He said he was a cop for thirty-one years, retiring in December of 1994. Back in 1983, he was working in the detective division of the department and would become the chief investigator for the Radio Shack murders. It was a case that would take up a month of his life and require considerable cooperation with several different law enforcement agencies. Hurley began by reflecting on the case. He said he would never forget the afternoon he responded to the call of shots being fired at the Beloit Mall. The former sergeant seemed to distinctly remember every small detail of the crime scene.

"When I walked into this store, I could smell gunpowder still fresh in the air. I was advised by officers there on the scene, they had two victims. It was later through our investigation determined the two victims to be the manager of the Radio Shack store, Rick Boeck, and a customer in the store by the name of Donald Raines. Rick Boeck at the time was 21 years of age, the Radio Shack manager. It was determined through investigation that he had five gun shots to his head and to his back, all shots fired at close range. The other victim in the store, through our investigation, Donald Raines, 26 years of age at the time. Investigation revealed that he had four gun shots to the back of his head and to his body," he said.

The Radio Shack crime scene had been quite a sight. There had been blood everywhere. When you shoot someone at close range, it makes quite a mess. The victim absorbs the full impact of the bullet's force as it catapults out of the barrel. The smell of sulfur and nitrate mixing with the air must have been an obscene aroma. These were images that stick in the minds of cops. I sensed that when Hurley talked about this investigation, he could still see the blood that decorated the walls of the store. He could still smell the acrid aroma that lingered in the air. He could instantly recapture a perfect picture of what the two men looked like lying lifeless on the floor.

This attack was a violation against an imaginary sense of security for the middle class. It is accepted that shootings are going to happen from time to time at gas stations and late night grocery stores, but malls were supposed to be safe. Of course, they aren't and never have been. Since the time they were invented, malls have been a magnet for thieves, killers and kid- nappers. Usually, the most dangerous part of mall shopping is the parking lot. It is rare to hear about a shooting happening inside a store. This truly put residents in the area on edge. Now, it was clear that this killer could strike anywhere at anytime against anyone. What made this violation of security so fright- ening was the degree of violence Ray Stewart used to accom- plish it. He didn't just shoot Donald Raines and Richard Boeck; he literally blew their brains out.

Hurley explained, "From my observation of the scene, it was very clear that the killings of these two men were execution- style, like they had been on their knees and then had gone down and shots fired. When the bodies were removed, brain matter was in the carpet on the floor of the store, to show how close the guns had been fired into the back of their heads. It is, by far, the worst homicide, the most brutal, I have ever seen in my police career, and I have not ever heard of any as brutal as these."

It is noteworthy that cops can often be nonchalant about very violent details. Hurley was describing the most gruesome case of his career, and was hardly showing any sign of emotion. His demeanor was very matter-of-fact-like. Hurley didn't have any notes, and wasn't reading a prepared statement, but it seemed like he was. His pace was slow. He carefully pronounced each word. He wasn't rambling. I would bet that prior to sitting down at the speaker's table, he knew exactly what he was going to say. Hurley appeared to be the kind of the guy who didn't like sharing his opinions. During his testimony, for the most part, he stuck to the facts of the case. With this case, the facts were enough. He didn't need to spice it up with his opinions, so his demeanor, though lacking emotion, was still effective. When he talked about the brain matter on the carpet, it was as if he was simply describing the room. He probably would have used that same tone to describe his living room to a stranger.

Hurley wasn't able to grab his audience's attention like Paul Logli and Tom Nimmo. But, that is asking a lot. The first two speakers against the clemency petition gave some very powerful testimony. However, Hurley was making a lot of good points and offering some decent insights into law enforcement's efforts to deal with this killer. In a way, he was the kind of speaker other cops might enjoy listening to more than Nimmo and Logli. Hurley wasn't using any theatrics as he told the board about the case. For the most part, he adopted the Jack Webb philosophy: just the facts.

"We proceeded to continue with the investigation on this. The victims were identified. Close range was something that showed these were intentional, very intentional, by the person responsible for these homicides. It was, through our investigation, determined two different weapons were used. These guns were recovered from the trailer down in North Carolina. The two different weapons, in my opinion, certainly indicated this was premeditated murder," he said.

Ray Stewart's modus operandi was much more consistent with an assassin's style than that of a serial killer. The killings were premeditated. Stewart walked into those situations with two loaded guns and no disguise. He knew he was going to kill and he did, without hesitation. The murders were quick. He walked into the stores, pretty much with his .38's blazing and then he quickly vanished from the scene. His motive was unclear. He wasn't taking any significant money or merchandise. His primary objective when he walked into Fredd's Grocery, Clark Oil, E-Z Go and the Beloit Radio Shack was to kill. The startling thing was that, with the exception of Willie Fredd, he didn't have a beef with any of his victims. He was completely detached from the Beloit victims. Richard Boeck and Donald Raines lived in a world completely different than Ray's. The only thing those two guys were guilty of was being in the wrong place when Raymond Lee Stewart decided he wanted to blow away two more people. They didn't stand a chance. They were blindsided by a man full of revenge and anger, who was half demented serial killer and half cold-blooded assassin.

The Beloit murders were clearly the most audacious ambush in the Ray Stewart killing spree. He had become dangerously comfortable with his new murderous habit. He walked into a predominantly white mall where several people could have spotted him and fired his loud pistols several times into Boeck and Raines, before walking out of the mall and getting into his car and driving away. He could have easily been caught. Some considerable time had passed before the bodies of the first four victims were discovered. In Beloit, police might have just missed Raymond Lee Stewart. As Hurley said, the gunpowder was still prevalent in the air when he arrived on the scene. It is possible that as he drove back to Rockford to load up his belongings before fleeing to North Carolina, he was listening to all the police excitement on the stolen radio scanner. Stewart knew how to quickly program a police scanner, and it was one of the many methods he used to try and ease his paranoia, or perhaps feed it.

That afternoon the Beloit Police Department didn't catch Ray Stewart. Later, they would be in on his arrest in North Carolina. In many ways, that afternoon changed the Beloit community forever. Once again, the board was hearing testimony about how this offensive episode had left deep and lasting scars.

Hurley explained, "The murders were of such unbelievable range that they still affect our community to this day. Members of our community have not forgotten it. Beloit Mall has not forgotten it. To this day, I still talk to people who have fears; in fact, they do not go up to Beloit Mall because of the terrorism of Ray Lee Stewart, the person who was later confirmed responsible for these brutal murders."

The sentiment was an oldie but a goodie in the Stewart case. For stateline residents, the Beloit Plaza remained a standing monument to the malacious murders. The jitters people felt in 1982 had faded, but a trace of the fear was still there. The impact of Stewart's crimes on Illinois and Wisconsin residents is truly immeasurable.

Detective Robert Hurley wasn't the best speaker of the day. The tone of his testimony was practically void of emotion. Still, he had some interesting insights. The Beloit murders, like the Rockford ones, were extremely brutal. The man the board was hearing about, for whatever reasons, went into these businesses with the intent of killing. The actual acts of murder probably only took a few minutes, but their impact is still being felt to this day. Raymond Lee Stewart is almost as notorious in some parts of Wisconsin as Jeffrey Dahmer is. The fact that Ray was responsible for the Radio Shack murders and was going to be executed in Illinois was another reason the media attention during his execution was so intense. Wisconsin news people don't usually get to cover executions.

The murders in Beloit insured Ray Stewart's secure position in the ranks of American serial killers. It was the city where one of the midwest's most feared serial killers added number five and number six to his inventory of victims. In Beloit, Stewart had added another state in the union to his ominous story. Stewart also expanded the long list of people who experienced fear because of his actions. After that fateful afternoon in 1982, Beloit, Wisconsin became known for more than just a town to buy fireworks and a place that had a great minor league baseball team. However, this is the kind of fame no community welcomes.

CHAPTER 14

*"There are two ways of exerting one's strength: one
is pushing down, the other is pulling up."*
                                   —*Booker T. Washington*

What notorious killers do after they have been caught and locked
up can bring to light what kind of people they are and why they
might have committed the crimes they did. Richard Speck, the
drifter who raped and killed seven nurses in a Chicago dormitory,
kept a large library of pornography in his cell. There is a famous
story about Speck nursing a sick bird back to health and beginning
to care for it like a pet. When guards told him he couldn't keep the
bird, he immediately killed it. After his death, a Chicago television
station broadcast a revealing home video of Speck. It showed Speck
engaging in sexual acts and apparently sharing cocaine with
another prisoner. In that shocking video, it appeared Speck had
been taking hormones to grow breasts. John Wayne Gacy, Chicago-
area sexual molester and serial killer of young men, spent a lot of
his prison time painting pictures. Several of these pictures were self-
portraits of him dressed as a clown. Before his capture, Gacy volunteered his time as a clown performer for children at local
hospitals. Afterwards, he was dubbed the "killer clown." The paintings sold for large amounts of money. Gacy was also an avid Cubs
fan who followed their ups and downs through the years. Gacy
spent a lot of time making collect phone calls to the media. He was
always trying out strange, new theories in hopes of proving his
innocence. Gacy hated the suggestion that he was homosexual, even

though he readily admitted to having sex with other men. Jeffrey Dahmer, a sexual killer of young men in Milwaukee who cannibalized the body parts of his victims, spent the first part of his prison years separated from the general prison population. He repeatedly asked to be put into the general population and was eventually granted the request. Shortly after that, he was murdered by another prisoner. Before that, he had granted Dateline NBC an interview. In that interview, he told reporter Stone Phillips he had rejected excuses like mental illness and an abusive childhood and was now accepting full responsibility for murdering and mutilating his victims. He was baptized six months before he was killed. The clergyman who performed the baptism said Dahmer was obsessed with trying to gain God's forgiveness for his sins.

There isn't a whole lot of information available about what kind of prisoner Raymond Lee Stewart was. The Illinois Department of Corrections does a pretty good job of keeping their condemned stars quiet. Until the end, there weren't any prison interviews with this man. What he had been doing to pass the time for the last 15 years was really a secret. I wanted to know what happened to the man who wreaked terror and fear in my community and my heart so many years ago.

I did know a few things about Stewart's life behind bars. In 1987, during one of his post-conviction proceedings in Rockford, he requested darning needles to use while he stayed in the Winnebago County Jail. He had taken up sweater knitting. The request was denied. Of course, there was also Stewart's oil painting hobby that caused such a stir with the Salvation Army in 1993. However, that was about the extent of information the public and I had about Ray Lee's life in prison. When I drove past Pontiac, on my way to this hearing, my curiosity was heightened. I was about to get some of the answers.

3:15 p.m.

Arlene Anderson leaned into the microphone and explained to the board that Captain Ed Houi would be her next witness.

She stated Houi was going to talk about his experiences dealing with Ray Lee Stewart at the Winnebago County Jail.

Captain Houi was dressed in full uniform. The uniform was different than the powder blue Rockford Police Department uniform Tom Nimmo was wearing. This outfit was a tan brown color. The shirt was neatly pressed. The shoes had a nice shine on them. His black hair was slicked back in a neat, short cut. He had a neatly trimmed mustache. He looked very official.

It didn't take long for Houi to capture the attention of everybody in the room. He politely introduced himself and his relationship to the case. After the formalities, he dove right into some gruesome and disgusting testimony. Houi quickly painted Raymond Lee Stewart as a monster behind bars. He said Stewart's behavior at times was subhuman. He also said Stewart treated the guards like they were subhuman.

Houi explained, "From the beginning, when he came in, he was throwing human waste on us. Telling us that he was going to kill us when he got out. I don't mean to be vulgar by saying these things that I am going to say. I want everyone to understand; human waste was human shit that he was putting on us. I know you all understand."

It was a pathetic image: a grown man throwing feces at guards who were just trying to do their jobs. Through the years, many of the victims' family members described Ray Lee as an animal. This nugget of testimony certainly lent credibility to their assessment. The behavior went beyond disgusting. The act of bombarding fellow human beings with human waste ranks as one of the worst imaginable deeds in terms of degradation and disrespect. It is hard to imagine that this kind of image wouldn't stick out in the minds of the board members who were listening intently to Houi's horrifying testimony.

In a way, I guess Ray Lee can be described as a creative psychotic. While he was in the Winnebago County Jail, he didn't have any access to weapons. He was powerless. Yet, he was still able to inflict suffering on the people around him. The only thing he had in his arsenal was his body's waste products, so he used it. This was a man who, even in the most dire of situations, was able to come up with some sort of modus operandi to push his agenda. His agenda, unfortunately, was hardly constructive. At the core of his objective was revenge, and he was clearly willing to use any evil and twisted tactic he had at his disposal to try and obtain it.

Houi continued by explaining what life was like while he was guarding Winnebago County's most infamous prisoner. During that period he was constantly on edge. He dreaded the times he had to go into Stewart's cell to deliver his meals or to move him for a court appearance. Houi said Stewart was always waiting for him. The attacks were non-stop.

"Everyday, we had to be careful. He would tie things on the bars, like his bed sheets, and tie the door up, and we would have to cut the things to go in. I would stand at the door and put a jumpsuit on, and he would take the human waste in his cups, because he would have cups all over the place, and pour it in my face and on my head all the time. Each time that we came in, I knew something was going to happen," he said.

It is a gross understatement to say this must have been difficult to deal with. Knowing beforehand you were literally going to get shit on by this man every time you had to deal with him had to have been extremely frustrating. It is hard to fathom the amount of dread Houi and the other jail employees must have felt. These men were coming to work everyday and having to face this monster behind bars. Between constantly tying up the jail bars with sheets and throwing his urine and feces around in the cell, guarding Raymond Lee Stewart was clearly a burdensome assignment. They were more like zookeepers than prison guards. I can imagine some of the guards probably even considered quitting their jobs. Stewart's abuse was extremely degrading to these officers. I think it is safe to say these guards wouldn't have minded executing the ultimate justice on this man back in 1982 and 1983. That they showed restraint is amazing, considering the circumstances. They had to hate this prisoner.

Back then, the local media never really picked up on Ray Stewart's lewd jail behavior. During the sentencing phase of the trials, prosecutors did use the behavior as evidence that defendant Stewart deserved the death penalty. The Rockford Register Star buried a small blurb about the behavior in the article that came out the day after the first death sentence was announced. In today's world, it is unlikely these incidents could have been ongoing without the media jumping all over it and making it a sensational blow-out story. Leaks to the press weren't as common as they are today. Furthermore, the story would have made great broadcast copy. This was the case of the century for Rockford, and gory details about Ray Lee's obscene behavior would have been a dream come true for local radio and television reporters. The accounts Houi was describing for the board were the kind of attention-getting details today's media thrives on. The story definitely would have been played up with colorful and punchy words. It would have been more than a blurb; today's media would have really done a number on Ray.

Raymond Lee Stewart was the most infamous character the Winnebago County Jail ever had the displeasure of accommodating. That fact plays heavily in the explanation behind the reason abused guards never retaliated against him. The powers that be in Winnebago County knew everyone would take an interest in any ugly incidents between guards and Stewart. The scrutiny would be intense. It could have even given Ray Lee some leverage during his trials, or possibly down the road during his appeals. For those reasons, they instructed their employees to adopt a strict hands-off policy.

Houi explained, "The Sheriff and the Chief Deputy had told us don't do anything to him. Treat him like you treat anybody normal. It was very difficult for us to have to deal with that everyday. You couldn't do anything to this guy. As much as, you know, at times I would want to, and I think anybody else would want to do something, but the bosses told us, don't touch him."

It was easy to relate to the predicament Houi experienced. I doubt many people could have kept their cool under those same conditions. Stewart had free license to abuse, and he probably knew it. The grave scenario was created by politics. It was an unforgettable period for this prison guard.

Houi continued, "During the time I have been at the sheriff's department, I have seen all kinds of people come through in the last 15 years. But, I have never seen anybody like him."

I think it is probably erroneous to state Winnebago County officials treated Ray Stewart like "any other prisoner." In reality, they treated him much better. It is naive to think jail guards never teach their unruly prisoners a lesson from time to time. As a jail official dealing with killers and rapists, you would have be extremely cautious. It would be foolish for them to think for a second that these people were not extremely dangerous. Ray Stewart hadn't been convicted of anything yet, but he did stand accused of six murders, and he also had a long rap sheet of convictions to his name. I can't say for sure, but I would be willing to put down good money that if some prisoner standing accused of low profile offenses started throwing his feces at guards, it wouldn't take guards long to put a swift stop to that behavior. But, this case was a very high profile one and, as a result, the guards, like Houi, who were assigned to deal with this man had no choice but to bear the brunt of Stewart's attacks.

Houi was a likable guy. His testimony was coming across as very honest and sincere. He isn't a fellow who is full of himself, and that came across to the board while he was talking. At the outset of his remarks, he introduced himself as "Eddie," instead of using Captain Houi. Eddie is a captain with the Sheriff's Department and is Superintendent of the County Jail. He is a big shot. However, the power clearly hadn't gone to his head. Houi came across as an everyday kind of guy. He was talking in a very casual, friendly tone. He wasn't talking in cop lingo. His observations and analogies were clear and to the point. It was easy to see where he was coming from. It was hard not to like this man.

Houi and Stewart spent a lot of time together. The con-
strained relationship had its moments. The pair saw each other
almost everyday. Several times Houi was responsible for taking Stewart back and forth during the trial. They probably did-
n't like each other too much. However, they couldn't help but
get to know each other a little bit. Houi took a moment to tell
the board about a time when Stewart offered him an explanation for his behavior.

"He talked to me during the trial. I was taking him out of his
cell, because I worked in Matz Hall, where we kept all the
felons, and he told me he wasn't throwing it all on me; he was
throwing it on the system. But, I didn't see anybody else there
but me. You know, I didn't see anybody else there but me at the
time," said Houi.

The room laughed at the incident Houi described. It was a
funny observation. One of the board members, Ann Taylor,
gave a wide grin and nodded her head. This was part of Houi's
charm shining through. Beyond its comical content, the story
cut through some of the outlandish thought processes that Ray
often used to defend his actions. By merely stating there was
no one else there at the time when Stewart was supposedly taking on the system, Houi was able to quickly and effectively
belittle Stewart's weak attempt at justifying his inhumane
behavior.

The amusing story was the beginning of the end of Houi's
roller coaster testimony. From using profanity in describing
disgusting details to his humorous observation, Houi's words
had flushed out a wide gamut of various emotions. It revealed
a fresh perspective on the Raymond Lee Stewart story. For the
most part, the information about all these crazy things Ray did
behind bars was never reported. That was going to change. I
knew the Register Star and other newspapers were going to
pick up on this angle of the story. Sure enough, Ed Houi's picture appeared in the newspaper during the Register Star's
extensive coverage of the execution. Beyond the horror stories,
the simple contrast between Stewart and Houi was an insight-

ful metaphor. Stewart was a vicious killer who seemed to thrive on terrifying the people around him. Houi was a straight arrow, a guy who played by the rules. You couldn't help but empathize with this living victim and despise his doomed assailant.

Houi finished by explaining he was not a babe in the woods. Like Stewart, Houi didn't exactly have an easy life. He understood a lot of the societal things which could tempt people like Stewart to jump off the deep end. However, he said Ray Stewart was a man who had drifted way past the boundaries of humanity. As a result, he created terror and fear in the quiet community where Houi had chosen to raise his family. Furthermore, Stewart had made his job a living hell. Houi pointed out all that played second fiddle to the fact that this man had killed six Rockford-area residents. These victims were people deeply loved by their friends and families. At the time of the hearing, Houi had recently lost his oldest son in a car accident. He knew what it was like to lose a loved one, and said he couldn't even imagine the terrible pain the family members of Stewart's victims must have gone through. The Ray Stewart story was truly an hideous blemish on his community.

"I came up out of the ghetto and tried to do everything I can and I understand some of those things. I understand how people are. I understand these things happen. But, how frightening it was for all of us for that week. I came to Rockford in 1973, and it was probably one of the better places at the time when I came to live there. It was quiet. Good place to raise your family. In that one week, I saw something that I never seen in my life; the people were so frightened; I mean, the whole city. People were afraid to come out of the house. I mean, even us who were real macho, all of us guys who worked inside the facility, we went and we stayed in like everybody else because this, out there, had frightened us," stated Houi.

It was a nice finishing touch by Houi. You had to appreciate a man who spoke up for his hometown and spoke out against any evil threats to that community's peacefulness. It is weird for me to hear good things being said about Rockford. It is easy to be negative about a mid-size, midwestern town. Rockford is consistently ranked as one of the worst cities to live in by Money magazine. Growing up there, all my friends ever talked about was leaving town as soon as they graduated high school. Most of those friends are still there. This guy sincerely loved Rockford. It still bothered him that his friends and neighbors were scared to death during Ray's rampage so many years ago. The image of the macho guys being scared, like everyone else, once again drove home the point of how far-reaching the fear connected with these murders really was. Houi was not the most polished or focused speaker of the day; however, a good argument could be made for him being the most likable. He was able to reveal some very unpleasant stories with a good degree of tact and poise. His friendly nature made the room a little more comfortable for everyone. Houi made it easy for the board members to relate to what his terrifying experiences with Ray Stewart were really like.

The testimony was beyond damaging to Ray Stewart's attempt for clemency. It was obvious that this convict, who was asking for compassion and mercy, was more than a killer; he was a deranged man who would stop at nothing to victimize the people around him. He kept his cell in squalid conditions and made the guards assigned to him suffer in ways unimaginable to most. His strange, selfish fight against humanity didn't slow down merely because he was behind bars. Ray used absolutely any means available to him, even if that meant succumbing to tactics like throwing human waste on guards. Ray supporters could have pointed to this behavior and said it was proof positive that Stewart was a troubled man who was in desperate need of psychological help. Joshua Sachs didn't address the jail attacks during his rebuttal. It would have been hard to counterattack the likablity of Eddie Houi, and it was probably best that Sachs just let his testimony die down versus bringing those images back up right before the board was going to meet to consider his client's fate. The truth was that the evidence against Ray being worthy of anybody's empathy was mounting quickly.

CHAPTER 15

"What lies before you and what lies behind, pales in
significance to what lies within you."
                                        —Ralph Waldo Emerson

The one thing that always attracted television stations to the Ray-
mond Lee Stewart story was the dramatic video of his daring escape
attempt. Television stations would jump at any opportunity to show
that tape on their air. It is hard to imagine viewers flipping the chan-
nel when this footage was being shown. Even in today's instant
media world, this tape holds it own in terms of drama. It is rare for
the media to be right on top of a scene like that, as it is happening.
The footage truly captures the chaotic scene. The police were every-
where. It was pandemonium. On the tape, you see officers scurrying
to the alley where Tom Gibbons found the escapee. The alley is full
of uniformed and plainclothes police officers who are running
around screaming into their police radios. Many of the officers are
visibly out of breath and are clearly emotional about the evolving
event. Finally, in the middle of all the frantic officers surrounding
him, you can make out Ray Stewart emerging from an alley in down-
town Rockford. The police are scrambling to secure the scene. Some
officers aggressively push the media out of the way to clear a path
to the waiting police vehicle. Tom Gibbons and Gary Reffett swiftly
escort Stewart to the van, while bright red blood drips off his blood-
soaked blue shirt from the gunshot wound on his right side.

If anybody ever invents a Rockford version of Trivial Pursuit, a
fine candidate for a question would be who shot Raymond Lee

Stewart during his 1982 escape attempt. If the game were being played in the living room of the average citizen's home, it would likely be a stumper. However, if the game were being played in the breakroom of a Rockford-area cop shop, it would be a gimme. The answer is Jim Kraut. This was the one guy everybody I talked to about the Ray Stewart case told me to track down. Kraut was the first name Fred Speer and Tom Gibbons mentioned to me. Over and over again, as I was calling around, tracking down information, Jim Kraut's name came up. His name always seemed to pop up during conversations about Ray Lee Stewart. When I went to Rockford with my camera crew, I wasn't able to locate him in time for my piece. Now, I was finally going to hear what this man had to say. His testimony was next.

He was dressed in plainclothes. He resides in Pecatonica, Illinois, which is a town of about eighteen hundred people that sits along the Kishwaukee River about 20 miles west of Rockford. For years, Pecatonica has been home to the Winnebago County Fair. The man from Pecatonica looked a little timid beyond the speaker's table. Kraut wasn't overly enthusiastic about appearing before the Illinois Prison Review Board. He didn't appear to be nervous, just a little tense. During his speech, he sat up straight and looked directly at the members. This was a story I am sure he has told a thousand times, but when he told it today, he was going to take an all-business approach. He didn't have any notes with him. He spoke in a clear voice and was able to settle into a nice pace. His straightforward presentation was easy to follow.

After introducing himself as an employee with the Winnebago County Sheriff's Department, Kraut didn't waste much time getting into his testimony. He knew exactly why he was there. He was there to tell the dramatic tale of Raymond Lee Stewart's escape, and he literally cut right to the actual chase. It was obvious from the outset that he carried strong memories from the afternoon of April 22, 1982. His testimony was detailed, and he was able to effectively construct a vivid picture of the events surrounding the wild escape.

Kraut told the story, "I was in plainclothes, as I am today. I was in the courthouse, going up a flight of stairs. I heard some guards hollering, 'Ray Lee Stewart has escaped. Stop him! He's leaving the courtroom!' Shortly after that, a person ran into me physically. I remember he had a blue suit on, the color of a robin's egg. I recognized him as Ray Lee Stewart. I drew my service weapon; he stopped at the bottom of the stairway for a short time. I remember he sunk down, put his hand to his throat, looked at me. I got about three feet away, and he didn't say anything, but he gave me that look, if you're not going to shoot me, I am gone. And, he did. He took off."

It was an amazing moment. Kraut had little warning that he was about to have a life-defining, face-to-face encounter with Winnebago County's most notorious killer. Suddenly, he was thrown into a situation where he needed to try and recapture the man who had terrified so many in his community. This was nothing like a police stop or a raid. He wasn't afforded the luxury of preparing himself, mentally and physically, for this kind of situation. He heard Ray Stewart had escaped, and a few seconds later he was staring right at him. Although his testimony was practically void of emotion, on that April afternoon he experienced a terrifying rush of adrenaline.

This was the kind of situation years and years of police training are supposed to prepare officers for. This was the moment of truth for Jim Kraut. The time when lethal force is absolutely justified, and a whole community is counting on your bravery and skills. Being a police officer is never a 9 to 5 job. Kraut's story is a perfect example of how cops can be called to perform above and beyond the call of duty in a moment's notice. It is safe to say a lot of people would have frozen in a situation like this, but Officer Kraut didn't. He was able to keep his composure and do what he had to do to try and put the kibosh on Stewart's escape attempt. As he talked, it was obvious he wasn't going to win awards for charisma, but if you were sitting in that room, you couldn't help but inch up on the edge of your seat. Kraut continued by explaining all of the factors that went through his mind as Ray Stewart was racing down the stairs of the courthouse. As I listened, I was impressed by the presence of mind he had at that moment. There were practically a million things to consider in those few seconds. Kraut knew the case. He knew how dangerous this individual was. He knew he had to do something.

"We continued down the last flight of stairs, I saw him opening the outer door to go outside. I knew of the case; I knew he had a death sentence in Illinois; I decided I had do something, so I fired a shot, as I was running down the stairway. I missed Ray Lee; however, I hit the door. That made the door go shut. Gave me time enough to get my footing at the bottom of the landing, and I saw Ray Lee's shoulder; the only thing that was inside the room was his right shoulder. I shot again and immediately saw a red mark where the bullet hit," explained Kraut.

As serial killers go, Ray was a lucky one. He was lucky that at the time of his escape, Jim Kraut had recently suffered a back injury and was on light duty. It is likely that a healthy Kraut would have killed Stewart right there in the courthouse. Stewart was also lucky that the bullet hit him where it did. Reportedly, if the bullet had been a centimeter over in any direction it probably would have killed him.

It was an amazing, wild scene in that courthouse. It was the kind of confrontation that usually only happens in the movies. There was confusion and screaming and shooting. The excitement all happened on a Thursday afternoon. The halls of the courthouse were crowded with all kinds of people. This wasn't a movie, and Kraut had to be careful not to jeopardize the safety of any civilians. A whizzing bullet could easily ricochet and injury somebody besides Kraut's intended target. At this point in the Ray Stewart story, the worst thing that could have happened would have been the deaths of more innocent people. Fortunately, no civilians were seriously injured. Unfortunately for Ray Stewart, the bullet that hit him would likely eliminate any chance for a successful getaway.

Kraut began telling how his encounter with Ray Stewart ended, "From there, we proceeded to another outer door to the street. I saw Ray run to a waiting vehicle. The vehicle was running; there was a female in the vehicle. The door was open. As he started getting into the car, I hollered, 'If you run into the car I am going to shoot you again.' Ray looked at me, got out of the car and ran around the block, to a mall where I lost sight of him. I went in and informed my com center of that. I was told later, of course, he was apprehended."

The waiting car remains a mystery. The car was a Chevy Vega station wagon. Chevrolet stopped making the Vega wagon in 1976, so it wouldn't have been the hardest car in the world to track down in 1982. But, the police never did. It is unclear if Stewart actually planned to escape that afternoon or if he merely took advantage of a situation on the spur of the moment. When I asked Stewart about that, he said he didn't remember trying to get into a car. When I pressed on, he suddenly remembered, but he refused to comment. Either he didn't want to incriminate his accomplice or, more likely, he wanted it to remain mysterious in hopes of somehow making him seem like a criminal who was more intelligent than he actually was. Kraut was concentrating on Ray Stewart and says he would not have been able to identify the driver. No one was ever charged with attempting to help Ray escape.

That afternoon there was a dramatic role reversal. Ray went from being the hunter to the prey. Back in 1981, it was Ray against the world. Now, it was the world against Ray. This was the first and only time Ray had every been shot. Now, he was learning what it felt like to be on the other end of a bullet. Since the media was already there to cover the trial, word spread quickly about the escape. Everyone was looking for him. Dozens of police from all kinds of different agencies were searching the downtown area for Ray. Everybody in the law enforcement business knew about this man. Nobody was a big fan. It would be foolish to underestimate how dangerous this fugitive was, and the Rockford area cops knew that. During the time he was at large, police considered him armed and dangerous. They weren't going to take any chances and put any more innocent lives on the line. He wouldn't have to give the cops much reason to shoot and kill him like he shot and killed Willie Fredd, Albert Pearson, Kevin Kaiser, Kenny Foust, Richard Boeck and Donald Raines.

After the capture, Tom Gibbons was getting the hero treatment by the media. Everybody was reporting how Officer Friendly found Ray Stewart hiding in a 55 gallon drum in the downtown alley. However, Kraut might have been a more suitable choice for heroic status. It is not impossible to imagine Stewart killing more people while he was on the lam. He was already facing execution at the time of the escape. He was a desperate man who had already crossed the line six times. During that period in Stewart's life he showed nothing but disdain for the families of his victims. He was obviously still a psychopath. He was still capable of murder. The fact that he was gushing blood from a gunshot injury insured it would be impossible for him to casually interact with potential victims that he might come across. By shooting him in the shoulder, Kraut might have saved some lives.

Furthermore, Kraut might have foiled the escape attempt. Stewart had a pretty good jump on the police. Witnesses say he was running extremely fast down Church Street. While talking with Ray, I was impressed with how accurate his geography of the city was, even after being behind bars for 15 years. He knew his way around, and he might have had a decent shot of commandeering a car and making a legitimate run for it. However, that is an extremely difficult task when you are leaving a trail of blood behind you. He was also hurt badly and that had to slow him down. Gibbons said that on the way to the hospital, he thought for a second that Ray was going to die in the van. You need a lot of energy and a lot of presence of mind to pull off an escape like that. The moment that Kraut's bullet pierced Stewart's shoulder his escape bid was over. It was just a matter of time before the cops would find the rock he was hid-

ing under.

　Everybody watching local television news that night saw what happened when the cops finally did find Ray Stewart. It took just over two minutes for the police to yank Ray out of the alley and walk him into the Rockford police van that took him to the hospital. All three stations had video camera people in perfect positions to get shots of the exciting capture. It is probably the most dramatic spot news video in the history of Rockford television. It was the first time I really got a rush out of watching the local news. Gibbons and Reffett are on each side of the handcuffed fugitive, holding on tight to each arm while they swiftly walk him through the alley. You can hear an out-of-breath Fred Speer giving his live radio report over his hand-held radio. Stewart's large eyes are haunting as he looks at all the commotion around him. He looks dazed and confused and tired. The blood has completely soaked the right side of his powder blue shirt. As he approaches the van, he ducks his head to clear the vehicle's side door. He immediately lays down and several officers hover above him and begin administering first aid. The sirens are turned on and the van takes off down the street. The show was over, but it would be replayed on video tape over and over again through the years.

　Beyond the escape attempt, Kraut was not directly involved in the case. However, at the conclusion of his testimony, he took the opportunity to throw his insights into the debate over whether the state should execute Stewart. To accomplish this, he revealed a moment when he overheard Ray taunting the family of Kevin Kaiser during the death penalty phase of the Kaiser trial.

　"I was also asked if there is anything that was said to me by Ray. I do remember when I testified, I told this story at his death sentence, the second one. As I got off the stand to walk out of the room, I got even to where Ray Lee was sitting. I remember he turned around, there was a lady, and I am sure it was Kevin Kaiser's mother, he looked at her and said, 'Yeah, I killed your kid.' And that is my whole involvement with Ray

Lee Stewart. I feel if he is not executed, he might flee again, and I think he definitely should be executed," said Kraut.

The escape is an important episode in the Ray Stewart story. First, it lends strong proof to the theory that Ray was an unremorseful, selfish bastard who would jump at the slightest chance to weasel out of justice. The unarmed bailiffs let their guard down for a second, and he was gone. He was already under sentence of death for killing Pearson and Fredd, and he should have no longer been a threat to the community. However, he managed to find a way to terrify everybody in the Rockford area again. For people who have been inside Illinois prisons, it is hard to seriously consider Kraut's comment about Stewart possibly fleeing again. Those maximum security, death row blocks seem impenetrable. Escape would be practically impossible, but it should have been impossible for him to get away the first time. When something like Ray's escape happens, suddenly, the promised guarantee attached to a sentence of life without parole falls short of the ultimate guarantee that comes with capital punishment. What if he gets away? What if he kills a guard or another inmate? These contingencies would have long-shot odds, but the thoughts had to creep into the minds of the Review Board members who were going to make a recommendation regarding Stewart's clemency petition. Could they afford the risk of letting their guard down?

Secondly, the escape incident is key because it proved what area police officials already knew. He may have been a psycho, but he was a fearless and intelligent psycho. "Life on death row is hell." I have never talked to a death row inmate who didn't utter that sentence. The worst part about it is that there is absolutely no light at the end of the tunnel. After living 14 or 15 years in those hellish conditions, you get strapped on a gurney and drugged to death. Stewart had nothing to lose by making a run for it. The moment he got the chance, he took it. He was running through a building packed with all kinds of gun-carrying cops. When Stewart bumped into Kraut, he forced Kraut to shoot him instead of giving up. Even with a gunshot injury, he continued his escape attempt. Stewart was one of those guys who just didn't have the capacity to be afraid. Once he was out of the courthouse and running down Elm Street, he knew that with his gunshot injury, his only chance to avoid eminent capture was to find a quick hiding place. He picked a good one. Stewart hid there undetected by the swarms of police and media people who were passing through the alleyway. The cops actually checked it twice and missed him both times, before spotting him the third time, thanks to a borrowed flashlight. For over an hour, the escape was successful. That was way too much time. For a man accused of brutally killing six people, the escape ranks as an Houdini-like achievement. In future Winnebago County Courthouse appearances, the security would be beyond excessive. They were never going to let Ray have a repeat performance.

Finally, the escape is so significant because it would forever make the Stewart case attractive to all-powerful television producers. The video footage is awesome, almost spell-binding. It doesn't rank with the likes of such sensational national stories as the shuttle explosion or Kennedy's assasination or the Rodney King beating, but for the local and regional media, it was priceless. When I first started gathering tape to put together a piece for WGN, this was the only footage from the Ray Stewart story that my station bothered to save. The footage was always perfect for teasing or advertising our upcoming stories. A good tease tugs at the curiosity of the viewers. Shots of a bleeding serial killer surrounded by cops easily accomplished that task.

Jim Kraut was the only man to challenge this killer face to face. Kraut took Stewart on eyeball to eyeball and was probably able to ruin his escape hopes by nailing him with a bullet. Stewart never afforded his victims the luxury of confronting him. He surprised them and quickly overpowered them with the help of his high-powered pistols. Stewart treated his victims like they were worthless animals. None of them ever had a chance. When he was originally captured in North Carolina, he was taken in a ruse by law enforcement officials from various departments. The feds were involved, along with police officials from Illinois, Wisconsin and North Carolina. It was all over in a matter of seconds. There was no chance of a struggle. Kraut looked a fleeing and desperate Stewart right in the eyes. He was able to keep his composure and do what he had to do. Taking Raymond Lee Stewart on, under those conditions, is a feeling that only Jim Kraut can relate to. Gibbons and Speer were right; he was the man to talk to.

CHAPTER 16

"There is no right way to grieve. There is just your way. It will take as long as it takes."

—Rusty Berkus

When Kraut finished his testimony, it concluded the law enforcement phase of the Attorney General's presentation. Now, it was time to hear from the victims' families. Arlene Anderson had a long list of family members who traveled all the way to Springfield to tell the Prison Review Board why Raymond Lee Stewart should not be allowed to escape his punishment. Everyone in the room was about to hear sad stories about pain and loss from teary-eyed family members. The speakers would surely be providing agonizing details of the ongoing, emotional torture they suffered because of Ray Lee's action. This part of the day promised to be very emotional. From the outset, it was exactly that. Arlene Anderson looked up at the board members and called her first family witness. His name is Alex Fredd.

Alex is Willie Fredd's son. The murder of Willie Fredd was senseless, but it wasn't random. Ray was definitely gunning for Willie. Back in 1970, Stewart held up Johnny-on-the-Spot Dry Cleaners. He got away with about fifty dollars. After the robbery, Stewart went to Fredd's store. At the time, the store was located at the intersection of Concord and Delaware. For some reason, Stewart revealed he had robbed the dry cleaners. It is unclear exactly how and why Stewart confessed this to Fredd, but Fredd quickly called the cops and Stewart was arrested. At the trial, Stewart pleaded guilty. Willie

Fredd never had to testify in court. Stewart waited nearly eleven years, but the reason he went into Fredd's Grocery Store was to get revenge for what happened in 1970.

Alex is a big guy. He is well over six feet tall and looks strong as an ox. Like me, he is a proud product of Rock Valley College. It took him a long time, but he finally got his Associate Degree. When he was younger, he sported a small afro; now his head was shaven. He is big, but his appearance is not threatening. In a way, he has an innocent look to him. When Anderson called his name, he slowly got up from the bench to take the stand. He took a moment to look behind him to make sure his mom and his grandmother were okay. Finally, he sat down in the empty chair next to Arlene. He looked nervous. Speaking in public was clearly not a chore he was used to. As he began to testify, his nervousness came through; however, it was obvious he was determined to tell that board his story.

3 p.m. Sunday, September 1, 1996

I first met Alex when I went to Rockford to put together our first Ray Stewart story. I met him at his house and interviewed him for that piece. The Fredd house is on the west side of Rockford, just a few blocks away from Fredd's Grocery Store, which was now a vacant building. When I pulled up in the news vehicle with my photographer, we instantly attracted a crowd of curious onlookers. As I walked up to the house to ring the bell, I could hear the voices of John Madden and Pat Summeral calling out the plays of a televised football game. I rang the doorbell, and Alex Fredd quickly answered the door. When I walked into the room, I saw Alex's mother, Sallie Fredd, sitting on the couch. We did introductions and then I asked Alex if he had a picture of his father. We needed to videotape a photograph of Willie Fredd to use for our piece. Alex ran upstairs to try and locate a picture. I sat down next to Sallie and began talking to her. She seemed happy to have company at the house. I wanted to interview her for the piece, but she declined, saying she was going to wait for the clemency hearing. When

*Alex returned, he was holding a large portrait of Willie Fredd.
It was a painting of him wearing a store clerk apron. It was
perfect. My cameraman, Marc Gerke, fired up the camera
lights and began to shoot the picture.*

*It is hard not to like Alex. He was very friendly and went out
of his away to accommodate us. I think he enjoyed the attention the media was giving him, but by no means was he show-
boating for the cameras. The mood was very relaxed at the
Fredd house. He laughed at my bad jokes about how terrible
the Bears' season was. He was very open about discussing the
murder of his father. From the first moment I talked to him, I
could tell he was deeply hurt by the crimes of Raymond Lee
Stewart. At the clemency hearing, it would be painful for me to
hear just how deeply hurt he was and how the murder of his
father really screwed up Alex's one-time promising life.
Despite the deep pain, Alex didn't come off as overly bitter. He
made it clear he wanted Ray to die for what he did, but the hostility was reserved exclusively for Ray. At the clemency hearing, he was very cordial towards the speakers who testified on
behalf of Stewart. I saw him giving a friendly hello to Joshua
Sachs and Shelly Sullivan as they passed him in the hallway.
Jennifer Bishop Jones, being a family member of a murder victim herself, told me she approached several of the family members to offer her sympathy for their loss. The Fredd family was
the only one that gave her the time of day.*

*Chicago anchorwoman Carol Marin had beaten me to the
Alex Fredd interview. She did a piece for WMAQ a week earlier and had traveled out to Rockford to do some interviews. By
the time I got there, Alex knew the drill. In a way, that helped
me. For the most part, I am a desk journalist. In the field, I
might be a little more skilled than our interns, but that is about
it. With Alex already being familiar with the routine, it took
some of the burden off me. At least one of us knew what to do.
He suggested we drive over to the grocery store and shoot the
interview there. Having the store where the first two murders
went down as a backdrop would be a nice touch. The Fredd*

house was dark, and the lighting would have been difficult. It was a nice day and Mother Nature could provide all the light we needed to shoot a high quality interview. We jumped into the news car and headed over to Fredd's Grocery Store on West State Street.

The store was a sad sight. I vividly remember the times my family drove past that location in the old station wagon. I grew up on the east side of Rockford, but I passed through the west side via State Street on several occasions. Both my brothers were bused out to Wilson Middle School where they were enrolled in programs for distinguished students. Whenever there was a soccer match or a concert recital, we would travel down West State to get to the school. As a child, Fredd's Grocery was an eerie place. I knew something terrible had happened there. I never passed by the store without thinking about Ray Stewart. For about a year, the Fredd family was able to keep the store open. Now, the building had been vacant for several years. It was boarded-up and run-down. Weeds were growing wild in the cracks of the paved parking lot. At the outer edge of the parking lot, a sign still hung from a pole identifying the store as Fredd's Grocery. Unfortunately, this is just one of many vacant, neglected buildings on the west side of Rockford. However, for the people who knew the history and the story behind it, it is much more than that. It is a constant symbol of the beginning of a terrible and horrifying crime spree.

Alex was emotional about being near the store. He was looking around, scouting out his old turf. I would catch him staring at the overgrown weeds and the boarded-up windows and shaking his head. This place was obviously special to him. As Marc set up the camera, Alex showed me around, and we talked about the store. The grocery store had a lot of memories, both good and bad.

"It is just so disgusting to see the store look like this now. We worked so hard to keep it nice and clean. This was my life here. I worked a lot of hours. If I wasn't in school, I was here. I never

will forget the day, January the 27th," he said.

It was tragic to think about what happened to the Fredd family. Alex told me they spent countless hours working at the grocery store. Education was important to Willie Fredd, and he insisted on his son going to school. However, the grocery business was what put a roof over the family. Alex had spent a lot of his youth inside the store, putting price tags on soup cans and bagging groceries for customers. The business had been successful and the Fredd family was on their way to prosperity. All of that was erased by the trigger finger of Raymond Lee Stewart.

We set up the camera in a parking lot, just west of the store. The shot was framed so the viewer could see the grocery store sign over Alex's right shoulder. I couldn't afford to lose time by doing a full-blown interview. I was on a tight schedule and under a lot of pressure to pull off this story quickly. To save time, my mother had graciously agreed to play courier for us and she was in the process of swinging by the local television stations and picking up the file tapes. The plan was for her to meet us at the grocery store and give us the tapes. As soon as I saw her pull up, I knew I was going to have to end the interview in order to insure we could get back to Chicago in time to put together this story.

During the interview, I wanted to try and extract the intense loss Alex felt as a result of his father's murder. Furthermore, to make the piece timely, I had to get his stance on the capital punishment issue. These two objectives were probably all I was going to have time for. I could have talked to him for an hour, but the time just didn't permit it. Despite the fact it was rushed and only touched the surface of his story, the interview was fascinating.

Kelly: *What was your father like as a person?*

Fredd: *My father was a hard-working businessman. He would work 17, 18 hours a day in our grocery store. We were just hard-working people.*

Kelly: *January 27, 1981, was a day that changed your life forever. It changed your family's life forever. Where were you when you heard that your father had been shot?*

Fredd: *I was at Rock Valley College, in a classroom, when a police officer from Rock Valley came to my class-room and got me out of class and took me back to the administration building. I didn't know what was going on. I couldn't believe it when they told me my father had been shot and killed. It changed my whole life.*

Kelly: *How did it change your life?*

Fredd: *My life, it seemed like to me, was pretty good. I was in school at the time, in college. I was getting ready to go into a four year school and I just couldn't cope with all of that anymore. This is something that has haunted me day in and day out, every day for the last fifteen years.*

Kelly: *Did you come straight here from Rock Valley College?*

Fredd: *I went home to see how my mother was doing and then I came here. I had to help clean up some of my father's blood. They had cleaned up most of it. Man, standing here now, it seems like yesterday.*

Kelly: *When I was between the ages of twenty and twenty-five, my father gave me some of the best advice of my life. I bonded with my father during that period. What was it like for you? What was it like not having a father at nineteen years old?*

Fredd: *It seemed like I jumped from nineteen to manhood on that day. I had to act like a grown man. I had to make decisions for my family. Things just changed dra-matically. My dad and I were very close. He wanted me to work hard and be an honest, law-abiding citi-zen and try to do the right thing in life. He was giv-ing me advice and all of a sudden, that was snatched from me. He wasn't there to give me advice anymore.*

I didn't have anybody to turn to anymore. I had to go out there and make decisions on my own.

Kelly: Has there been a time when you can forget about what happened, or is this constantly on your mind?

Fredd: I believe after the execution takes place, I believe I can go ahead and get on with my life.

Kelly: You are looking forward to this execution, aren't you?

Fredd: I am looking forward to it. I am going to be there. My family is going to be there and we are looking forward to this.

Kelly: How does killing Stewart bring peace to you?

Fredd: It just brings back a peace of mind that the guy who killed my father is paying the price, and justice will be served.

Kelly   How would you describe Stewart?

Fredd: He is an animal. He is a vicious animal. He is a very vicious animal that needs to be executed. This guy can't be rehabilitated whatsoever. If they turned him loose tomorrow, he would be right out there doing the same thing again. He would pick up right where he left off. This is something that needs to be done.

Kelly: Where were you the day he escaped? What were you doing?

Freed: I was in the courtroom when he escaped. I heard gunshots and I remember the State's Attorney saying everybody hit the floor, just don't move. Somehow, we didn't know what had happened. Me and my brother were in the courtroom. When we found out what happened, we went looking for Ray Lee Stewart in the Rockford area.

Kelly: What would have happened if you would have found him?

Fredd: There wouldn't be any need for an execution. It would have been over with. If we would have found him, it wouldn't have gotten to this point.

Kelly: *Take us back to 1981. Willie's death and Albert's death in the shooting at the store here. I am sure that you are following the media reports closely. All of a sudden, you hear about the 17-year-old kid shot dead at a gas station and then the other murders.*

Fredd: *I remember the investigation. The police were doing a lot of forensic science to see if these murders were linked together. Finally, the tests came back, and they said these murders were linked. I couldn't believe what had happened. I mean we had a serial killer running around loose in Rockford and they better find him. I just couldn't believe it.*

Kelly: *Your father had a gun in the store?*

Fredd: *He had eight of them. He couldn't get to them. Ray Lee Stewart executed my father; he killed my father; he butchered him. He killed my father by surprising him; my father didn't have a chance. It is unbelievable that Ray Lee Stewart had fifteen years of chances, of appeals. It is unbelievable. I believe the justice system needs to take a look at this case, and this ought to be a case they can learn something from.*

Kelly: *Anything you want to add?*

Fredd: *I will be glad when it is all over.*

   The interview was nothing to write Barbara Walters over, but it was effective at accomplishing my needs for the piece. Alex gave some really good sound bites. The interview was going well, and I was actually a little disappointed when I saw my mom's car pull up, my cue to wrap up. He was very emotional about this case, and that showed on the videotape. I learned a few thing as well. It was interesting to find out that he actually went looking for Ray Stewart after the 1982 escape. He looked up to his father and spoke of him with pride and reverence, saying that he was an honest, hard-worker who would sometimes put in seventeen hours a day. In that inter-

view, Alex was able to really drive home the point that Ray had snubbed out a man who was deeply loved and in doing so, absolutely devastated the family members who were left behind. Alex is a living testament to the devastation that happens, not only to the victim, but to the survivors of a homicide.

The Alex Fredd now sitting in front of the Prison Review Board was a lot more nervous than the Alex Fredd I interviewed outside the vacant grocery store. He was shaking as he sat in the wooden chair. He began by asking the board to bear with him because he was nervous. In Rockford, I suspect I was able to set him at ease. He was in his house watching the football game, and I came in and struck up a conversation about the game. I was wearing blue jeans and a baseball cap. It was a very non-threatening outfit in comparison to the suits everybody in the Capital Building was wearing. All sorts of strangers were staring at him with their pens poised. Like Alex, I knew the story inside and out and was able to immediately understand things he was talking about. As an interviewer, you are always in a much better position when you are familiar with the subject matter. I think it sets the mind of your interviewee at ease. Despite his nervousness, his presentation was far from a disaster. In fact, the nerves probably magnified his anguish. At the beginning of his speech, I felt he was not going to able to finish without breaking down. Once again, Arlene Anderson was opening a phase of her presentation with her strongest, and most emotional, witness.

Alex began by telling the board the details of how he found out his dad was dead and the impact that terrible news had on his life.

"Ray Lee Stewart, when he killed my father, he didn't only kill my father, he killed me spiritually. He tortured me. I have been through torture. January 27, 1981, I was just beginning to go to college. My first semester of college at Rock Valley College. I will never forget it. I was a full-time student at Rock Valley. I was majoring in Business Administration. I was going to my classes everyday. I made good grades in high school.

Real good grades. I never will forget the day, January the 27th, when a Rock Valley Police Officer came to the classroom and told me he wanted to talk to me."

It is truly a tragedy that Alex let Ray torture him so much. It is hard for non-victims to understand how a murder like this could have, as Alex said, killed him spiritually. That is a very strong statement. I guess most of us could not imagine such lingering pain. One would think that after a tragedy like this, you grieve for a period, you try different things until you can find peace and you live on. That is the way it usually works in the movies. In real life, it is a much different story. After a crime like this touches your life, it is impossible for things to ever get back to normal. The loss is permanent and the nightmares seldom fade. It is a thing that only people who have gone through it can truly understand. This is why there are support groups for such people. Like recovering addicts, the victims of crime often need to interact with people who can really relate firsthand to the emotional roller coaster they are on. Many survivors never find peace. Alex is still struggling with it.

The image of a police officer interrupting a class to tell a young man that his father was murdered is a frightening one. Alex had no idea this interruption in his life was going to last for years and years. I imagine the events of that afternoon play over and over in Alex's mind, just like the scene of him cleaning up his dad's blood from the grocery store floor. These are haunting images not easily forgotten.

Alex continued, "I didn't know what he wanted to talk about because I knew I hadn't done anything wrong. I had never been involved with the law in no kind of way. He immediately took me back to the administration building at Rock Valley College. On the way up there, I asked him what had happened: 'Do you know? Can you tell me? What did I do? What has happened?' He said, 'Alex don't worry, you haven't done anything.' When I got back to the administration building at Rock Valley, I was greeted by Stu Nelson from the Rockford Police Chaplain's office and a uniformed police officer."

Stu Nelson and his wife graduated from Rockford East High School in 1964. They were in the same class as my mother. There were several times when I was developing stories on Raymond Lee Stewart where I sensed that I was only a couple of degrees of separation away from everybody involved. Once again, there was a coincidental connection. Nelson is well-known in the community. He is actively involved in several youth programs that are sponsored by the Rockford Police Department.

Alex Fredd vividly remembers the details of that afternoon. His testimony about begging the police officer to explain why he was being pulled out of class shows his human reaction to the event. It is natural to suspect trouble when a cop turns up at your door. The classmates who didn't know him well probably did think he was in trouble. The testimony also demonstrates how well he remembers what happened. Alex Fredd could probably tell the board what he was wearing, what the weather was like and what the lecture topic was that afternoon. When something tragic like this happens, you tend to remember all kinds of nitty-gritty details. There is something about hearing horrible news that temporarily sharpens the senses. It is unlikely Alex will ever forget anything about that afternoon.

Stu Nelson had a terrible job to do. This is the one thing all cops hate. What made it worse was that Alex had no idea what was coming. Never in a million years could Alex have predicted what Nelson was about to tell him. There was no way to sugarcoat something like this. The best Nelson could do was to be blunt and then try to help him deal with it. The news devastated Alex.

Alex described what happened, "Stu Nelson told me he wanted to talk to me in a conference room. He went in there and he told me, he said, 'Alex, your father has been shot and killed.' When he told me that, I forgot everything. I looked at Stu, and told him, I said, 'Stu, my life is over. I can't live without my father. I cannot go on.' I told him, I said, 'I just can't make it, Stu, I can't.' He told me, 'You can make it Alex, you can.'"

The feeling that your own life has ended after hearing something like this is natural. For Alex, though, it wasn't simply a knee-jerk reaction. He would never fully recover from losing his father. The police in that conference room could not possibly have known how close he was to his father. With his death, Alex's promising life was about to go into a bona fide tailspin. When he told Nelson he couldn't go on, he really meant it. Of all the victims I have ever interviewed, Alex seemed to be the most deeply hurt. This instantly changed everything for him. Alex was going to spend the best years of his life drowning in despair.

At this point in the presentation Alex was showing signs of losing his composure. His voice was cracking, and it was obvious he was holding back the tears. He wanted to be strong in front of all these people, but the pain was still very much alive in him. When he talked about his father, the agony surfaced. As a journalist, it is hard to divorce yourself from stories you become intimately involved with. I liked Alex, and I felt for him as I watched him struggle through his testimony. Up to this point, his testimony was focused and organized, but as a side effect of losing his composure came a sudden lack of direction.

"I was 19 years old at the time. At that time, I had to try to bring my family together, my brother and sister, my mom; I had to become a man. I had to do the responsibilities of my father. I was scared during that time; I was really, really scared. Essentially, after going to bed that night at home, come to find out another person had been killed, Kevin Kaiser. I was really scared, I couldn't believe it. I went to the store from Rock Valley College. I even cleaned up some of my dad's blood. I thought, I just couldn't believe it," said Alex.

It was disturbing to listen to Alex jump all over the place. It reminded me of Ray's sister, Faith Crocker, who also started losing it on the stand. Alex was rambling from topic to topic without any sense of direction: from having to take over the helm of the family, to the Kaiser murder, to cleaning up his dad's blood. He was losing focus and trying to throw in every little tidbit that he thought the board needed to hear. For Alex, it wasn't always easy to talk about this, and it had to be incredibly difficult to discuss in front of a large and diverse audience. The signs of pressure were starting to show on Alex. Giving this speech was a lot to ask from a young man who had been through so much. It was just a matter of time before he was going to hit the point where he couldn't go on.

For now, Alex was going to try and continue to struggle through. It took some willpower, but Alex was able to regain his composure and began to tell the board about his father. As he talked, the board was getting a clear picture of what Willie Fredd was like from the man who knew him best, his son. From all appearances, the contrast between Willie Fredd and Ray Stewart was a stark one. Ray was a life-long criminal, who never really got his act together. Stewart was incapable of sticking to anything for too long. When the going got tough, he usually sought the easy way out. Stewart killed Fredd for doing his civic duty. Willie Fredd was a man who probably worked too hard. Willie labored to achieve his long-term goals, day in and day out. He desperately wanted to provide for his family. To accomplish that, he would put in long, back-breaking hours. Willie Fredd carried the burden that comes with unselfish living.

Alex explained, "I was brought up in a real good environment, my family was close. I had a pretty good life, real good lifestyle. Ray Lee Stewart took all that from me. My family had a pretty good business. We did a lot of business at that store. We helped a lot of people. People who weren't able to pay for their groceries, my dad would give them credit, and they would come into the store and pay later. There were a lot of people in poverty and despair where my dad's store was, and he helped those people. Not only did Ray Lee Stewart hurt my family, but he hurt those people also."

As I listened to Alex talk about his father, I thought about how refreshing it was to hear somebody saying good things about their parents. In today's world, it seems like the trendy thing to do is blame your parents for all the screw-ups in life. This man openly adored his family. It is too bad he wasn't given the opportunity to make his dad proud.

Once again, the theory that Ray Stewart's actions impacted countless people was supported. I never put much thought into what the west side community lost as a result of Willie's death. Losing a dedicated grocery store owner would have an immeasurable impact on people's lives. That area of the city was not a spot where a lot of businesses were popping up. The double homicide couldn't have helped the neighborhood's reputation in the business community's eyes. When Fredd's Grocery finally closed its doors, it created a void for families who shopped there. A lot of residents were now forced to travel a considerable distance in order to buy food for their children. During that time, the economy in Rockford was terrible. Jobs were simply not around. People needed to be cut some slack, like being able to buy some groceries on credit from time to time. That was never going to happen at the supermarkets. Alex was right. Ray Stewart hurt those people too.

The saddest moment of the afternoon was when Alex started to talk about the impact his father's murder had on him. What he was about to say was shocking and depressing. He could barely get the words out. Everyone in the room was about to unknowingly witness a major stepping stone in Alex's road to recovery. At this point, everyone knew that he was devastated, but now they were going to find out how deep and damaging the devastation was. Alex had gone from Rock Valley to rock bottom since the death of his father.

"My life has been a living hell since then. My grades in college went from B's to F's. I had to drop out of school. I didn't go back for awhile. I started to drink alcohol very heavily. This is the first time I ever told anybody this: I became an alcoholic. I hated alcohol because I knew what alcohol could do. I never took a drink of alcohol until after my father got killed," said Alex.

When Alex revealed he was an alcoholic, several people in the audience gasped. It was the most noticeable audience reaction during the hearing. This was the first time Alex made this revelation in a public forum. Many of the family members from the other families had watched Alex grow up through the years, seeing him at various court proceedings. In the last few years they had seen much of each other. Now, those people were learning what happened to Alex. Sadly, he had turned to the bottle in a futile attempt to escape the pain. More than anything, he turned to booze out of despair.

The road to recovery is a long one. Alex took a major step by telling a roomful of mostly strangers that he was a drunk. Coming out in public like that was not a small feat. It took a lot of guts. Some recovering alcoholics never get to this point. Alex was attending Alcoholic Anonymous meetings and trying to get his life back to normal. It is safe to say Ray Stewart's actions probably triggerred a lot of this behavior. However, Alex did do this to himself. He caved in to despondency and started to drink heavily. Nobody held a gun to his head. He was starting to realize he needed to take responsibility. Alex needed to start undoing some of the damage Ray did to him and his family. More importantly, he needed to start correcting the damage he was doing to himself.

"I got some help, I sought counseling, I went through treatment. I still go to meetings today. I did finally graduate from Rock Valley College. I did receive my Associate's Degree in Business Management. I am determined not to let Ray Lee Stewart wreck my life anymore. He has done enough. My mother's health deteriorated after this. My grandmother's health deteriorated after this."

While hearing Alex's story, I got a feeling that he was going to be okay. He was finally going to find his way after all this time. Going back to college and earning his diploma is proof that he is committed to making something out of his once-ruined life. There must have been a thousand desperate moments for Alex. Growing up is usually painful, but for him it was unbearable. There were times when he was really on the edge. He felt alone. Few people could have fathomed the complicated emotions going through his mind. There were even times when he thought about ending it all.

Alex explained, "One day, I wanted to kill myself at the park. I went in to call a friend and told him flat out that I was going to drink and drink, and I just didn't want to live anymore. Everyday, every single day, for the last 15 years, I have been thinking about what has happened to my father. I hope nobody else in this room, if you haven't experienced it, I hope you never experience what I have experienced."

It said a lot about Alex's character when he said he wouldn't want anyone else to experience what he went through. Alex went through hell. Raymond Lee Stewart tortured him and Alex tortured himself. For years he walked through life in a painful trance. What is so sad is that his tale is not all that uncommon. There are thousands of family members who struggle for long periods of time after a relative is murdered. Too often, stories like Alex's are forgotten. Society has built a strong immune system to the constant violence that plagues our street. People just don't care anymore. Alex's story and stories like his need to be told. Even for the most cold-blooded individuals, it is difficult to listen to his experiences and not be touched. Maybe if more people listened, they wouldn't be so quick to pull the trigger. Maybe before picking up a pistol, people would think about all of the repercussions. I wouldn't wish Alex's plight on my worst enemy. Thankfully, Alex didn't kill himself. He didn't let Raymond Lee Stewart make him number seven. For the first time in years, Alex feels alive again.

Alex truly believed killing Ray would finally give him closure. It was the one thing he needed to complete his comeback to humanity. He hated Raymond Lee Stewart for what he did to his father. Furthermore, he hated Stewart for what he did to him and his family. He hated the fact that Raymond Lee Stewart was still alive. Even if you are against the death penalty, it is hard to blame him. The reason he came to Springfield was to make sure Raymond got what he deserved. I suspect he would have gone off the deep end if Stewart would have been awarded executive clemency. The very thought of that possibility haunted Alex.

"I am pleading with the board, please, begging, please, don't let this man escape this punishment. He deserves the death penalty. He has to pay for what he did. Not only to my father, but to me. He killed my mother, me, my sister, my brother, and the rest of the victims that are in this courtroom. I can't . . ."

Alex was crying, and he quickly got up, rushed back to his seat and hid his tear-soaked face. He was finished testifying.

The death penalty was incredibly attractive to Alex Fredd. In a way, he was thirsty for Ray's blood. I suspect he would have liked the execution to have been more painful. His story is the strongest case that pro-death penalty folks have. Why should a man who has killed and hurt so many, be allowed to live? This is where the notion of an eye for an eye comes into play. Ray Stewart viciously gunned down Alex Fredd's father. Stewart shot him twice at point blank range. Victims can never be allowed to decide the punishment of criminals. If that were the case, people would probably be getting executed for driving violations. However, Alex truly believed this was going to be the end of a long, harrowing chapter in his life. He truly felt that when the execution was complete, he could finally get on with his life. It is hard to come up with reasons not to let Alex have his closure. Regardless of how anyone feels about the death penalty, it is hard to give a damn about what happened to Ray Stewart after hearing Alex's testimony. Alex almost made it all the way through. It was the most emotional exhibition of the day. At the end, Alex had everybody in the room emotionally involved. It was very sad. I noticed one of the board members shaking her head with an obvious frown on her face. Alex's testimony had clearly touched her. At that moment, I knew there was no way this board was going to recommend commuting Ray's sentence to life in prison. In a few days, Ray was surely going to be executed and Alex was finally going to get his closure.

Alex Fredd had a bright future. He was a decent student in high school who was attending a decent junior college. He had inherited a strong work ethic from his family. Most of all, he was a nice person. He was a likable guy with promising prospects and a good chance at becoming somebody important in the community. Then, Raymond Lee Stewart walked into that grocery store and blew away his father. Suddenly, Alex was lost. He took a lot of wrong turns. He didn't have anybody there to push him back on track. In the whole Ray Lee Stewart story, Alex Fredd is one of the saddest victims. If Raymond Lee Stewart hadn't killed his old man, I think things would have been different for Alex. Maybe he would have been derailed by something else farther down the track, but there's no way to know that. Nor is there any way to know how successful this young man may have become if Ray Stewart had not taken Willie Fredd's life. Ray Stewart destroyed Alex's future, and now Alex lives his life one day at a time. For now, that's the best he can do, and even that is a struggle.

CHAPTER 17

Then Job arose, and rent his robe and shaved his
head, and fell upon the ground and worshipped. And,
he said, 'Naked I came from my mother's womb, and
naked shall I return; the Lord gave, and the Lord has
taken away; blessed be the name of the Lord. In all
this, Job did not sin or charge God with wrong.
—Job 2:20-21

There was a slight delay in the proceeding after Alex stormed off
the witness stand. Sallie Fredd was the next scheduled speaker, and
it took the Fredd family a few minutes to regain their composure.
There was some hugging and back patting to get out of the way.
Arlene Anderson didn't bother introducing Sallie right away. She
respectfully gave the family some time to regroup. When Anderson
thought they were ready, she quickly introduced the board to Sallie
Fredd by simply stating that Willie Fredd's widow was the next witness. In a way, her son's testimony was introduction enough. The
Fredd family had staked out a spot on the left side of the hearing
room. After a minute or so, Sallie emerged and started making her
way to the microphone.

I have seen old pictures of Sallie from the early 1980's. She
looked completely different now. Sallie always used to wear a large
hat with a big brim to the court appearances. After the 1982 escape
attempt was foiled, reporters rushed up to her to try and get her reaction to the dramatic event. She looked confused and bewildered. She
simply told them she didn't have any comment and then walked

away. Back then, she was an attractive middle-aged woman. At the clemency hearing, she had a very motherly look to her. It appeared she had some trouble getting around. She didn't need any assistance, but it took some time for her to reach the speaker's table. I got the impression she didn't go out all that often. The trip to Springfield probably took a lot of her energy.

This was an emotional moment for Sallie. She had just finished listening to the heart-wrenching testimony of her son. It wasn't easy for me to listen to; I can't imagine what it was like for her. Still on the heels of that emotional experience, she was going to have to tell the board about the worst event of her life: the day she became a widow because of Raymond Lee Stewart. Her emotions had to be high. However, she didn't show signs of being extremely nervous or having any lack of composure. In fact, she seemed very focused as she began to tell the board her unfortunate story.

Sallie began her presentation by telling the board how she found out about the murders that shocked the Rockford area and changed her life forever.

"I didn't know about it until after it was on the news. I got a call, and someone asked, 'Sallie, what on earth is going on at the store?' I said, 'What do you mean.' 'I see a lot of policemen there.' I said, 'Well, no one has called me.' I hadn't heard anything about it. So, I got on the phone and called up there and the phone rang a long time and finally a police officer answered. I said, 'What is going on.' He said, 'Who are you?' I said, 'Willie Fredd's wife.' He sighed, and he said, 'Well, an officer is on the way out to get you.' And so, he came and got me. They had taken Willie to the hospital, or somewhere. Anyway, I didn't see him. He was gone. He had been killed."

It was a tough way to find out the news. She slowly learned she was now a widow through a quick and confusing chain of events. It must have been terrible for her to be gathering bits and pieces of the story, until someone finally told her that Willie was dead. I believe women have an intuition about this sort of thing. The second she took the phone call about the police being all over the grocery store, she probably knew what they were going to tell her when she arrived there. The event is a testament to how fleeting life can be. One moment she is safe and sound at home. Her son is in school. Her husband is at work. All of the sudden the phone rings, and everything she knows has suddenly changed.

The murder turned her life upside down. Willie Fredd was a smart and hard-working man. He saw to it she was taken care of. He was a good husband and a good father. Now, he was gone forever. Her kids were going to have grow up without their father. At that time, it seemed like she was coasting through life. Alex was a smart boy. The family had a flourishing business. Then, along came Raymond Lee Stewart. He fired two bullets into Willie Fredd. The bullets probably killed Willie in a matter of seconds. After that, Sallie was no longer coasting; she was fighting to survive. Sallie had to take on strange, new demons. She had to deal with problems she never thought her family would face.

Sallie explained, "Ever since that happened, I have been struggling, trying to keep my family together, and we have had problems. My son just got through talking; he said he would never do alcohol, because he wouldn't drink. He didn't do any of that when he was in school and when my husband lived. He would start drinking and start getting out and doing things he didn't have any business doing. He started sleeping in the park, and he would come home and talk to me. He would say, 'Sallie, I have been out to the park; I was out there sleeping.' He would say, 'I just can't live.' He thinks about his father all the time because he has worked with his father ever since he was big enough to work."

Not only did Sallie have to face the burden of losing her husband, but in the years that followed she watched her one-time promising son destroy his life. Mothers relish even the smallest accomplishment that their children achieve. Alex wasn't accomplishing anything. He was taking these weird trips to the park and drinking like he didn't want to live. Several times, the police sent him home from that park, which is a few blocks away from their home. Most of the Rockford cops knew his story, and they probably cut him some slack from time to time. Sallie was forced to try and guide this boy into adulthood by herself, and he was completely freaking out on her. What do you say when your son tells you he doesn't want to live? Willie was the rock in that family. Sallie wasn't used to setting the example. She didn't know what to do. She didn't know who to turn to. Sallie tried her best, but her son's life had become a wild tailspin, and it just kept getting more and more out of control. All the time, Sallie had to deal with this as a single parent. It was a heavy burden to bear.

Alex isn't the first kid to trade in his books for the bottle. At that age, it is more the rule than the exception. Every year lots of kids flunk out of college because they discover booze and simply lose control. Those kids' parents have to deal with that scenario. But, Alex's case was different. It was much more severe than a young person's experimentation with liquor. Alex wasn't drinking to have fun. He wasn't trying to be cool. Alex was drinking because he was severely depressed. Depression and alcohol are a deadly duo. Dealing with this problem goes way beyond the capabilities of most parents.. Alex needed professional help. As his mother, I bet there were times when Sallie knew her son was on the edge. She just didn't know what to do about it. Sallie had to be asking herself why all this was happening to her. Why was she being put to the test like Job? Luckily, she was strong and made it through. Fortunately, so did Alex. Now, she can finally relish the accomplishments, both big and small, of her son.

Before the murders, the Fredd family had a lot to be proud of. The store was constantly getting bigger and better. Alex was bringing home great report cards. This was a family that was finding its way. The Fredds had tasted success and the sky was the limit for them. But, it would all come to a crashing halt on that fateful January afternoon. In a matter of seconds, all of their hard work quickly disappeared in the smoke that Ray

Stewart's pistol left behind. According to Sallie, that moment ended a long winning streak for the Fredd family.

"His father started a grocery truck, and after the grocery truck started going good, he opened up a little business. We were the first blacks to open a business on West State Street. We never had any burglaries or robberies or anything until the incident happened with Ray Lee Stewart. When he killed my husband, he killed me and my three children. He left me without a companion. My children do not have a father. I have to do all the business. At the time my husband was the provider, and I didn't have to do anything. He took care of everything. All of that fell on me."

Willie Fredd was a trailblazer of sorts. People could have learned a lot from him. I imagine being one of the first black grocery store owners in Rockford wasn't always easy. Somehow, Willie found a way to succeed. He was one hell of an entrepreneur. In the 1960's, he started in the grocery business by selling fruit off of a truck trailer. He would drive the truck through the west side neighborhoods looking for customers. He saved his money, and eventually opened a snack shop at the corner of Delaware and Concord. Finally, he opened the store on West State Street. Three years later, he would die in that store. According to his family, the key ingredient to his success was his dedicated work ethic. He lived to work and he rarely complained about the long hours. He didn't deserve to die like he did. Ray Stewart couldn't have picked a more decent man to kill.

Sallie is a lonely woman. When she said she had to go through the rest of her life without a companion, it really pulled at the heartstrings. She comes off as so unselfish and so concerned about her fatherless son, that it is easy to forget she lost her man. In this world, it is so difficult to find someone you can really spend the rest of your life with. Sallie found him, but Ray Stewart took him away from her. Willie and Sallie were robbed of the joy that comes with growing old together.

Sallie was in the courtroom when the jury came back and

recommended the death penalty for Ray. She heard Judge John Sype pronounce the sentence of death immediately after the jury read their recommendation. Now, it was fourteen lonely years later, and she thought it was time for that sentence to be carried out. Sallie wanted her husband's killer to finally get what was coming to him.

"I just feel like he did it, and he should pay the price. I don't know why he killed my husband. I really don't. I don't have anything else right now. I want to see justice done. If he is not executed, I bet that will send a message out to all these other people who are doing a lot of killing, and let them know they can just go on killing and nothing will be done about it. I want to see justice done."

It was interesting that Sallie included an argument about deterring crime in her plea for Ray's execution. This was an excursion from her mostly political-free, straightforward presentation. It struck me as strange that she suddenly asked the board to make an example out of Ray Lee. Death penalty opponents are quick to point to all kinds of stats that suggest the death penalty is not a deterrent to crime. I seriously doubt Ray was focusing on his potential punishment when he decided to go on his spree. However, Sallie had been through hell and she was looking for answers, not for herself but for other potential widows. I think she is a compassionate person. Though she obviously did not have any compassion for Ray, I think she did have compassion for victims. She truly wanted this punishment to be an example to other potential killers who might be out there. She didn't want anyone else to go through the horror she went through. She believes the threat of the death penalty might be a step in the right direction. In her mind, she thought there was a chance Ray's execution might stop at least one man from killing somebody like a Willie Fredd in the future.

Sallie's desire for Stewart's death did not equal Alex Fredd's. I don't think she needed the execution for closure. She wasn't really seeking revenge at this point. At the heart of her request was the notion that fair is fair. The facts are Ray killed

Willie and he was sentenced to die for it. Right or wrong, Illinois has capital punishment. It is the penalty the state reserves for its most heinous offenders. Ray Stewart's murder convictions top the list of heinous crimes. Sallie simply felt it was time for the state to finally punish her husband's murderer. For her, there was really nothing personal at this point. I suspect she just wanted it to finally be over. No more court proceedings. No more appeals. No more hearings. Sallie wanted the state to commence with the designated punishment, and put an end to the Raymond Lee Stewart saga.

When Sallie was through with her testimony, Arlene called Dorothy Shaw to the witness chair. Shaw had flown in from Atlanta, Georgia for the hearing. She described Willie Fredd as an affectionate, Christian man who was well-liked by the entire family. She asked the board not to commute Ray's sentence. Shaw had taken in Alex's younger brother, William, after the murder. Sallie thought Atlanta might be a better place for him. He ended up going to school at Devry Institute in Atlanta. William still lives there and has been working at Delta Airlines for close to ten years. The youngest member of the Fredd clan is Thelma Demetra Fredd. She stayed in Rockford, and is now raising a family there.

The last member of the Fredd family to testify was Willie Fredd's mother, Thelma Crawford. Alex got up to help Thelma to the witness chair. Somebody else in the audience also got up to lend Alex a hand with his grandmother. Obviously, coming to this hearing was a burdensome affair for Thelma, but I could tell she wouldn't have missed it for the world. She was an old lady, but she was still sharp as a razor, and she didn't waste much time getting right to the point.

"I am Willie Fredd's mother. Oh, Jesus. I know everybody wants to go to heaven, but nobody wants to die. My son did not want to die. But, Raymond Stewart took his life, and now he wants to live. But, I don't think he should live. As far as being abused, I took chastising from my parents, and I didn't call that abusing. It is the parent's duty to chastise their children, and even though my parents abuse me, that doesn't give me any right to go and kill somebody else."

There seemed to be a spiritual force guiding Thelma's testimony. Her delivery was not unlike that of a preacher's. In a way, she was delivering a sermon to the board members, the media, the audience and especially to Ray's family. If anybody in the room was dozing off, they perked right up when she delivered that line about going to heaven. This kind of language was foreign to the hallowed halls of the Capital Building. For Thelma, this was very serious business, but I couldn't help cracking a smile. Her sermon was going to be short, but it was going to be full of passion. This woman really knew how to grab the attention of a room.

Thelma Crawford had no reservations about going right after Joshua Sach's arguments for saving Ray's life. Her counterattack against the abused childhood theory was a little thin. I am convinced there were clearly two very different degrees of abuse at hand. The folks on Ray's side of the room weren't talking about the occasional spanking. However, Thelma's assertion was that past abuse cannot equal an excuse for murder. There are a lot of abuse victims out there. Frankly, many abuse victims suffer far worse torture than Faith Crocker described. The impact of terrifying, ongoing abuse can be severe, and it is a serious problem for the victims. However, most of them do not end up killing all kinds of innocent people. We can't simply give abuse victims a license to kill.

Thelma Crawford ended her testimony by asking the board to deny clemency for her son's killer. She stated, "I have heard it has been said that the living don't know what the dead is doing, but the dead know what the living is doing. If that be the case, I know my son, which I love dearly, knows that I am here today in hopes of Raymond will not be granted clemency for taking his life. And what can I say, I just hope that it will not be granted."

It is an eerie notion to think about the murder victims watching this hearing from beyond. Perhaps many people in that room felt the presence of the deceased victims. Thelma Crawford and Constance Mitchell were the only ones who brought it up. As far as capital punishment is concerned, it would be interesting to know what the six victims thought about executing their murderer, Raymond Lee Stewart. However, the question will always remain unanswered. Mere mortals can only guess and speculate about things like that. Entertaining theatrics aside, Thelma Crawford's testimony definitely forced people to explore uncharted waters about the spirituality surrounding the issue before the board.

The Fredd family did quite a number on Ray's bid for clemency. All four speakers gave compelling reasons for executing Stewart. They had a noticeable influence on the board members who listened patiently and intently to what they had to say. Nobody on that board had spent much time, if any, on the west side of Rockford. None of them ever shopped at Fredd's Grocery Store. Prior to this hearing, they had no idea who these people were or where they came from. To them, Willie Fredd was just the first name on their list of murder victims. Now, they knew who he was. The Fredds had painted them a clear picture. Now, they knew how much damage inmate number A-11739 had done. I think it is a safe bet to say that, at this point, they also knew what their recommendation to the Governor was going to be.

CHAPTER 18

He shall have judgement without mercy that hath shown no mercy.

—James 2:13

In the files department of the Rockford Public Safety Building, there is a huge folder with hundreds of pages of notes on the Raymond Lee Stewart investigation. Included with those notes are pictures that police photographers took at all four Rockford crime scenes. These pictures are beyond disgusting. They show exactly how Ray Stewart left his victims. Their bodies are destroyed with bullet holes. Pools of blood surround their corpses. You can see blood on the walls and all over the rooms. Matter from the victim's organs and brains are visible. While working local news in Chicago, I have seen a lot of murdered bodies. None of those compare to the images found in that folder. Of all these photographs, the ones of Kevin Kaiser are the most disturbing. Stewart truly butchered that young man.

It cannot be stressed enough how brutal Ray's attack on Kevin Kaiser was. Kevin was shot five times at pointblank range. This was his most vicious crime ever. The first bullet went through his hand and into his body. Police believe that to be an indication Kaiser was begging Stewart to spare his life. Cops think he raised his hand in a futile attempt to stop the bullet. It is a common reflex for people who know they are about to be shot. The last bullet was fired pointblank into his face. The injury from that last bullet was a non-bleeding wound. Kevin's heart had already stopped. It was a unnecessary exclamation point on his assault.

Now, the Prison Review Board was going to hear from the family of that murdered teenager. They were going to find out who Kevin Kaiser was before Ray Stewart got to him.

Kaiser came from a big family. He had two brothers and six sisters. Originally, seven of them were going to testify. The day of the hearing, they decided three of Kevin's sisters would talk on behalf of the whole family. Kelly Reeverts was sitting in the middle of the room by herself. When Arlene called her name, she quickly got up and took her seat at the speaker's table. Kelly is Kevin's twin sister.

It was uncanny that the victim's twin sister was now sitting in front of the Review Board. That alone was a look at what Stewart took away from the Kaiser family. Of course, they are fraternal twins. The similarities between the two would be the same as the similarities between any brother and sister who shared the same gene pool. However, if Kevin were alive, he would be the same age as Kelly. Somehow, you couldn't help but think that you were looking at a living image of Kevin.

Kelly Reeverts was in her early thirties. If I were a bartender, I would card her. She looked a lot younger than she was. Kelly was dressed very casually. She was wearing jeans and tennis shoes. I don't know if it was just the burden of that day, but she seemed to have a very serious look about her. When she talked, I got the sense that she felt like she had to do this. She wasn't particularly excited about the whole affair. When she was sitting in the audience, she kept to herself. It was obvious she wasn't interested in talking to anybody else in the room. I didn't see anybody from the media try to engage her in a conversation. If they had, I doubt she would have obliged them. Kelly was giving out clear signals that she wanted to be left alone.

She was holding several sheets of loose-leaf paper in her hands. The papers were full of words she had handwritten with an ink pen. Kelly had prepared what she was going to say and read her statement from the paper. She was the only witness who did this. She didn't look nervous, but she was clearly emotional. Her words were shaky, and she seemed to be holding back tears. Kelly read quickly. The impact Kevin's murder had on the family was both emotional and physical.

Kelly explained, "My mother was devastated. My sisters, brothers and myself, our lives were altered forever. One sister couldn't eat for days. I myself vomited uncontrollably because a part of me had died with my brother. My brother Mark was in total denial because they had been inseparable. All of us remembering different things: Christmas, birthdays, Easter, silly things we did to each other. No one believed this could or had happened to us."

It was obvious the Kaiser family was absolutely crushed by the news of Kevin's death. Considering the brutality of the crime and the young age of the victim, their desolation was completely understandable. Kevin was just a teenager. His adult life hadn't even begun. All violent deaths are tragedies, but when the victim is a teenager, it seems to really hit home in a hurry. The memories of him being a little kid were fresh in the minds of the surviving family members. It might have been easier to absorb if it had been a car wreck or a freak accident. This wasn't an accident. It was intentionally caused by a sense-less murderer. The sting had to have been tremendous. What is worse, family members couldn't help but imagine what his ter-rifying death was like. It is likely they constantly relive the hor-ror Kevin felt during those few moments before Ray Stewart gunned him down. It is a family's worst nightmare.

When Kelly talked about the memories, anybody with a family had to be touched. It is too easy to take holiday time and goofing around for granted. When you hear about stories like the Kaiser family's, it really begs at you to cherish the moments you can have with your own family. Those things are truly what people work and live for. Ray Stewart took Kevin away from his family forever. He could no longer be a part of those special moments. It left a void. I bet weddings and grad-uations and holidays were all dampened by the fact that Kevin couldn't attend in person. It is really amazing how long-lasting was the damage from Ray Stewart's actions. You couldn't even count the number of times the Kaiser family longed for Kevin to be a part of something they were doing. After a funeral, you simply don't stop missing a brother like Kevin. In fact, you probably could never stop missing him.

Reeverts continued by telling the board what happened on the morning of the murder. The events of that unbelievable day still haunt her. She had lost her brother forever. Furthermore, her mother was never going to be the same again. Everything she knew about her family had quickly changed.

"I will never forget when our mom went to see him. She was gone for hours. When she returned home, her life had been drained from her. She had to see one of the children she had fought to protect, laying alone, gone, and never able to tell of his love for her again. After that day she was never the same. Some of us, to this day, find it so hard to believe this has happened to our family."

The mental image of a mother standing over her murdered son is a ghastly one. What a horrible thing to have to go through. It is easy to understand why she was never the same. Something like that is beyond traumatic. It is catastrophic. Especially since the attack was so brutal. Kevin's body was mutilated. I could barely stand to look at the photos; I can't imagine being the boy's mother and looking at the actual body. This testimony was extremely emotional. The way Kelly described this scene was very touching. You can't help but feel compassion for a mother who could never hear the words 'I love you' from her son.

All this pain and disbelief was due to the selfish act of one demented individual. Kelly Reeverts didn't mix words when she talked about Raymond Lee Stewart. She outright hated him. To Kelly, he was someone who was below human standards. Whatever he was, Kelly made it clear she thought it was time for him to die.

"Today you are here to decide the fate of his murderer. I am sorry, I can't use the word man because Raymond Lee Stewart, in our opinion, is no man. An animal, yes. A murderer, definitely. Does he deserve to live any longer than he already has? No. He has lived off of taxpayers since the day he was captured. We paid for his medical expenses after his escape during his trial for our brother's murder. And yet, you are here to decide if he deserves clemency. We say no."

Kelly's disgust for Ray Stewart was burning through in bright, fiery colors. She was really letting her brother's murderer have it. She wasn't holding back at all. She called Raymond an animal, and it was obvious she absolutely believed that. This man gunned down a complete stranger, who happened to be her twin brother, in cold blood, for no apparent reason. That murder was one of six he admitted to commiting. During the trials, Stewart openly taunted everybody, but he was especially cruel to the Kaiser family. By calling him an animal, Kelly Reeverts wasn't trying to make the decision easier on anybody. She truly believed he was an animal. Man or beast, Kelly believed he had to die for his repulsive crimes. Justice had to be served up in the form of a lethal injection. She also belived it should never have taken this long.

I think the whole Kaiser family was frustrated with the entire process. They didn't seem to believe there was any real need for this hearing after all that had happened in the past. Why should this man be allowed to beg for leniency? As for his execution, what was taking so long? Ray Lee Stewart used every possible stale tactic to delay his death. He almost spent more time behind bars for the murders, than Kevin did on this planet. The only Ray Stewart event the Kaiser family wanted to attend at this point, was his execution. They were sick of the appeals and the court appearances. They were sick of the art shows and the controvery. They were sick of Raymond Lee Stewart avoiding the punishment designated for him.

The day Ray Stewart was sentenced for killing Kevin Kaiser was supposed to be a day of justice for the Kaiser family. The man who violenty took their young Kevin away from them was getting what he deserved. He was going to die. Raymond Lee Stewart shocked people in the courtroom that day. He took the opportunity to taunt the family of his victim. He made a mockery out of the event.

Reeverts explained, "The day his death sentence was handed down, he turned to my mom, my brother Mark and my sister Michelle, and said, 'I did it.' And he then smiled and mouthed, 'at least eight or ten years' to my mom. Well, he was wrong. It has been fourteen more years. Enough is enough. We ask you to show no mercy, carry his sentence out. Raymond Lee Stewart does not deserve to live one more day, one more month, one more year or one more decade."

It was a clear case of adding insult to injury. It wasn't enough that he brutally killed Kevin; he had to be an asshole to the Kaiser family, too. Their day of justice turned into another demonstration of Ray Stewart's cruelty. The only comfort the Kaiser family could walk away from the courthouse with was that it wouldn't be so funny to Stewart when he was strapped down to a gurney with a needle in his vein.

When the police make an arrest, they read Miranda rights to the alleged offenders. It is the arresting officer's responbility to make it clear that anything they say can later be used against them. What Raymond said in that courtroom in 1982 was now coming back to haunt him. At that point, he had had over a year to think about the crimes he had committed. Instead of showing any sign of remorse, he chose to flaunt his stature as a feared criminal and pick on the poor victim's family. His courtroom statements didn't help his clemency case at all. In 1982, he was almost baiting today's players into expediting the procedure. I bet nobody wanted to prove him more right than he already was about the system's lengthy appeals process. I don't know if Ray Stewart had a lack of vision, or if he just didn't care, but his courtroom antics were crushing to his clemency petition.

Kelly Reeverts was on her last sheet of paper. She asked the board to take a close look at the disgusting photos in the Ray Stewart file. That is what this killer did to her twin brother. In a way, she was asking the board to show Ray the same amount of mercy Ray showed Kevin.

"We hope, as you consider your decision, you will think of a 17-year-old boy who was shot not once, not twice, but five times. Look at the pictures of him when the police got there. I have seen them, and they will always be in my mind. Think of my mother, who lost her youngest son. Of six sisters and two brothers who lost a sibling, a twin, a friend. Of nieces and nephews who were never able to know their Uncle Kevin. Of grandparents who had to say good-bye to their youngest grandson."

I don't know if the board even had access to those photos, but it was still an effective sentiment by Reeverts. With all this hoopla about abuse and rehabilitation, the fact of the matter is those photos do not lie. Ray did that. It is hard to imagine just how gruesome the images on those crime scene photographs are. It is hard to fathom what it must have felt like for Kelly to see those pictures. Imagine one of your own relatives with their face blown off and their body riddled with bullets. It is a truly terrfying thought.

I liked the way Kelly listed all the various people in her life who felt a sense of loss because Kevin was gone. Killing a person is an endless chain reaction of hurt. I imagine the list was incomplete; there were probably other relatives and friends. It truly lends evidence to the notion that murder is one of the worst crimes against humanity. The repercussions of a single homicide are astonishing. The impact goes beyond counting the heads of the family members and victims. When a loved one is murdered, it is difficult not to be hardened by the experience. Psychological problems are common. Relationship problems are common. After a crime spree like this, everybody in the community becomes a little less trusting. The damage that Ray Stewart did can really never be measured, but it is safe to say that he affected hundreds of lives.

Kelly ended her presenation by talking about her mother.

"My mother's only wish in life was to see the execution of her son's murderer, Ray Lee Stewart. Unfortunately, my mother passed away in 1991. But she asked not to let people forget our brother, and we won't. In conclusion, my family has drawn up a petition and taken it to businesses in Rockford, and within a week-and-a-half, we have collected over 900 signatures wanting the death sentence to be carried out."

It was sad her mother didn't get to fulfill her final desire. It was even sadder she wanted to live to see a man die. What Raymond Lee Stewart did changed a lot of people's lives. Because of his actions, people's priorities were out of whack. Kevin's mother should have been able to spend the last years of her life relishing the huge family she was blessed with. Instead, she spent much of those years hoping she would live long enough to get revenge on Raymond. She had been through the worst imaginable experience a mother can go through. It is a terrible thing to have to bury one of your own kids. It is especially terrible when that child is murdered. The family had to live without her now, just like they have had to live without Kevin since 1981. I don't pretend to know much about the afterlife. I don't know if she got to see Ray's execution or not. I hope she got to hear Kevin say the words, 'I love you,' again. The Kaiser kids were carrying the burden of their mother's last wish on their shoulders. There was no way they were going to let her down, by letting their guard down and giving Raymond Lee Stewart a shot at escaping his punishment.

The list of signatures demonstrated how dedicated the Kaiser family was to avenging Kevin's murder. That project took some effort. I suspect they anticipated what people on Ray's side were going to pull at the clemency hearing, and they wanted to make sure the Review Boad members knew this man really had few friends. I bet they easily could have gotten nine-thousand Rockford residents to sign that petition. It is hard to find too many folks in Rockford who didn't want this man to die for his crimes. For business owners, he represented something petrifying. He walked into four Rockford-area businesses and blew away everybody who was inside. I doubt it was too difficult to find area business owners who were willing to sign. After fifteen years, there was still plenty of anger in my hometown. In fact, one pizzeria in town actually had a sign with a countdown to the number of days left before the execution.

Chairman Williams asked Kelly to submit the list of signatures to the board. Williams nodded at the clerk, who got up and headed over to the speaker's table. Afterwards, Kelly got up and returned to her seat. It was quite an accomplishment for her to make it all the way through her presentation without breaking down. I thought there were times when she was on the edge. But, she was prepared and determined. She found a way to do what she had to do.

There are no two ways about it, Kelly Reeverts has a lot of hostility. Losing Kevin was a bitter pill she is still trying to swallow. I really got the feeling a big part of her did die when Ray Stewart pulled the trigger on that fateful Wednesday morning in 1981. All of the Kaiser family probably felt like a part of them had died, but for Kelly that unpleasant agony was amplified. This was her twin brother. She probably knew more about him than anybody. She could probably tell what he was thinking. Kevin was probably Kelly's archrival and her best friend. For the last fifteen years, she had to find ways to live life without him. She never got to confide in him again. She never got to compete against him again. They never got to tease each other again. They had identical backgrounds. I am sure it would have been extremely interesting for Kelly to see what Kevin ended up doing with his life. Now, all Kelly Reeverts had left were some memories, both good and bad, and some pictures. Some of those pictures are actual developed film, but most of them are mental images. Some of them are ugly. For her sake, I hope that someday she only remembers the beautiful ones.

CHAPTER 19

"I looked over Rockford and what did I see? It was the Kaiser family, with pain in misery, coming for to carry me home."

— Raymond Lee Stewart

That quote is taken from a phone conversation Ray Stewart had with Jennifer Bishop Jones on the night of his execution. He replaced the words to 'Swing Low, Sweet Chariot.' The quote can be taken a lot of different ways. Jennifer believes it was not intended to be hostile towards the family he hurt so much. I suspect the Kaiser family finds that hard to believe.

The Kaiser family had been visible throughout the Ray Stewart saga. The day Ray was sentenced to die, they came out and told the media about the antics he pulled in the courtroom. During the Salvation Army controversy, Stewart believed they were the main force blocking the show from displaying his work.

Regardless of the meaning behind his lyrics, Ray Stewart definitely had a distaste for this family. When I talked to him the night before his death, he was still outraged at what had happened during the 1993 art show. Stewart thought it was unfair that they pulled his work, but not the work of other death row inmates. He said he no longer felt anger towards the Kaiser family, and that was proof he was no longer a vengeful man. However, I could tell he didn't care too much for them. The feeling was obviously mutual.

There were two others sisters who testified on behalf of the

Kaiser family. They were Kevin's older sisters, Laura Davis and Margie Burza. They were testifying at this clemency hearing to insure this matter was going to end, once and for all.

Laura Davis began her testimony by attempting to refute some of the earlier testimony on behalf of Ray. There were a lot of nice things said about this killer. People testified he had changed and killing him now would be a tragedy. Laura didn't believe any of that.

She explained, "This man has lived long enough. He has lived longer than my brother, longer than the other victims. He asks to live another day, and breathe another hour, but he didn't give my brother that choice, or any of the other victims. If this man is such a gentle man, what happened to the gentleness fifteen years ago when he shot my brother five times and the last shot had to be in the face when he was already dead? Tell me why he had to do that, if he is such a gentle and caring man."

Davis was obviously taking a shot at what Jennifer Bishop Jones had said earlier. I imagine Laura was squirming in her seat as she listened to Jennifer describe the Ray she knew as a gentle and caring man. The clemency hearing was starting to get a little ugly. The only Ray that Laura knew was the Ray who gunned down her kid brother. He was the only Ray she needed to know. For that crime, Laura was convinced he needed to die. To her, it didn't matter what he had been doing for the last 15 years. All of that was moot. Kevin had spent those same 15 years dead and buried. Her family had spent those same 15 years living without him. The fact that maybe he was a gentle man today didn't really matter. For her, Ray still hadn't paid the price for his lack of gentleness in 1981.

You could tell Laura had a lot of hate in her heart for Ray Stewart. Like Kelly, she didn't hold much back. Laura was displaying her anger for everyone to see. Her voice got louder when she talked about how Ray shot her brother five times. Several times, her testimony was peppered with emotional shifts in her speaking tone. It had been years since her brother's death, but the hurt hadn't gone away at all. Laura absolutely hated Ray Stewart for what he did. Time had done nothing to fade that hatred.

Like several members of the Kaiser family, Laura attended many of Ray Stewart's court appearances. Those long court proceeding were emotionally draining. Because she so frequently attended court, she knew the case backwards and forwards. In fact, she knew some things a lot of people had forgotten about. For Ray, her expertise proved to be a dangerous weapon. Laura knew this wasn't the first time Ray Stewart had petitioned for leniency. She shared with the board a moment she remembered from the sentencing phase of the Kaiser trial.

"I remember during the trial when it was brought up that he had been in jail before, and he sent a letter to the judge saying, 'I have changed. Please let me out. I will show you how much I have changed.' Well, he showed this judge when he showed him the six victims. Now, you are telling me this man has changed again and deserves clemency to live another 15 years? So, he can breathe and say, 'I have changed, please think about letting me be paroled'?"

Ray got an early out on his first felony conviction. In 1970, he was sentenced to a five to fifteen year prison term for robbing a dry cleaners. Ray only served 14 months.

Like the revelations about Stewart's cruel courtroom antics, this was damaging stuff. Could the board risk making the same mistake the judge made several years go? This blunder of justice demonstrated how risky it was to believe anything Ray Stewart said. He had already pulled the song and dance routine about being a reformed man once. Later, he went out and killed six people. Now, Stewart's attorney was filing for clemency. Laura was telling this Review Board to seriously consider his past track record. She was asking them not to let this man fool the system again.

I think most people in the room knew Ray Stewart did not have a chance in hell of getting clemency. This whole afternoon was more of a procedural thing than anything. The media was already making arrangements for covering the execution. The Department of Corrections were making their preparations. Hotel rooms in the Joliet area were getting booked up. Nobody really thought Edgar was going to commute this serial killer's sentence. However, it seemed to me the Kaiser family was genuinely concerned his life might actually be spared. I guess in the Ray Stewart story, anything is possible. After all that had happened, they weren't taking any chances. They were tortured, ridiculed and insulted by the man who killed their young Kevin; at this point, they wouldn't be able to cope with any outcome other than his death. The idea of parole for Stewart was completely unrealistic. However, for the Kaiser family there was only one to make sure of that. With Stewart's death, the Kaiser family knew for sure he would never be able to get out and do this to another family.

Laura finished her testimony by asking the board to shoot down Stewart's clemency bid, stating that Ray Stewart's crimes absolutely warranted the death sentence.

"This man deserves the death sentence. He deserved it fifteen years ago, and he deserves it today. He is a cold-blooded murderer and in my heart, I hate his guts. And all I ask is that you deny clemency."

There was absolutely no ambiguity in Laura's closing remarks. The statement, 'I hate his guts,' leaves little room for interpretation. In a way, it was painful to be exposed to the degree of anger she was carrying. For that split second, when the intense remark took me by surprise, I believe I really got a sense of the pain Laura felt. I think the audience really got a sense of the anger she felt. For a moment, she let everyone in that room see one of the darkest corridors in her heart. Laura didn't ask to become the sister of a murder victim. I doubt she liked carrying this darkness in her persona. However, it was there. Ray Stewart put it there. She hated him, more than she thought it was possible to hate a single individual on this planet. The outburst wasn't theatrics. Laura Davis was simply showing some of her true, uglier colors.

The media jumped on the "I hate his guts' bite. It appeared in a couple of newspaper articles on the clemency proceedings. It was perfect for the press. The words are short, sweet, and right to the point. It reminded me of the way the media handled Jeffrey Dahmer's sentence hearing. During that proceeding, a family member of one of Dahmer's victims screamed uncontrollably at Dahmer for a long period of time. The memorable incident epitomized the hurt Dahmer inflicted on his victim's family. In a way, the media reduced Laura's testimony to that short statement. But, it was much more than that. It was a very honest, intelligent, and moving presentation. It was obvious Laura deeply loved her brother Kevin. It was obvious Laura deeply loved her family. After listening to her talk, her hated for Raymond Lee Stewart was understandable.

Margie Burza was the final member of the Kaiser family to talk. She is the oldest of the Kaiser kids. Because of that, she was entrusted with the unpleasant duty of calling up several family members and breaking the shocking news about Kevin. It was an emotionally and mentally draining task. It was something she never got over having to do.

Burza explained, "I had to call my aunts, my uncles. I had to find my brother-in-law, to call my sister; I had to find my sisters; I had to track down my brother, who lives in Ohio, through my mother-in-law. The only people I didn't call, because I didn't think it would be safe to tell them over the phone, were my grandparents who lived in Florida. They had a police officer go to the house and tell them. Later that day, I had to go to the airport to pick them up and tell them everything I knew about Kevin's death. I am the oldest sister. I am the oldest child. I think that is a lot to ask for anyone to have to do, to break that kind of news, telling the family."

It is easy for anybody to relate to how heart-rending it must have been for Margie to have to call people she loved and tell them the Kevin they all loved had been murdered. I can't even imagine where she found the strength to pull that off. This murder was completely out of left field. The people she had to call had no idea she was about to tell them that healthy, 17-year-old Kevin was gone forever. I imagine as she spoke to various people and repeated the shocking news over and over again, it was still only just beginning to sink in with her. Margie had to help her family members cope with this tragedy, as she was simultaneously trying to cope with it herself.

Margie says to this day she is still trying to explain what happened at that gas station to members of her family; to both the family members who knew Kevin, as well as the ones who never got to meet him. Because Kevin was working the day Ray Stewart walked in, her family will now always be incomplete.

"I had to tell my children their uncle had died. They were the only niece and nephew he knew. We now have a much larger family, lots of nieces and nephews who don't know their Uncle Kevin, but they see pictures, and they are obviously at the ages now, that they know a little bit about what is going on. I mean, a whole piece of my family is missing and we can never have it back"

The thought of the Kaiser family introducing their kids, born after 1981, to the memory of their murdered uncle is touching and curious at the same time. They weren't trying to put this behind them forever. Kevin was still very much a part of the family. His framed picture still sits out in their living rooms for their kids and visitors to see and ask questions about. It is important for kids to know their family's history. Kevin Kaiser was not an unfortunate part of that history. His murder was. It must be a tricky tightrope to walk as a parent, when your kids start asking questions about something like that. Especially considering that a conversation would surely open up a plethora of painful memories. They weren't hiding it, and that is good. I don't envy this added burden to their parental experiences. Clearly, the murder of Kevin Kaiser by Ray Stewart created several bizarre and awkward moments for years and years. Once again, the scope of the damage Ray did proves to be astonishingly far-reaching.

It was during the trial for Kevin Kaiser's murder that Stewart was able to sprint away from two guards and escape from the courthouse. The courthouse was electrified by the events. Nobody really knew what the hell was going on. Gunshots were fired. People were screaming. It took the police several hours to piece together all the events of that exciting afternoon. For the Kaiser family, it was an exasperating eternity.

Burza remembered, "I was in the courtroom the day he escaped. We felt terror when they told us to call our families and tell them to stay in the house until he was recaptured."

The escape incident was truly a terrifying time for the Kaiser family. It must have been a kind of fear few people experience. They were going to court and seeing the man who killed Kevin. He was already under a sentence of death for the first two murders. He would come into the courthouse wearing handcuffs. There were guards assigned to watch him. The building was full of cops. They thought they were safe. Then, they heard the ruckus. Suddenly, they found out Raymond Lee Stewart was on the loose. Millions of turbulent thoughts had to have been racing through their minds. Not only was there a possibility their brother's killer might get away, there was a possibility he might hurt another member of the Kaiser family. Considering his revenge motive for killing Willie Fredd, it was not totally preposterous to think Ray Stewart might try and go after a member of the Kaiser family. And, after talking to Stewart about the Kaisers, I don't think that is a crazy notion at all. A lot of the family members were down there in the courthouse. Those people naturally would have felt the presence of danger in the air. That they called up other family members and warned them about the escape demonstrates how thoroughly terrified that family was of Ray Stewart. They knew all too well what he was capable of. They were smart to not take any chances. Fortunately, Ray was captured. Less than a week later, the Kevin Kaiser trial ended, and he was sentenced to death for the second time.

Burza continued, "I was also sitting there the day he turned to my mother and admitted what he had done. My mother always felt she should have never outlived one of her children. It was a very hard thing for her to accept. She wanted to be able to go to the execution; obviously, that won't happen."

When Kevin's mom, Delores Clark, died, it was an especially sad moment for the family. Of course, they had to cope with the pain that comes from losing a beloved mother. They also had to deal with the unrealized wish she carried to see justice done to the man who killed her son. Margie was the second Kaiser sister to mention this with regret. It really hurt them that their mother wasn't going to be there in person next week when they killed Raymond Lee Stewart. Stewart's actions devastated her life, and the one thing she wanted was to see him get what was coming to him. The family wanted her to be there. The surviving members of the Kaiser family still wanted revenge, but it wasn't going to be as sweet without Delores.

Margie ended her testimony by telling the board not to believe all the hype about this man being changed after all these years. She had sympathy for the magnitude of the decision the board members had to make. Still, she desperately wanted them to deny clemency to the man who killed her brother.

"Lastly, I just don't think he is capable of change, but I know that is a decision you have to recommend. It is not in my ballpark to do that. But, I ask that you recommend carrying out the sentence a jury of his peers recommended."

Margie didn't envy the job ahead for the Review Board. Making a recommendation about whether someone should live or die, cannot be taken lightly. At times, it had to be a soul-searching experience for those people. No sane person could possibly enjoy carrying the weight of being involved in a decision like this. Margie was the only one who acknowledged the moral difficulty that comes with the board's task. I thought that was an important moment. I don't believe she had any second thoughts about what should be done to Ray Lee. I don't think she was questioning the morality of the death penalty. I think Burza, more than the others, recognized and respected the potential ethical complications attached to being a party to this serious and permanent punishment. Margie saw that, in a way, some of Ray's blood was going to be on the hands of the Illinois Prison Review Board. Those men and women hovered around the horseshoe desk looked like secure and stable enough people; but they don't have all the answers to life. They don't know for sure how they are going to feel about this years from now. They can't know for sure if they are ever going to have to answer for their decision. That afternoon, every one of them would probably leave the Capital Building with some amount of psychological baggage. For that burden, Margie seemed to have sincere empathy.

The Kevin Kaiser murder was a terrifying moment of enlightenment for Rockford Police. I doubt, up to that point, anyone could have predicted the magnitude of the two newest cases for the department's homicide division. But, some red flags were starting to sail, and the cops were beginning to sense they had a big problem on their hands. Then, when they saw the next murder victim annihilated with bullet holes in that manner, it was a safe bet the perpetrator was acting out of an emotional motive rather than an objective motive, like robbery. Usually, robbers don't make their victims kneel and then shoot them five times at close range. So, when the investigators saw the Kaiser body, they knew they were now looking for some sort of deranged killer. They were probably starting to think about a serial killer suspect. For the most part, detectives don't put a lot of stock into the notion of coincidences. Back then, homicides were rare. When the Kaiser murder happened on the west side, right after the two murders at Fredd's Grocery, they were definitely thinking the two crimes were linked. The murder of Kevin Kaiser was the beginning of the revelation that Rockford might be under attack by a trigger-happy maniac. After the Kaiser murder, a strange fear started to grab hold of my hometown community.

That fear would quickly tighten its horrible grip as the death toll continued to rise. From the Kaiser murder on, it became clear it was time to watch your back. There was a killer on the loose in Rockford.

The Kaiser family was well-represented at this hearing. They were intelligent people. Their presentations were well-organized. They spoke with passion. Their stories were easy to relate to. In comparison to others, their presentations were short. I imagine they could have talked about this for hours. Instead, each of them only talked for a few minutes. I think the short length strengthened their testimony. In keeping it short and to the point, their effectiveness didn't wear as their presentation lingered on. In a way, I pictured them as brave siblings rushing to the aid of their kid brother who was being picked on by a big bully. All three of those ladies should be proud of what they did. It takes bravery to stand up and give your opinion about a difficult issue that has personal and emotional attachments. They showed true poise and self-control. This hearing could have easily turned into a bloodthirsty circus, but it never did. For the most part, the participants were civil. Obviously, there was a mixture of people in that room which could have been explosive. The Kaiser family handled their end of the hearing with class and decorum. Delores would have been proud.

For the Kevin Kaiser family this was the swan song out of the publicity and the controversy that had so often dominated their lives for the last fifteen years. Their testimony was the final sayonara to the murderer all of them hated so much. Kevin is gone. It is not fair, but the fact is he is never coming back. They will never again get to enjoy spending time with him in this world. I doubt anything could fill that void. However, they did have plenty to live for. Kelly Reeverts, Laura Davis and Margie Burza are three intelligent, beautiful women with a sense of family that is actually rare in this day and age. It was obvious the emotional trauma that came with Kevin's death left deep scars. With Raymond out of the picture, I now hope hate has taken a permanent vacation from their souls and their hearts are filled with only love and peace.

CHAPTER 20

"A mother's love perceives no impossibilities."
—Paddock

I suspect the joy of all joys for mothers is seeing their children all grown up and succeeding in life. It must be immensely delightful for mothers to witness their adult babies working hard towards building careers, homes, relationships and families. As a good mother, you have to invest years of thankless and constant effort to insure that your child has what it takes to make it in this competitive world. There are diapers to change, doctors to visit, homework to help with and heart-wrenching discipline to enforce. It is a badge of burden that fades with age, but never really disappears. When your child hits adulthood, hopefully in exchange for the burden, parents start to reap joyous rewards. The burdens Rosemarie Boeck endured to raise her son Rick were especially intense. From the outset, baby Rick required all of her motherly effort and energy. The hard work was just starting to pay off when Ray Lee Stewart ended it all, by killing Rick when he was in the prime of his life. Ray walked into the Radio Shack and shot the manager, Rick, along with one of his regular customers, Donald Rains. He didn't take much in the way of material possessions. Stewart swiped a radio scanner and a small amount of cash. For Rosemarie, he took a lot more than that. On that Monday afternoon, he robbed her of the glory that comes with cashing in on years of exceptional child-rearing labor. Her middle child, Rick was dead. Her other two children would never be the same.

Rick Boeck was twenty-one years old. Despite his young age, he was already the manager of the Radio Shack store. It was a job that held a lot of promise. The Tandy Corporation was molding their chain of Radio Shack stores into a retail powerhouse. Radio Shack was just coming off a boom in CB radio popularity and was starting to lead the way into the affordable computer age. Rick was beginning to build a name for himself as the store manager. In the Rockford Register Star article that reported the shootings, there were numerous quotes from neighboring store employees who were devastated when they heard Rick had been murdered. It seems he was liked by everybody at that mall.

Rosemarie is the proud mother of Rick. During her testimony, she openly boasted about her son's success and determination. Often, part of a mother's life is lived vicariously through her children. It was obvious this was the case here. Rosemarie was thoroughly prepared for her presentation. She was armed with a folder full of papers, a framed picture, and several newspaper clippings. She came across as a smart woman with a lot of common sense who had a sweet, small-town aura about her. Her testimony was full of emotion. It was obvious she had an intense connection to her murdered son. This wasn't an easy chore for Rosemarie, but she was organized and, in turn, was able to provide an effective speech for the board.

Rosemarie began by thanking the board for letting her talk. She had traveled down from her home in Baraboo, Wisconsin, and was grateful the State of Illinois allowed her to take part in this event. The only murders the Review Board could officially look at were the three for which Stewart received convictions in Illinois. The Kenny Foust murder (which never went to trial) and the Beloit, Wisconsin, murders were merely background information. It was a gesture of respect for victims that permitted Boeck to testify to the Illinois Prison Review Board. The State of Illinois would also allow the Wisconsin victims to witness Ray's execution via closed circuit television, if they wanted to.

Wisconsin is one of twelve states that does not have the death penalty. Wisconsin was the first state to ban the death penalty, and they haven't had an execution there in almost 150 years. When serial killer Jeffrey Dahmer was caught in Milwaukee, the court handed down the worst punishment they had: life in prison without parole. Like the Dahmer case, the Ray Stewart case reopened the debate over capital punishment in Wisconsin. The Beloit Daily News ran some editorials blasting the state for not being able to dish out death to this man like Illinois was doing. Some Wisconsin residents were appalled by the fact that in order to get the appropriate justice for this man, they had to give him to the Illinois authorities. The overwhelming sentiment was that Illinois knew how to handle killers like Ray Lee, while Wisconsin didn't have a clue. On the other hand, death penalty abolitionists praised Wisconsin's method for dealing with Ray Stewart, calling their idea of punishment civil and humane because it stopped the cycle of violence. The Governor of Wisconsin, Tommy Thompson, is for capital punishment and continues to try and persuade the state legislature to adopt a death penalty.

Rosemarie wasn't the smoothest speaker of the afternoon. She was a little overwhelmed by all the different people who were listening and watching her. As she talked, it was obvious Rosemarie was shaking off a few nerves. Despite that, it only took her a few seconds to gain the attention of the entire room. Rosemarie opened her presentation by slamming a framed picture of Rick on the speaker's table. It was a very effective attention-getter.

"I have always appreciated that Illinois includes all of the Wisconsin victims in all of their activities with this. Oh, this is really something. I brought a picture of Rick. I wanted you to see how beautiful he was, so there he is. That picture was taken three weeks before he was murdered. It is not a studio picture. It is just a snapshot, but it's Rick. We didn't have time, I guess, to get a portrait shot before he was murdered," she said.

There he was, the murder victim, sitting in a frame next to

his heartbroken mother and staring right at the board members. It was a chilling moment. Rosemarie was literally showing the board members the face of her son, one of Ray's victims. It was just a snapshot, but the board members could see what his eyes looked, how he combed his hair and what his face looked like. If you were sitting in that room you couldn't help but stare at the picture. Not simply because it was resting next to the speaker, but because the image of that young man was so alluring that it seemed to work as a magnet for the human eye. That picture is one of a few, lifeless things of Rick's that Raymond left behind for Rosemarie. She continued by explaining where her son's murder came into play during the terrifying Raymond Lee Stewart saga.

"I am the mother of Richard Boeck, the sixth victim of the Ray Lee Stewart murders; a week-long rampage that terrorized those residents of two states involving several towns in and around Rockford, Illinois and Beliot, Wisconsin. My son's life was violently taken from him, his family, and all who ever knew him, as well as all who will never know him," she said.

The Beloit murders further changed the complexion of Ray's killing spree. No longer was this just a series of homicides in Rockford. Now, the entire stateline area was under siege. Towns all over the area went on high alert. It sure as hell wasn't just a west side thing anymore. This killer on the loose could strike anywhere.

It is interesting that Rosemarie, like the Kaiser family, cited a sense of loss for people who never got to met Rick. It is hard for non-victims to understand the depth of loss that family members of violent crime victims feel. Rick was very much a part of Rosemarie. The fact that she could no longer show off her son to new people she met was disheartening. It would be hard to bring up the topic of Rick, without bringing up the terrible reason he was no longer alive. Any discussion about him would surely produce painful memories. Furthermore, it is impossible to go through the major events in life, like weddings and graduations, without wondering how the moment would be different if Rick were there to participate. It is a never-ending weight on Rosemarie's heart. I suspect it is difficult to predict when a moment would trigger a sad sensation of loss. Dealing with Rick's death is a life-long challenge for Rosemarie.

Raising Richard Boeck was also a challenge. Rosemarie Boeck was not blessed with a healthy baby. Rick had all kinds of medical problems that kept doctors busy for years.

Rosemarie explained, "Our Rick was very ill for the first two years. He was born allergic to my milk and allergic to water. He spent his first year in and out of hospitals. After lots of research, the doctors finally decided that Rick would be able to tolerate bananas. So our son survived 18 months on bananas. They were smashed and creamed and holed and diced and in some sort of a liquid state, fortified with vitamins. He was a smiler. He kept on smiling and he lived. At his first birthday, he was a whopping one and a half pounds larger than his birth weight, and he lost all of his hair and had no teeth. He looked pretty much like a little old man; yet, always smiling. He survived. By his second birthday, he had developed quite normally. Full of unbelievable energy. Energy that nearly wore his whole family, friends and neighbors all out. Our private joke was it had to be those bananas."

There has to be something special between a mother and child when the child is born sick and miraculously makes it through to healthy adulthood. At the very beginning of the kid's life, the mother has to face the reality of what it would be like if the child dies. When the baby turns out to be okay, there is a fantastic sense of accomplishment and even a belief in divine intervention. The mother and child faced death and pulled through; now, they can take anything the world can dish out. Unfortunately, it doesn't always work out that way. There was no way of seeing Raymond Lee Stewart coming.

I found the story about all the problems Rick had early in his life to be very touching. Usually, people don't share little family nuggets like the Boeck's belief that those bananas had some magical power that filled young Rick up with energy. The audience was being treated to a special peek into the usually concealed family realm. Rosemarie was really sharing her feelings with the board. This takes some courage. She ran the risk of sounding like a lunatic. Rosemarie was able to pull it off quite nicely, though. Instead of sounding loony, she came off as a very endearing mother. I think she sounded like a sweet, sincere, and incredibly honest person who was painting a marvelous picture of the relationship she had with a son whom she dearly loved.

The energy those life-saving bananas seemed to give Rick didn't disappear as he grew up. Rick went from being a sickly baby to a driven young man. According to Rosemarie, that high level energy was with Rick right up until the day he was murdered.

She explained, "I had spoken with Rick at midnight, the night before he died. He was very high, because he had just come back from mailing in the results of the inventory he and his employees had completed that evening. He was very proud of the tallies he had just turned in. He had been a manager for this store for only a short time and already he could see an open swing in sales. When Rick was satisfied with results, everybody knew it. It was really big, because this child of mine had such high standards for himself, but he nearly wore us all out just hearing about them. His humor, his energy, his drive was infectious to anyone near him."

The board was getting a clear picture of what the man in the snapshot was all about. It is easy to relate to the image of a young man making sure everyone around him knew when he was having success in his life. As I listened, I really felt like I began to know Rick Boeck.

The impact of Rick's death on people around him is immeasurable. It is sad to say, but it seems like there are few people in this world who actually aspire to try and do better. Rick really took pride in his work at Radio Shack. It is rare to find a person who is so pumped up about improving sales that they immediately call their mother to share the good news. Young people like that are invaluable to our society. Usually, the sky is the limit for such people. Rosemarie was right about that kind of energy being contagious. It is likely Rick could have been a role model for his co-employees. When you work around a manager who really cares and really has his act together, it tends to motivate you to emulate that effort. Unfortunately, Rick and the people around Rick never got to see how far his work ethic was going to take him. Raymond Lee Stewart denied Rick Boeck the opportunity to be a complete success story.

It was a sad contrast to hear about the difficult time that Rick had coming into this world in comparison to the senseless way he left it. Rick had survived all of his infant health problems only to be murdered. Ray Stewart cut him down, right when he was cleared for take-off to the top of the world. He never got to reap the rewards for his hard work.

"Rick was only allowed to be old once in his life, and that was his first year on this earth. Life was over for him at the age of 21 when he should have been receiving awards for his efforts. Not death. He already won that battle once before, with death. Now, he lost. There would be no more smiles. No more dreams and no more anything. He is just gone, and gone from us forever. You know, he is really gone."

The murder of Rick had an especially devastating impact on his older brother. Robert Boeck was 23 years old at the time of his brother's murder. It seems there was some role reversal at work between the two brothers. According to Rosemarie, Rick was the one who was acting as a role model to Robert. With Rick's death, Robert temporarily lost his sense of direction. For several months after the murder, Robert disappeared from his parents' view. For a long time, Rosemarie thought Raymond Lee Stewart had taken both of her sons.

Rosemarie explained, "He couldn't deal with Rick's death, not with us anyway. Bob was a more content child. Honestly, in some mother's eyes, depending on who you measured him by, Rick was a doer and Bob was a non-doer. But, it was Rick that kept Bob moving. It was this younger brother who nudged Bob constantly to just get with it and go for it, Bob. Go for those bananas. Don't settle for anything less, he would tell him. We had been led to believe this killer had killed both our sons, but it was after five years, slowly regaining the relationship back with Bob, that he told us he treated us like this because he was afraid he could never live up to goals Rick had set for him. I didn't even know these brothers had these goals."

What a petrifying prospect for Rosemarie back in 1982. She must have felt like her world was coming to an end. First, she loses Rick. Then, she had to face the possibility that her oldest son was going to permanently slip into a world of despair. Just when she had guided her boys through the rigorous terrain of adolescence, along came Raymond Lee Stewart. Rick was gone forever. I suspect Rosemarie had to, for family survival purposes, be the first Boeck to come to terms with that tragedy. Rosemarie was the glue that held the Boeck family together through that dreadful period in their lives. Fortunately, Bob found a way to deal with losing his younger brother, Rick. He is now married and working as a Corrections Officer at a state prison.

The relationship between brothers who are close in age is usually more complicated than it appears. It didn't surprise me that Rosemarie was unaware of the secret goals Bob and Rick shared. Not even the most involved mother could possibly know and understand the many dynamics that surround a relationship between two brothers. Brothers like that would undoubtedly share the same frame of reference. They would talk the same language. Growing up together, they could almost tell what the other brother was thinking by just looking at him. They would love each other deeply, but usually keep that love on an understood basis. There would also be a competitive overtone to the fraternal relationship. In a way, the brothers would serve as clones to measure themselves against. I don't doubt that Rick would have done anything to help Bob find the path to success. When Ray Stewart killed Rick, Bob truly lost a best friend, a loyal coach and a loving brother.

Robert Boeck wasn't the only one that lost a brother when Stewart shot and killed Richard Boeck. Rick's kid sister, Crystal, was completely floored by the murder.

Rosemarie explained, "My daughter was 15 when she lost her brother. He was her idol. There were five years between her and Rick, and you'd've believed they were twins. They looked alike. They thought alike. Her every gesture, decision, and every word is still totally the essence of Rick. One difference though, she became more selfish with her goal-setting and was not as contagious as Rick. I know that Ray Stewart took that extra sparkle from her."

Crystal is now part of the police brass for the Phoenix Arizona Police Department. Her husband is a cop with the neighboring Scottsdale Police Department. To Rosemarie's dismay, they have chosen not to have children. Rosemarie believes that Crystal is afraid of bringing a child into this world, because of what Raymond Lee Stewart did to Rick. Rosemarie said Crystal couldn't bear the thought of going through what she went through: having to bury one of her kids because of a murderer.

It is interesting that members of the Boeck family chose to adopt a law enforcement lifestyle. I hope that in their work, none of them ever encounters a criminal as vicious as Ray Stewart. Certainly, they have acquired the training and skills to deal with someone like him, though. Why would the siblings of a murder victim seek a career in law enforcement? They might have chosen those career paths anyway, but it could be because they had felt the sting of violence firsthand and they were dedicating a part of themselves to helping reduce the number of people who have to go through the same kind of hell they went through. It could also be that because of the anger they felt for Ray Stewart, they were waging a personal war against violent criminals like him. I doubt even they know all the reasons behind it. Clearly though, the murder of their brother had a long-term impact on their lives. Like so many others, they were a part of that enormous, ongoing chain reaction that started when Ray Stewart went on his killing rampage.

Rosemarie has a really tough time dealing with the fact that she doesn't have grandchildren to spoil. Like Crystal, Robert Boeck and his wife haven't had children. Rosemarie thinks that is also because of what Ray did. The grandparents of Rick Boeck had a tough time dealing with the loss of their grandson. Both of Rick's grandmothers are still alive. They are in their eighties. Through the years, they have seen a lot. Despite that, they were still confused by the senselessness of Rick's murder.

Rosemarie explained, "My mother is a little torn up because her daughter has had to suffer losing her child. Something, she believes, is the hardest loss of all, losing a child. She has trouble that Rick's death was a man-made choice, not God's choice. My mother-in-law is very familiar with death. She has lost four husbands and twelve siblings all through war and the aimlessness of old age. But, the hardest for her, yet today, is understanding that Rick's death is by murder. After 15 years, she goes into a state of shock and anger when she thinks of this devil, Ray Lee Stewart."

The perspective that Rosemarie's mother and mother-in-law had on Rick's murder is an interesting one. Here were women who had observed and survived all kinds of death through their eighty plus years on earth, and yet, to them, nothing seemed as senseless as Rick's murder. Even the craziness of wars couldn't compare to Raymond's random act of violence. Rick had done nothing wrong. He was at work, doing his job. He should have been safe there. It is understandable that they thought of Raymond Lee Stewart as the devil. It was as if Satan did send one his soldiers to wreak havoc on their family's life. Rick's death was something they could never get over. In all their years, I suspect they never witnessed anything so unfair.

For the most part, Rosemarie's testimony was focused on who her son Rick was and the lingering damage his murder had on her family. Towards the end of her presentation, she took the opportunity to directly attack the man who killed her son. She had a clipping from a recent interview that Raymond Lee Stewart had done with the Milwaukee Journal Sentinel. In that article, Stewart apologized for his actions and tried to explain why he did what he did. Rosemarie wasn't buying his reasons. In that interview, Stewart said he accepted the death penalty the moment he pulled the trigger at Fredd's Grocery Store. If that were true, Rosemarie wanted to know why he killed five other people, including her son Rick, whom he didn't have any beef with. Stewart also said the reason he went up to Radio Shack was to get back at white people for what they did to John F. Kennedy. To Rosemarie, this was just some race card hoopla a condemned man was using to conjure up support from people who might be sympathetic to him because of racial tension in this country. She pointed out that half of Stewart's victims were black and half were white. Stewart also told a story about stopping in a Tennessee park on his way to North Carolina. There, he was going to discard the guns. Ray said he didn't, because he no longer wanted to get away with his crimes. Stewart said, at that point, he was ready to face the music. If that were the case, Rosemarie wanted to know why he didn't just drive to a police station and end it all. Instead, he continued his flight from justice into North Carolina.

Rosemarie had some good points. It is safe to say most people would have a difficult time understanding the perplexing thought processes of Ray Stewart. The way he thought is much different from the way most people think. His rationalizing abilities were as creative as they were crazy. What Ray told the Milwaukee Journal Sentinel reporter did seem a little farfetched. It would obviously be foolish to take anything Ray Stewart said as the gospel. The evidence suggests Raymond Lee Stewart spent years trying to escape punishment for the killing spree. This was a killer who, throughout his trials, always pleaded innocent. When he had an opportunity to escape, he took it. During his years on death row, Raymond Lee Stewart had a remarkable ability to find ways to incorporate images and issues into his story that would spark emotional reactions from people on the outside. That is what the whole art show thing waš all about. That is why Joseph Cardinal Bernardin would eventually be lured into the story. I suspect that is what the sudden John F. Kennedy motive was all about. Rosemarie thought his theories and explanations were self-serving. To her, this was just a vicious killer who was trying out a new strategy in his continuing effort to escape justice. She wasn't about to let him get away with it. As far as his apology, Rosemarie wasn't impressed.

"His sorry and regrets just come too late for me. It comes only when it is convenient for him. I don't believe he has repented or feels any measure of sorry for us victims. Only sorry and regrets that he didn't get away with it. Even now, he is working very hard with his telephone calls to the media to merely gain sympathy from anyone who wants to believe he might be worthy of keeping alive. There were 36 jurors involved in Mr. Stewart's life decisions here. And three different judges. They heard all the evidence, and they all found him guilty beyond a reasonable doubt."

Rosemarie was quickly establishing herself as an bona fide expert on this case. She knew the facts inside and out, and it was obvious she had thoroughly prepared herself for this hearing. Rosemarie was making sure the board understood that the decision to execute Ray Stewart was not made haphazardly. It went through a lot of people. The state's attorney had to decide to seek the death sentence. The jurors had to unanimously make the recommendation. The judge had to sentence him. The death sentence also survived a rigorous appeals process. Rosemarie truly believed that now, after all that, it was time. It was time to rid the world of this devil. It was time to execute Raymond Lee Stewart.

"They sentenced him to be executed for the deaths of three of the four known Illinois victims. Please let these sentences be carried out; let us survivors have our celebration of justice. I think we're ready for it. Rick's father and I remain simply parents of a murdered child because of Raymond Lee Stewart. Just let us go on with life, wearing this title in peace. Peace that will only come after this murderer has paid the consequences for his actions."

Rosemarie Boeck's testimony came near the end of the clemency hearing. Everybody in the room was already drained from being bombarded by the words of several emotional speakers. Yet, she was still able to capture the attention of the entire room. Beyond being very emotional, her story was compelling because it was genuine and easy to relate to. Listening to her, you really felt like you knew where she was coming from. When she talked about the different relationships Rick had with his family members, you couldn't help but think of your own brothers or your own sons. Rosemarie was a master at making the images of her deceased son real for the audience. For people who were listening to her on that afternoon, Rick Boeck was no longer just victim number six. After listening to Rosemarie, you really felt like you knew Rick. Now, he was a flesh-and-blood young man, who died before his prime and left behind loved ones who will always miss him.

For non-victims, it might seem strange to view an execution as a celebration of justice. For Rosemarie, she needed and wanted this chapter in her life to end like the jury decided it should end, with the death of the murderer who killed her son so many years ago. With the execution, she would no longer have to deal with the evil, vicious man who killed her innocent son. With the execution, there would be no more media interviews and no more appeals. With the execution, Rosemarie could finally start forgetting about Ray Lee Stewart, and focus exclusively on loving memories of Rick.

Sandy Jensen also testified towards the end of the clemency hearing. Jensen is a life-long friend of the Boeck family. The one thing she really tried to drive home for the Review Board was that Raymond Lee Stewart might have cost Ernie and Rosemarie the joy that comes with being grandparents. Through the years, the Jensen and Boeck families celebrated all kinds of events together: birthdays, holidays, and family get-togethers. Now, Sandy is noticing a strain in her relationship with Rosemarie. Sandy was blessed with a grandchild. The fact that Rosemarie doesn't have any grandchildren makes Sandy feel guilty and reluctant to share that joyous part of her life. Like Rosemarie, Sandy is convinced that Raymond Lee Stewart is the reason behind Rosemarie's children's decision not to raise kids. Sandy asked the board to not grant clemency to Ray Stewart because of all the people he killed, including Rick. Furthermore, she was asking the board to consider all the long-term ramifications of Stewart's actions. In her eyes, Raymond Lee Stewart also needed to be punished for the babies who will never be born and the grandparents who will never be.

Richard Boeck was deeply loved. His family and his friends were looking forward to big things from him. I suspect he would have surpassed their expectations. However, he never got a chance. This young man was in the wrong place at the wrong time. It caused an avalanche of hurt. I sensed that the Boeck family was just starting to find their way to the surface from the bottom of that avalanche. Rick is gone forever. Since the beginning of time, bad things have happened to good people. Monsters like Raymond Lee Stewart have always been around. It is important not to let them take over. I know Rick would have wanted his family to vigorously live on without him. It is easy to preach this, but hard to achieve it. It is foolish to think this family could ever forget about the past. At the same time, at some point, you have to put some of that behind you. Otherwise, Ray completely wins. You have to find a way to continue to go for those bananas.

CHAPTER 21

"There is no such thing as justice, in or out of court."
— *Clarence Darrow*

The closing arguments marked the end of a very long afternoon. It was also was the end of the road for Raymond Lee Stewart. This was it. In a few moments, the people were about to permanently rest their case against Raymond Lee Stewart. Undoubtedly, there would be those last minute appeals to the U.S. Supreme Court as the execution date grew nearer. However, those appeals would more than likely be disregarded as routine, last-ditch efforts. The fact that this man had killed six people made it unlikely the appeals would be given much consideration by any court. In reality, this was Raymond Lee Stewart's last stand. It was the last time the awkward mixture of victims and family members would collide in a room to discuss this gruesome case.

The people who testified against Raymond Lee Stewart's clemency petition did a remarkable job. The law enforcement officials and the family members of the victims really did a number on Ray. If you sat in that room for those hours and listened to those stories, it would be impossible for you to ever forget them. Most of the speakers only talked for a few minutes; however, in those few minutes they shared stories that were vivid and tragic. I will never forget the teary-eyed Alex Fredd telling the board about how Raymond ruined his life. I will never forget Captain Ed Houi describing the abusive and disgusting behavior Ray demonstrated in jail. The pain Raymond Lee Stewart caused people is real. It is easy to forget that, when you merely look at newspaper clippings and court documents. But, sitting in that hearing room, the point was painfully driven home time and time again.

There were three times as many pro-death penalty speakers as there were anti-death penalty speakers. I thought Joshua Sachs did a pretty good job presenting his arguments for saving Ray's life. However, it seemed like days ago since we had heard from speakers on Ray's behalf, like Constance Mitchell and Faith Crocker. Clemency hearings are very serious business. A man's life is on the line. It shouldn't be an issue over which side won, and which side lost. It should be, and it was, a forum to present all sides of the issue before the Governor makes his important decision. The fact of the matter is, though, the speakers against the clemency petition were damn good. Their combined testimony lasted over two hours. During that two hour period, there was not one single dull moment. Afterwards, it would be challenging for anyone to justify lifting a finger to help this man. Raymond Lee Stewart's fate was sealed years ago. It was hand-delivered that afternoon.

Arlene Anderson had to be feeling good about her case. Her presentation was organized and efficient. Everything went very smoothly for her. Anderson had handled a number of clemency hearings for the Attorney General's office. With the closing arguments, she would put the finishing touches on another successful one. When she started this case, Anderson was far from an expert in the Raymond Lee Stewart saga. Now, she was friends with a number of people whose lives were destroyed because of this petitioner. Anderson came off as all-business, but I got a sense that this case had become more than that for her.

Anderson explained, "Two months ago, I knew very little about Ray Lee Stewart's victims, beside their names and their jobs. In fact, I am a little embarrassed to admit I didn't even know the names of the Wisconsin victims. Now, after talking to family members and friends and reading all the letters that have come in asking that clemency be denied in this case, I feel like I know them personally. One thing that keeps hitting home as I deal with victims' families, not only in this clemency hearing but in others, is that no matter how strongly the defendant claims he has repented or has become rehabilitated, the pain in the family members remains."

What a crash course education Arlene Anderson got on the Raymond Lee Stewart case. Through the years, the State of Illinois has had a rather colorful inventory of inmates. Everybody knew about famous Illinois cases like Richard Speck and John Wayne Gacy. This case wasn't as famous, but the Stewart case certainly had elements that gave it a certain brand of unique luster: the escape, the high number of victims, the two-state spree, the lewd behavior and the consistent controversy. It was quite a story. As Arlene began investigating this case, she was surprised to find all the different variables that went into it. This wasn't just another routine capital punishment case. As she quickly learned, it truly was a saga.

I thought Arlene had a interesting position in the Attorney General's office. Handling the appeals for death penalty cases is an awesome responsibility. When cases like these come up, it must be a tad mysterious to dig through the court documents and take notes about victims and investigators. Later, meeting those victims' families and seeing how the inmate in question impacted real people's lives must be an almost esoteric experience. For the most part, criminal appeals is a paper-shuffling act. For a legal professional whose forte is criminal appeals, it has to be wild when you start talking to and meeting real people who are entwined in a case like this. It has to be a demanding, but fascinating and rewarding, occupation.

The bulk of Arlene's closing arguments came in the form of a letter from a person who was unable to attend the hearing because of her poor health. The letter was from Rick Boeck's grandmother. In the letter, she reminisced about what the Christmas holiday was like at grandma's house, when Rick was still alive.

Arlene read from the letter, "The last Christmas they came, I took the last picture ever taken, while he was alive. He said, 'Grandma, you have taken all these pictures all these years, and I have never seen them.' I told him after dinner, I would get them out so he could see them. But, after dinner he went to take a nap before the long drive from Will County back to Beloit to lock up the store at closing time, and I didn't get to show him the pictures. I always regretted I didn't go and get them right then. It seems we never have time, but you should-n't put things off, because it might be too late. He told me that last Christmas, before he died, a little after New Year's, how he had enjoyed coming to my house for Christmas and how he loved my good cooking, and he did enjoy Christmas cookies."

Arlene Anderson's case was successful because, for the most part, she adopted a hands-off approach to the hearing. She knew nobody really needed to hear from her. The stories from the loved ones of Ray's victims would be ten times more effective than any argument she could make in front of the Review Board. Throughout the presentation, she utilized quick introductions and let her speakers tell their entire stories with-out interrupting them or asking questions. Even in her closing argument, she yielded to quoting the victims. Touching images of a grandmother remembering how her murdered grandson loved her homemade cookies would create a level of effective-ness which a lawyer who was not personally attached to the case could never come close to. Arlene's case was strong because she completely let the victims' families tell it.

The story sold itself. Raymond Lee Stewart left an amazing legacy of pain: all the problems that the Fredd family had to cope with, the deeply hurt sisters of Kevin Kaiser, the sad story of a proud mother, Rosemarie Boeck, who lost her promising young son. It is mind-boggling that a single man can snap and, by his demented actions, start a domino-like reaction that just continues to go on and on. The stories we heard just scratch the surface of the pain Ray Stewart left behind. Two of the victims, Donald Rains and Kenny Foust, didn't have anybody there to testify. After so many years and the often intense media scrutiny, I can understand why family members might not be interested in coming to Springfield. That doesn't mean their lives are without impact as a result of the murders. I imagine Kenny and Donald are still deeply missed. As far as the family members who did testify, they were just representatives for a larger number of people who are still devastated by what happened back in 1981. The number of people affected by that week-long rampage is truly astonishing.

The letter-reading was the dramatic conclusion for Arlene Anderson. When she finished, one of the board members asked her a question about the legal issue Stewart's attorney had vigorously pursued. This was the issue about the jury not being told that the sentence of life without parole was an option in the Stewart case. Since the Stewart case, the law has changed and, today, juries have to be told that the death penalty is not the only way to insure a man will never get out again. Anderson felt the crimes Ray Stewart committed were so heinous, that giving those instructions to the jury wouldn't have changed anything.

She explained, "To me it's a very technical rule. This is a case in which the defendant is clearly guilty. Ray Lee Stewart is admitting at this point in time that he has committed these crimes. Now, he is trying to make us feel guilty by saying that since he was convicted, since his trials, there has been a new law that has come into effect. And, that because of that law, he did not receive a fair trial. Ladies and gentlemen, he did receive a fair trial. He is a person who has continued to show violent tendencies while he is in the penitentiary. During his trial, he tried to escape. If this is not a person who has demonstrated his future dangerousness, I don't know who would be. The evidence is so overwhelming that how can there be any question that the death penalty should not be imposed at this point?"

Anderson stumbled a little with this question. This was not a court of law, and it was an out-of-place question. She handled it fine, but this was the only time during the whole afternoon where it was obvious she was a little off balance. This particular legal issue speaks only to the sentencing phase of the trial. The jury would have been given those instructions after they had already convicted Stewart for the murders. It is not an issue about guilt or innocence. It is an issue about punishment. Anderson was smart to remind the Review Board about the escape attempt and the discipline problems in prison. This clearly was a technical issue that Stewart was attempting. People have been executed in Illinois for far less. In the end, it wouldn't change anything. For Arlene Anderson, this was an awkward ending to a successful presentation.

Joshua Sachs was sitting in the audience on the left side of the room and was busy taking notes throughout the afternoon. His naturally messy hair was starting to become more and more frenzied. The man in the bow-tie had been quiet for two hours. Sachs stood up and, while trying to juggle a number of notepads and pens between his two hands, asked Chairman Williams if he could have a short recess to prepare his rebuttal. Williams refused the recess, saying it had already been a long afternoon. He told Sachs he would be patient for a few minutes while he prepared his notes. Sachs, recognizing that the board was anxious, only took a few seconds before beginning the rebuttal on behalf of Ray Stewart. So, without a break, Sachs was forced to dive right in. He began the rebuttal by acknowledging this had been a difficult afternoon.

Sachs explained, "We have had a lot of very painful things to listen to. Mr. Stewart caused a great deal of harm. This is obvious. Why is it, then, that we have heard from many people all day who have been scarred by what he did, why one person responds with a deep sorrow and conviction that justice requires he be put to death, and another person responds with anger and hatred, and another person responds with forgiveness, and a fourth person responds with a feeling of being called to some sort of reconciliation? I don't know. The emotional responses to this, that people have to this horrible situation, defy the ability to pass judgment. We have nothing to do but be in awe of the people who have suffered this way, whatever response they come with."

It is noteworthy to look at the different ways people whose lives are touched by violence react to the issue of punishing the criminal. In the godawful Oklahoma City bombing case, there were a handful of victims' family members who came forward and said it would serve no purpose to execute Timothy McVeigh. There is definitely no uniform human response to tragedy. There are people, like Alex Fredd and Kelly Reeverts, who are absolutely convinced that capital punishment is the only way to deal with killers like Ray Lee Stewart. There are people, like Constance Mitchell, who can't see what good it would do to kill another person after so many people have already been killed. The majority of the victims' families leaned towards one side on the issue of punishment, but, deep inside, did have some slight reservations about being a party to the killing of another man, even a man as evil as Raymond Lee Stewart. It is impossible for non-victims to ever know for sure what their reaction would be in that situation. It is an emotionally confusing ordeal. Only one thing seems to be certain: this is an issue that is never going to go away.

During this part of his rebuttal, Sachs was clearly walking a tightrope. I think he is a caring man, who sincerely had respect for the victims. At the same time, his agenda for the afternoon was to try and get this serial killer, his client, off of death row. He was choosing his words very carefully. The slightest slip on Sachs' part, would make him come off as insensitive to the victims in this case. That would be the worst thing he could do for his client. Sachs adopted a very scholarly-like presentation on the capital punishment issue. By pointing out the different reactions all of the witnesses had to the case, he was quietly attacking the belief that capital punishment is now a completely accepted practice in society. It was a tricky balancing act, one which Sachs was able to masterfully accomplish. Obviously, he wasn't successful at accomplishing his goal for the hearing, but he did handle the entire hearing with a respectable level of decorum.

The main obstacle Sachs had to overcome during the rebuttal was to remind the board members of the compelling witnesses who testified on Ray's behalf at the outset of the afternoon. Witnesses like Constance Mitchell and Jennifer Bishop Jones gave some very moving testimony, and it was important to Sachs' case that the board members left the hearing room with those stories fresh in their minds. There were a lot more witnesses against the clemency petition, and these witnesses had the luxury of speaking during the second half of the hearing. It was important to remind the board there were two sides to this story.

During the rebuttal, Sachs chose to especially focus on the testimony of Ray's sister, Faith Crocker. It was a strange selection for Sachs, because, of all the speakers that afternoon, she was probably the most incoherent. Sachs felt that lack of composure was actually essential evidence of a brutal upbring that should be considered when deciding whether this case merited clemency.

Sachs explained, "In a way, I think the most compelling witness today was Ray Stewart's sister Faith. You get disciplined, you get severely disciplined when you're young, you get chastised, that doesn't necessarily make you abused. On the other hand, there is a difference between chastisement and being beaten bloody, thrown up against the wall, thrown into a garbage can and hit with a garbage can lid. We know something for sure; there was something very, very, very sick about what happened to Ray Lee Stewart when he was young. When he grew up, he killed six people. We saw his sister Faith, who came in here an attractive and self-possessed woman, and inside of ten minutes, we saw that she was hanging by her fingernails to the last vestiges of her sanity. Mr. Chairman, I think if you hadn't stopped her, she would have gone off the deepend right here. What these people went through when they were little, what Ray Lee went through when he was little, leaves scars as ugly and as deep and as horrible as the cuts that did them."

There is no way around the fact that Ray definitely was not a stranger to abuse and neglect. After listening to Faith, that was obvious. Her true emotional colors did break through that afternoon. Faith's testimony was more revealing than she could ever comprehend. The things that happened to Ray Stewart in his childhood should never have happened. The community should not have allowed it to happen. Someone along the line should have taken the time and energy to stop it. The police should have put a stop to it. The State of Illinois should have put a stop it. It was wrong, and there is no way any child could grow up to be normal in that kind of environment. The motivation behind the killing spree is still hazy, but one thing is clear: this was not about robbery, this was definitely the result of a bizarre mental breakdown. In a way, a man who kills exclusively for money is more deserving of the death penalty than Ray Stewart was. Faith Crocker described frightening, constant abuse. According to her, Raymond Lee Miller openly molested Ray's sisters. When Ray tried to stop his drunk father from beating the hell out of his mother, he got beaten to a bloody pulp. A confused, teen-aged Ray Stewart was forced to face the world alone after he was nearly beaten to death and kicked out of the family home forever. Ray Stewart's childhood was undoubtedly a recipe for disaster. Unfortunately, the disaster wasn't confined to his own self-destruction. Instead, he took six people's lives, along with his own, and in turn hurt hundreds of other people.

The abuse and neglect are important to understanding what happened, but by no means does it excuse what Ray Stewart did. Sachs was careful not to call Ray's troubled childhood an outright excuse. Sachs acknowledged that Ray was responsible for many shameful things and should definitely be punished, but this was an execution clemency hearing, and, as his attorney, he needed to point out all of the extenuating factors that may have contributed to the breakdown that caused the killing spree. This could not have been a particularly comfortable position for Sachs to be in. There was no way the many victims in that room could view him as anything but a bleeding heart liberal attorney who didn't truly understand the pain his client had caused them. Joshua Sachs is a lot more than that, though. To me, Sachs came off as a brave man with a strong sense of principles who stood up and spoke his unpopular beliefs while maintaining the respect owed to his client's victims. The evidence of abuse is strong and the consideration for clemency on those grounds was valid; it was important that somebody said it for the record.

Unlike Arlene Anderson, the issue of jury instruction was critical in Sachs' mind. This was not a court of law, and the court had already spoken (by refusing to hear the case) on this issue. However, Sachs took the opportunity to underline his belief that the conditions under which Ray received the death penalty were unfair. Sachs also took an opportunity to challenge Arlene Anderson's earlier comments on this matter.

"On this jury instruction question, I don't think Mrs. Anderson meant to confuse the issue, but the only question anyone is talking about is whether there is an execution. There hasn't been, for a very long time, any question about whether Mr. Stewart committed the crimes. He clearly did. The door is about to close forever on this case. This is the last lap. Whether Mr. Stewart goes to his death next week, or whether the Governor commutes the sentence to natural life without parole, the door is closed; he is never coming out of that prison alive. Whether he comes out dead on the 18th of September, or sometime in the future when the Lord calls him, as Mrs. Mitchell said, he is not ever coming out alive. The jury thought, was told, he could get out and kill another person, something that still haunts people today, as you heard. The law in the State of Illinois says no. Never. That is not a technicality. This is a matter of fairness."

It was a technicality, but as technicalities go, it was a pretty good one. The important thing to remember is it only takes a single dissenting juror to avoid the death sentence. It can be hard to get twelve people to agree on the same thing. I don't think it is too far-fetched to reason that part of the motivation behind the jury's decision was to insure Ray Stewart was never able to get back on the street. Somebody on that jury might have been satisfied with a life sentence, if they knew for sure there was no chance for Stewart to get paroled. The fact that those jurors were faced with the alternatives of killing him or risking his possible future release, was deplorable. It wasn't fair. That is why they changed the law. When the U.S. Supreme Court changed it, they created a valid appeal for criminals, like Ray Stewart, who were sentenced under the old rule. It is unlikely this would have made any difference. Stewart's crimes are almost the textbook example of what society deems as worthy of the ultimate punishment. However, it is vital that when life and death decisions like these are made, society has, at the least, a process which is indisputable, fair, and can stand up to the most intense scrutiny. The punishment is final. There is no room for mistakes or regrets.

Sachs ended the rebuttal by quoting in Yiddish an ancient doctrine called the Restatement of Punishments. The doctrine served as guidelines to judges who enforced the Biblical criminal code in what is now Jerusalem. The quote says carrying out a death sentence is devastating to society. It is the kind of severe punishment that should only be called for once in a seventy year period. Even then, it is a monumentally grave deed. The quote provided a spiritual tone to Sachs' appeal. It confirmed my assumption that Sachs was a man who was motivated by his personal, moral convictions. Clearly, times have changed a lot in the last two thousand years. It probably didn't have any impact on the board, but it was a nice finishing touch to a classy appeal for clemency on behalf of a condemned man.

After the reading, Chairman Williams asked the board if they had any questions for Sachs. Ann Taylor raised her hand and Williams called on her.

Taylor asked, "With reference to the abuse in Ray Stewart's

family, are there any other of his siblings in prison, who were also abused?"

Sachs responded, "If you give me a moment, I can verify that."

The attorney then got up from the speaker's table and walked over to Faith Crocker. The two whispered to each other for about a minute. Afterwards, Sachs returned to the speaker's table to answer the question.

Sachs continued, "I asked the question of Faith Crocker; she said, 'No. Nobody else.'"

Taylor responded, "So, they somehow managed to go on and lead productive, or reasonably productive, lives?"

The room instantly went completely silent. And then, all you could hear was the sound of pens scribbling on notepads. It was a quick peek into what the board members were thinking, right before they were about to decide their recommendation. It didn't bode well for Ray Stewart. If the abuse was so bad that it triggered the killing spree, how come none of Ray's siblings, who had to have experienced the same abuse, didn't turn out to be a vicious criminal like Ray? It was an intelligent question, one Sachs couldn't possibly answer. It practically crushed his abusive childhood defense. Chairman Williams recognized this was a dead end for Sachs and instructed him not to answer the last question. Ann Taylor had made her point. It had already been a long afternoon, and there was no need to dive into the issue at that late juncture. Williams felt the board had a decent grasp of the pros and cons of the Stewart clemency petition. The board didn't need to hear any more testimony. It was time for them do their jobs. It was time for them to meet, decide what they were going to tell the Governor and then close the book on this matter forever.

Like Arlene Anderson's presentation, Joshua Sachs' presentation ended on a sour note. It was another anti-climactic conclusion to an otherwise productive presentation. When they executed Ray Lee Stewart next week, I wasn't going to feel much sadness for him. However, I did a feel a connection to the speakers who spoke on his behalf at that hearing. This execution was going to be crushing for them. For them, I did feel sadness. No matter how evil a criminal is, or how heinous his crimes against society are, there are always people who are going to be hurt when he is executed. Before the hearing, I had no idea what kind of defense somebody like Raymond Lee Stewart was going to be able to come up with. I never thought it could be as impressive as it was. I guess there is always another side to a story. The speakers were able to outline the other side of this story with emotional and truly thought-provoking testimony. I doubt they changed anybody's opinion, but they definitely made some people think twice. In this case, that is a remarkable feat.

For journalists, obsession can be like a passionate love affair, dangerous and doomed. For me, the drive to Springfield was like a mad dash back into haunting history. When I was a child, Raymond Lee Stewart left his mark on my psyche. By going to Springfield, I was looking for answers. I did get some answers, but more than anything, I came out of there with more questions. When I got to the State Capitol Building, I quickly realized there was more to the case than I ever imagined. In my hometown community, there were people like me who never forgot about this story. The impact this man had still amazes me. At the hearing, I saw people whose lives were ruined during that terrible week in 1981. I found people with unique perspectives. I found myself desperately wanting to find a way to tell these stories. Although I denied it a million times to a million different colleagues and friends, I became obsessed with this case. I ran the risk as coming off like a demented death freak. To some, I probably am. There was something about being in that hearing room on that afternoon that drove me to dig further. I knew the execution was going to be a big story. I had to have every available piece of video. I had to cover every event related to this case. I had a personal connection to this story, and I fervently wanted to beat everyone else's coverage. Leaving Springfield, I knew this was going to dominate my life, not just for the next week, but for a long time. It was quite an afternoon.

CHAPTER 22

"Don't judge any man until you have walked two moons in his moccasins."

       —Native American proverb

11 a.m. Sunday, September 15, 1996

The small auditorium on the campus at Loyola University looked like a Socialist convention. In the old Chicago days, the meeting would have been infiltrated by members of the Chicago Police Department's Red Squad, which used to spy on hippies at political get-togethers. The folding table with the xeroxed propaganda was on the right side of the room. Grunge students, hippy throwbacks, political activists and a handful of those Karl Marx dress-a-likes had shown up. For an anti-death penalty rally, it was a good crowd, about fifty people. The room was decorated with the usual anti-death penalty banners. They read, "Stop the Death Penalty, Now!" and "The Death Penalty is Dead Wrong." Constance Mitchell was sitting alone in the back of the room. Jennifer Bishop Jones was standing next to her husband who was fiddling around with a camcorder.

It can be difficult to get a crew for a weekend story. Usually, there isn't as much news on the weekend; the courts are closed, stock markets are closed, no city council meetings, and no rush hour delays. Because of all that, news stations scale back the number of photographers and reporters. The skeleton crews on the schedule have to shoot a lot of different stories in order to fill an entire newscast. After some politicking with the managing editor and the weekend assignment people, I was awarded a crew to cover this death penalty rally. The same videographer who had to drive all the way to Rockford with me, Marc Gerke, would be my guy for the death penalty rally.

The clemency hearing for Raymond Lee Stewart failed to propel Ray's case to the forefront of the Chicago media's interest. The Rockford media all did stories on the event. The Rockford Register Star gave their coverage of the hearing the full-spread treatment. The television stations all ran stories. But, in Chicago, the hearing was mostly ignored. The Chicago Sun Times ran an article on Constance Mitchell in their Sunday edition. Carol Marin's station, WMAQ, ran video of the event with a sound bite. That was it. There were people at the station who doubted my news judgment on this story. Frankly, some of my colleagues thought I was nuts, chasing a non-Chicago story because of a personal demon. But, the death penalty rally ended up being the beginning of a coverage explosion for the Chicago media. At the rally, Jennifer Bishop Jones would reveal that Joseph Cardinal Bernardin was going to visit Ray Lee Stewart on the day of his execution. Suddenly, everybody would be interested in the story I had been developing for weeks and had been following for years.

The news media was invited to cover the rally. Despite that, I couldn't help but feel somewhat unwelcome by some of the organizers and participants. The news media tends to be a natural enemy for political types who fancy themselves as subversive activists. Usually, when a news crew walks in a room, the place is abuzz with excitement that the event is going to be on television. Even today, people still get excited about getting their faces on the tube. That wasn't the case at this rally. Marc and I were greeted with undeniable scowls. The only buzz in the air was the sound of the not-so-quiet whispering of sneers about the media. Finally, Jennifer Bishop Jones spotted me and walked over with her hand extended out to shake mine.

Jennifer couldn't wait to tell me her big news. At the clemency hearing, she hinted that Joseph Cardinal Bernardin was going to get involved in Ray's case. Now, she had received confirmation that Bernardin had agreed to visit Stewart at Stateville Prison. In addition to the news about Bernardin, another major Chicago religious leader was going to throw his name into the Stewart story. Earlier that day, Jennifer met with the Reverend Jesse Jackson at Operation Push Headquarters on the south side of Chicago. Reverend Jackson told her he was going to attend the vigil outside the prison on the night of the execution. It was obvious that with religious heavyweights like Cardinal Bernardin and Reverend Jackson going to bat for Ray Stewart, this was going to end up being a big national story. Suddenly, I found myself right in the middle of a huge news event. It was all kind of surreal, but at the same time, I fully expected this sort of thing to happen. Ray Lee Stewart knew how to find his way to the lead story slot.

I asked Jennifer to introduce me to Constance. I didn't have an opportunity to talk to her during the clemency hearing. That was a disquieting gathering of people down in Springfield. I felt that talking to a person on one side of the death penalty issue in plain sight of family members who were on the other side of the issue, might somehow alienate me and compromise my ability to get both sides of the story. It seems petty, but in the field you have to trust your instincts. It is not how journalism is taught in the textbooks, but in the real world, it's sometimes the way the game has to be played.

Constance was a very sweet, simple lady. This was a big production for her. She was just a 63-year-old grandmotherly woman from the mid-sized midwestern town of Rockford, Illinois. Now, she was in the big city about to address a roomful of bright, colorful young people. The lights from the Chicago television cameras would be on her full blast as she explained her story. This was quite a morning for her. I had asked Jennifer to make sure Constance brought a photo of Albert, so my videographer could shoot it. Constance had a wallet size picture of Albert that Marc scotchtaped to one of the banners. He then set up his tripod so he could get a nice, tight shot of it. I was slightly disappointed when two other news crews arrived, saw us shooting the photograph, and began setting up their gear to do the same. I felt like I had done the legwork to insure that the photograph was going to be at this rally, and now they were able to leech off my efforts. There was nothing I could do or say about it. That is all part of the game, too.

I made small talk with Constance and Jennifer until the revival was about to begin. Then, as they took their places at the panel table, I walked up to the podium, placed my tape recorder on it, and found a seat next to where Marc had set up the camera. I wanted to be close to him, so I could instruct him on what we needed shot. Otherwise, I would have sat in the front row (as I did at the clemency hearing), so I could hear everything.

The master of ceremonies for the rally was a young woman who was with the campaign to end the death penalty in Illinois. Her name is Sara Coty. She had long, black hair which kept falling in her face, forcing her to shift her body or swipe at it with her hand. Sara seemed to be driven by a nervous energy as she talked. Despite that, she came off as somewhat intimidating. As she spewed out the typical anti-death penalty rhetoric, she adopted a speaking style that was only a couple of octaves shy of outright screaming. Everybody in the room was pretty much anti-death penalty; otherwise, it might have been the scene of an interesting and loud debate. I don't think she was angry, although at times it was hard to tell, but she was definitely passionate about this issue.

The arguments Coty was so ardently spelling out for the audience were the oldies but goodies for the anti-death penalty folks. In 1972, the U.S. Supreme Court abolished the death penalty because of evidence that suggested it was applied disproportionately to African-Americans and Hispanics. It was reinstated at the federal level in 1976, and today the racial disparities are still suspicious, according to Coty. The death penalty also tends to be society's way to deal with its poorest criminals. Coty said that if you are accused of a capital crime and have a good attorney, chances are you are not going to be sentenced to death. Coty also pointed out several recent cases where innocent people were sent to death row and freed after years of court appeals finally revealed they were not guilty. The 1995 Crime Bill that was Bill Clinton's pride and joy, limits the habeus corpus appeals process in an effort to speed up executions. Coty saw this as a recipe for disaster. In her eyes, it was likely that, sooner or later, Illinois was going to end up executing an innocent man. Finally, Coty pointed to studies that show the death penalty does nothing to deter crime. According to her, the leading state in capital punishment, Texas, has had a 46 percent increase in violent crimes from 1982 to 1991. Coty also cited the FBI study which shows that states with the death penalty have a higher crime rate than states without the death penalty.

With the stats and classic arguments out of the way, she introduced the audience to Constance Mitchell as a mother of a victim, who, despite her loss, still rejects the eye-for-an-eye mentality.

It looked like Constance was taken aback by the loud applause she received as she approached the podium. She was dressed in black. Her ears were decorated with large gold ball earrings. Constance wore big glasses that covered most of her small face. I could tell she had dressed-up for the occasion, but there was nothing overly fancy about her outfit. The room had big windows and the late morning sunlight was glaring from behind the podium towards the audience. The light was hitting the faces of the people sitting in the folding chairs, but not enough to cause squinting or discomfort.

Constance began by telling the audience that even though her Albert was dead, he was still very much a part of her life.

She explained, "Sometimes, I can see my son in this paradise of a place. It is so beautiful there. Beautiful trees, flowers, the grass is green as can be, the river flows through there, and it is as blue as the sky. That is with my heart. That is not with the naked eye. I can see him sitting there; sometimes he is walking around, and I know he is okay, and I know he is with

God. You don't have to worry about people when they are with God, because you know they are being taken care of. So, his spirit is all around me, and I carry him in my heart. I talk to him. He talks to me, but he doesn't talk to me like I am talking to you. He talks to my heart. Ray Lee Stewart painted a portrait of him and sent it to me. It is just like he is jumping off of that canvas. If you could see that. I talk to him (Albert) every night, and I believe he is an angel on my left shoulder that God has sent to take care of me, every day. I thank him every night for taking care of me."

Constance had a unique perspective on her dead son. When people start speaking about seeing visions and talking to the dead, they're often dismissed as slightly insane by their audiences. That wasn't the case here. Constance had a blatant sincerity about her convictions, and I doubt anybody in that audience was failing to take her seriously. On the contrary, I suspect most of the people listening to her were deeply touched. This was an old, harmless woman who had lost her son many years ago, and was speaking from the heart about living without him. The details of the vision of Albert in paradise surroundings are so vivid and intense that it is hard to disregard them as unbelievable. The way Constance described it and the words she chose were almost perfect. Constance really provided the audience with a clear picture of a truly magnificent place. I hope it is real. I hope Albert is there. That place is where I want my loved ones to go when their time on earth is through.

How interesting that Constance accepted a portrait of Albert from the serial killer artist. It shows she truly had abandoned ill-will against her son's murderer. I suspect many of the victim's family members would be extremely offended if Ray would have chosen their deceased loved ones as subjects for his artistic efforts. Constance wasn't offended at all. In fact, she liked the portrait. Constance didn't harbor hatred for this man. To her, the painting was simply a beautiful picture of her son. It was just paint on a canvas in the image of Albert. The fact that it was painted by his killer didn't add any negative connotations to the artwork in her mind. Constance knew sometimes actions are only controversial if you decide to make a big deal out of them.

Despite the collect phone calls, the letters, the paintings, and the plea to save his life, Constance made it clear she was not a huge fan of Raymond Lee Stewart.

"It is not that I want to break bread with this man or sit at the table with him. I am not saying that. But, I do not want him to die this way. To me, it is an inhumane way to die, and it doesn't deter crime whatsoever. Because, I tell you one thing, if a person has years of hate in their heart for you, they are not going to stop to think, am I going to be electrocuted? Am I going to die for this? They don't stop to think what is going to happen to them. I think we better start forgiving people. We need to get all that hate out of our hearts and put some love there, because God is not about hate."

When you hear about a case like this, the mother of a victim forgiving the criminal, you might come to the conclusion that the mother may be compensating for her dead son by adopting the criminal as her new son and becoming like a surrogate mother. In those cases, the victim is often looking to fill a void and the criminal is looking for some kind of redemption. This kind of victim-criminal scenario is hardly the norm, but it is not completely uncommon. However, it was not the case here.

Constance did not want to be a mother to Ray Lee Stewart. She never met him face to face, and I doubt she would if given the opportunity. Ray didn't do anything extraordinary to win Constance over. In fact, he didn't do anything at all. At the core of Constance's plea to save his life were her moral objections to capital punishment. She forgave Ray because she truly believed that was the Christian thing to do. Constance imagined the pain Ray's mother must have been feeling, and decided to try and do something to help. Part of the laborious task of forgiving meant she had to have a relationship with the killer. Constance didn't long for any kind of deep relationship with Raymond Lee Stewart, and she definitely never wanted to see him back on the street where he would be in a position to kill another young man like Albert. A cornerstone of the Christian religion is to study how Christ lived his life and use that as an example. When you think about it, it is hard to imagine Jesus, who was executed, doing anything but fighting against the execution of another man. This was clearly Constance's motivation.

Constance believed criminals like Ray Lee Stewart would be eliminated or greatly reduced if parents did a better job raising their kids. In her eyes, too many parents these days were not being good role models for their children. Constance was troubled by all the violence in the world, and she suspected lousy parenting was the culprit. She wanted to send a message to the parents of the world: raise your kids right, or the world is not going to be worth living in.

She explained, "If we start when they are down there, and bring them up like God intended for us to bring them up, we won't have any Ray Lee Stewarts. We are not going to have a future, because all the kids who are supposed to be our future are going to be on death row or they are going to be in somebody's prison or they are going to be dead. Where is the future, then? Where is the future? I hope all of you in here, and some of those out there, will really please listen, look and listen, and bring up your child the way God wants him to be brought up. Then only, can we get rid of the Ray Lee Stewarts."

By the death penalty activists' own admission, we are a long way from having all our children on death row. There really hasn't been an increase in violent crimes nationwide in the last twenty years. It just seems that way. Constance was right about one thing: if we don't stop our children from getting involved in gangs and drugs, we are going to have a big problem on our hands. That is obvious.

The solutions Constance proposed during her speech were hardly innovative. The notion that the world would be a better place if our children had better role models has been around forever. Across the board, it is a pretty common sentiment. That doesn't mean it is without merit. On the contrary, I think it's obvious that Ray's childhood was void of any role models. If old man Stewart hadn't been such an abusive and atrocious father, who knows if Ray Stewart would have done what he did. Surely, the abuse didn't help. However, there are plenty of killers who had storybook childhoods packed with excellent role models. Jennifer Bishop Jones had to have known that, seeing that the kid who killed her sister, David Biro, came from a very privileged upbring. Having good role models is definitely an important start, but the problem of eliminating killers from the world is more complicated than that. Ray's motives were a mixture of long-term revenge, deep-seated hatred, and intense frustration. There were a lot of people who grew up under similar conditions of abuse and never went off on a killing spree. It would be a gross oversimplification to suggest that Ray's killing spree was solely due to his unfortunate upbringing.

The rally was billed as a forum for discussion and debate on the death penalty. There wasn't a whole lot of debate, but several of the audience members made lengthy comments, and a few even asked questions. For the most part, the people in the crowd were trying to throw in their two cents against the death penalty. Nobody spoke out for the death penalty. One audience member, who looked like a student, gave a long soliloquy on the inhumanity of war and how most people in society fail to appreciate the value of life. He talked for about five minutes. Ultimately, he was asking Constance if she thought executing Ray Stewart was equivalent to murder.

Constance answered, "I think it is murder. God didn't put us here to judge each other. I think He is the one who is supposed to judge us. People see in the Bible, an eye for an eye. They interpret that as what they are supposed to do, but it is not. It is what God is supposed to do. I don't want to see this man out on the street, don't get me wrong. I would never want him to do this to another person. I would never want another person to go through what I have gone through. But, I would like to see him in jail for the rest of his life, and not be killed like this."

Ironically, the kid's question yielded the most important comment of the afternoon. The eye-for-an-eye justification is the number one argument used by people who are for the death penalty. Constance gave one of the best rebuttals to that I have ever heard. To her, an eye for an eye doesn't mean what most people think it means. It was a difference in how you interpret the Bible. More than that, Constance had a completely different outlook on life than most people. For a lot of people, church is a nice place to spend a Sunday morning. It is rare to see people sacrificing and struggling to follow the example of Christ. There are a lot of folks who try to customize the Bible's message into a convenient fit for their own lives. That is not the way it is supposed to work. In Constance's life, that is not the way it is. When I interviewed her one-on-one, I got the feeling that she really didn't enjoy talking to Ray Stewart. In addition, I don't think she was particularly fond of public speaking. These were things she felt she needed to do because of her religious beliefs. They were not things she wanted to do. Constance did a great job bearing this cross in her life.

There was a reporter from another television station who showed up right after the rally began. Like most reporters would have done, she asked a question that was searching for a news angle. The reporter was on a b-roll/sound bite patrol; meaning that she went to a lot of different press conferences and events and picked up little stories (or pacers) for the broadcasts, instead of focusing on and developing a single, big story. The reporter asked Constance if she thought Ray's chances for clemency were hurt by the fact that he followed the Guinivere Garcia case, where Governor Edgar had used his executive clemency power to commute her sentence to life in prison without parole. There were some serious questions about Garcia's mental condition and she was the victim of an extremely abusive marriage. Edgar took the position that her case was not the kind of case for which the death penalty was intended. As far as the Stewart case was concerned, the thinking was that if Governor Edgar commuted another death sentence, which would make two in a row, it would hurt him politically because he would look soft on crime. This question was inappropriate for someone like Constance Mitchell. Constance was not a "player" in the state political games. I doubt she knew much about Guin Garcia. Constance explained the only thing she really knew anything about were her personal beliefs and the case of the man who had killed her son.

"I am not active in this sort of thing; I'm really not. I am just a simple person, and I forgave a man that I thought needing forgiving, because that is the type of person I am. I really don't keep up with who is on death row, and who is in jail. I just think we need to be more forgiving of other human beings. I thought maybe it would take a little bit of whatever his mother was worried about, away from her, and make her feel a little bit better if she knew that one of the victim's mothers had forgiven her son. That is all that I am about."

The answer did sum up everything that Constance was about. Instead of fueling the flames of hatred, she chose to extend her hand and reach out to the heart of Ray Stewart and his family. It is a simple, but amazing story.

When Constance was through answering the reporter's question, Jennifer Bishop Jones, who is a "player," quickly chimed in. Jennifer stated she did think the timing of Ray's execution (right after Garcia was granted clemency) was unfortunate. She told the audience she had written letters to the Governor asking him to give serious consideration to this case. However, she wasn't expecting Edgar to use his clemency power because of the potential political ramifications. That didn't mean she was giving up hope. Jennifer asked the audience to write their own letters to the Governor. At this point, Jennifer also took the opportunity to applaud Constance Mitchell for her strong faith.

"I have to say this on Constance's behalf. She really, truly has found the secret to peace of mind. I know this from personal experience. When I listened to people on Thursday at the clemency hearing who were for Ray's execution, who had had somebody killed, they were all in agony. Fifteen years later, they were all still in agony. There is a peace that comes in knowing the only way you are going to find healing is to find a non-violent solution to violence. Until somebody who is a victim of violence, stops and says, 'No more, it ends with me,' then, the cycle is just going to keep going on and on," said Jennifer.

Jennifer was absolutely right-on about Constance. I don't think this audience of liberals was expecting such a spiritual presentation. During her remarks, Constance touched on everything from Bible interpretation to angel spirits to Christian child-rearing. These topics are hardly the norm for a death penalty rally. Usually, these types of rallies are packed with anti-government, anti-media and anti-justice system rhetoric. This was a very different and special approach. It is impossible for Constance Mitchell to be a part of something that doesn't take on a religious spin. For someone like me, who has had to sit through a few of these death penalty rallies, it was truly a breath of fresh air. Although it could not have been what the audience was expecting, I doubt that anyone in the room was disappointed. It was a good speech. It was a brilliant sermon. Constance's beliefs are probably not in the center of the beliefs that society holds as a whole. Frankly, she said some things that bordered on bizarre. I doubt that anyone could totally agree and believe in everything she says and believes in. However, I do think anyone who listened to her at this rally would have to agree that Constance Mitchell is truly a tower of spiritual strength.

When Jennifer Bishop Jones stepped to the podium, the rhythm of non-typical anti-death penalty discussion continued. Like Constance, Jennifer was also dressed up for this occasion. She was wearing a dark purple blazer over a floral pattern blouse. Her bright, blond hair was slightly messy from having to run around all day. Jennifer was not only a speaker for this rally, but, as the chief advocate for Ray's case, she also had a large role in organizing it. For her, this would be one stop of many on a very busy day. Before this rally, she was at the Operation Push breakfast with Jesse Jackson. Afterwards, she was going to go to another rally for Ray at DePaul University. Jennifer had a nice speaking pace. She didn't talk to the audience like she was giving some big, grand speech. Instead, she adopted a very conversational style. Jennifer is a teacher, and that experience showed as she talked to this group of mostly college-age kids. It was obvious she was much more comfortable with public speaking than Constance was. Jennifer was also much more politically inclined than Constance. She tied in a lot of current news events into her presentation. Although she didn't dwell on them, she also had all the typical anti-death penalty facts down pat. Jennifer only used those facts for seasoning in her speech. For the most part, she stuck to the thing that made her so unique: she probably knew Ray Lee Stewart better than anybody.

Jennifer began her presentation by telling the crowd about her sister's murder in 1990. Jennifer explained her sister and her brother-in-law came home from her father's birthday celebration to find David Biro waiting in the living room with a loaded .357 magnum. Jennifer said Biro first shot her brother-in-law in the head at point blank range. Afterwards, he shot her pregnant sister in the stomach. Jennifer told the audience she was actually happy when she found out her sister's killer was too young to be eligible for the death sentence. This unfortunate crime really did give Jennifer credibility on the death penalty issue. No one could say to her, "wait until it happens to someone you love." It did happen to people that Jennifer Bishop Jones loved. It was a terribly brutal and truly senseless crime. Despite that, Jennifer didn't waiver in her belief that capital punishment was the wrong answer.

The editorial Constance Mitchell wrote to the Rockford Register Star is what brought Jennifer into the Raymond Lee Stewart story. Somebody brought the article to her attention and she decided to investigate. I believe Jennifer was trying to find a sense of reconciliation. The issues of forgiveness and punishment had become paramount in her life. David Biro never showed any signs of remorse for his crime. In fact, he never has admitted to it, despite confessing the murders to a high school buddy and police finding the gun in his room. Biro was supposed to appear via satellite on the Geraldo Rivera show with members of Jennifer's family, but the arrangement fell through at the last minute. So, in the murder case that rocked her life, Jennifer has to live with a lot of unanswered questions. She couldn't talk to David Biro; however, she could talk to Raymond Lee Stewart. Jennifer stated that the differences between Biro and Stewart had become a defining point in her life. While she was looking at Constance, Jennifer told the audience she would give anything for David Biro to have the presence of mind Ray Stewart had.

It is rather eerie for one victim to envy the killer of another victim. Jennifer didn't want to ever hide from that sorrowful chapter in her life. She realized the terrible tragedies that touched her life and Constance's life could never be erased. The killer cannot undo his murders. For the victims, it is suddenly good-bye, forever. For Jennifer, the only way to live in peace was by courageously confronting every demon that came along. David Biro was the biggest demon to ever touch her life. I suspect she longs to hear an apology from David. I believe she wants to explain to him just how much pain he caused. At the core of Jennifer's being is love and compassion, but she feels a great distance from those personal beliefs when she thinks about the man who murdered her baby sister. I believe that makes her uncomfortable. In the back of her mind, I think she has hope that one day those important sentiments will surface in the most unlikely relationship of her life. Jennifer is not the kind of person to leave things unsaid.

The audience seemed interested as she told her story. Jennifer stated the Raymond Lee Stewart she knew was a compassionate man, who is living with a great deal of regret and remorse for his actions.

Jennifer explained, "Ray is very, very changed and very, very sorry, now. I know there are people out there who will say, 'Well, sure, you are on death row facing execution; of course you are sorry. Everybody finds God on death row,' right? But, I have worked with this man closely, and I know he is truly only living now to try and make up for the wrong he has done. He has spent the last 15 years trying to make up for the wrong he has done. He is contrite and remorseful. We have ministers with whom we have been working, who are for the death penalty, who are saying, 'Look, I have never seen anybody more remorseful.' This is a very good and respected man. He is a moral leader in the prison. He is a friend to the guards and the prisoners alike. He tries to keep people behaving when they are misbehaving. He has a lot of wonderful qualities."

I don't know if the audience really understood how bizarre it was that Raymond Lee Stewart was being described as a person with great qualities. The people at the rally were only hearing one side of this story. None of them were down in Springfield when family member after family member of his victims testified to the contrary. None of them grew up scared to death because of the shocking stain he left on an entire community. I do believe Jennifer was speaking from her heart; she did truly believe Ray had grown up and changed into a decent human being who couldn't erase his horrific past. On the day of the execution, Jennifer told me she thought Ray was going straight to heaven. When I talked to Ray, he did express remorse for what he did. However, his apologies were hardly forthcoming. Ray was very angry about a lot of things. He was still furious that his artwork got pulled from the Rockford show. He was angry at the Attorney General. I don't believe Ray accepted his eminent death until the last few hours. In addition, I got the feeling that the revenge mentality had not completely vacated his soul. But, somehow, when Jennifer talked, all the anger Ray had and all the victims who are still hurt by his crimes seemed a million miles away. That is why

Jennifer Bishop Jones was such a fantastic advocate for Raymond Lee Stewart. Without her on his side, his execution would have surely passed with minimal mention. Jennifer was tactfully painting the most flattering picture that could possibly be composed on behalf of a man who killed so many innocent people.

In the middle of her presentation, Jennifer told the audience about the horrendous abuse Ray suffered as a child. Ray Lee Stewart grew up in a dirty, run-down house that didn't have electricity. The threat of abuse from Ray's alcoholic father constantly loomed. Jennifer said Ray didn't like to dwell on this, but he did share a story with her about one incident when Ray came home and found his mother on the floor, beaten-up with several broken bones. When Ray tried to help, his father hit him over the head with a concrete brick. Jennifer also described in gruesome detail the sexual abuse Faith Crocker and the other sisters had to endure. Finally, she told the audience about the fateful day when Ray was nearly beaten to death by his father, thrown in a garbage can and kicked out of the home forever. Jennifer was careful not to use this abuse as an excuse for the murders, but she did insinuate that the abuse left unhealed wounds on his psyche and really pushed him down the wrong path in life.

The fundamental problem with the death penalty in Jennifer's eyes is that it is a reactionary solution instead of a holistic one. Most of the audiences she talks to are for the death penalty, and, she said, the main thing those people want is revenge. In Jennifer's eyes, a more productive approach would be to look at ways to avoid violent crime altogether. Instead of simply reacting afterwards, she was calling for a more complex approach that focused on organizing to try and fix things. Jennifer pointed to the numerous studies that show the death penalty is not a deterrent to crime and actually costs the taxpayers more in the long run. Jennifer felt an anti-crime agenda which simply reacted after the fact, didn't do society any good. To her, the death penalty was an easy, ineffective answer. Jennifer wanted people to strive for more complex, useful solutions aimed at preventing the environmental conditions which she felt bred violent criminals. Furthermore, Jennifer was calling for an absolute denouncement of murder. To her, it was an hypocritical contradiction to tell the killers of the world that killing is wrong, so we are going to punish you for killing by killing you.

Jennifer believed the way to win abolishment of the death penalty was down the avenue of education. The main obstacle against abolishment are those opinion polls which show that over 80% of voters favor capital punishment. Politicians look at the numbers, and their hands are basically tied. If they decide to enter an election with an anti-death penalty plank as part of their platform, their chances are greatly reduced. Jennifer thought educating the voters and changing those polls were the only real chances at ending capital punishment in the United States for good. Jennifer believed if more people were given the options between the death penalty or life without parole, more folks would side with the life without parole choice. Not all states have the life without parole option. Jennifer challenged the audience of young people to go out and help educate people about the realities of the death penalty. For most people, the end of the death penalty in this country seems very unlikely. For Jennifer, it was just a matter of getting people to read up, wake up, and act out. Jennifer Bishop Jones embodies the epitome of the die-hard activist who truly believes attaining her seemingly impossible, and unpopular, goal is not futile.

The rally was a successful one. The audience listened carefully to every word the speakers had to say. The media had a lot of good sound bites to choose from. I don't know that Jennifer and Constance swayed too many people's opinions, but I think even the most cynical pro-death penalty person would have come away from this rally with a certain amount of respect for what they were standing up for. The people who spoke out on Ray's behalf at this rally are special. Perhaps more special than Ray deserved. They truly made a strong case for a killer most people would have believed had absolutely no defense. It's disconcerting how you can listen to one side of a story and in your heart feel so convinced, and then, when you listen to the other side, doubts slowly creep in. The death penalty is one of those issues where it is difficult to truly get a handle on your personal beliefs. There are two distinct, compelling sides to this controversial issue. Jennifer finished her presentation and the rally by asking the audience for help.

Jennifer concluded, "I am teacher, so I always ask you guys to give me the answers. I want to know how you can get people to let go of sound bites and tough on crime as a winning political issue; get people to let go of that and embrace a more complex, less black and white, less easy, reality. Crime is really very complicated. And, it really is environmental. We know if you spend just one dollar on a head start program, you save $30 in the prisons later on. Why is it we can't get people to see that? That is why education is so important. So are your ideas of how to get people to let go of simple, easy, formula, sound-bite type thinking, which is becoming so much a way of life. People really don't want to think for themselves. It is the product of the television generation. It really does scare me. They don't want to look for more complex answers; they want the easy answers. You all are the educated generation; you have to save us. Save us."

CHAPTER 23

*"Man does not weave the web of life. He is merely a
strand in it. Whatever he does to the web, he does to
himself."*

—*Chief Seattle*

September 16, 1996

The first time Ray Stewart called my house, the call didn't go
through. It was the day before the scheduled execution, around 6:30
in the evening, and I picked up the phone to hear the automated
operator say it was a collect call from Ray Stewart. I accepted the
charges and then all I heard was a dial tone. I was furious. I threw
the cordless phone across the room in anger and frustration. The
phone hasn't quite worked the same since. Then, I waited for him to
call back. Hours passed and there was no word from Ray. I thought
I had blown my chance to interview the man who terrified me as a
child when he went on a murder rampage in my hometown in 1981.
I felt sick as I watched WMAQ's news that night. Anchorwoman,
Carol Marin, had an 'exclusive' interview with Ray. Finally, after
10:00 at night, he called back.

The setting for my one-on-one showdown with Ray was hardly
suitable for an official interview. Since word of Bernardin's visit,
the execution of Ray Lee had become the major story of the week.
Because of that, I was working around the clock on the story. The
constant work had taken its toll; I was exhausted. When the phone
rang again, I was sleeping. On the first ring, I jumped out of bed and
darted into action. This time I didn't bother with the cordless. First,

227

I picked up a legal pad with some prepared questions and then the telephone receiver which I had placed close to my bedroom door. I did the interview in my boxer shorts on the cold, hardwood floor of my Chicago apartment.

As a journalist, I have been in various situations with celebrities and politicians. From time to time I have fired difficult questions at some powerful people. Rarely do I get nervous in those situations. When I heard Ray's voice on the other end of the phone, I was outright trembling. The telephone receiver was shaking in my hand. I had to concentrate on my breathing pattern to insure I would be able to squeeze questions out of my vocal cords. In part, this was because of the unconventional nature of this interview situation. However, more than that, my nervousness was a side-effect of how terrified I was of Raymond Lee Stewart. It is almost embarrassing to admit how scared I was. Demons from your childhood aren't easily slain.

In order to get some decent information out of Ray Stewart, I needed to handle the interview with a considerable amount of tact. Eager as I was to quickly take Ray on and really ask him the hard questions, I thought the better strategy would be to make him a little more relaxed and trusting before diving into uncomfortable territory. This was a convicted serial killer, and I knew too well how evil his crimes were. It is not that I wanted to extend him any sort of courtesy, but I needed to treat him with kid gloves, at least in the beginning, until he got comfortable with me. This is another journalism tactic that isn't found in college textbooks. This was the real world, and the fact was that, at any moment, Ray could hang up and end it, and I would have nothing to show for the effort it took to get him on the phone. Before I risked everything, I wanted to make sure I at least got a couple of useable sound bites.

On that day, Governor Edgar's press office had faxed out a statement on Stewart's request for clemency. In the statement, Edgar is quoted as saying that "the death penalty is an absolutely appropriate punishment for this mass murderer," and that "this case has had a full, fair review by our legal system, and it is time for the penalty to be carried out." I began the interview by asking Ray for his reaction.

Stewart answered, "In the statement he (Edgar) made today as far as the statement that was released on the media, which basically said that since Mr. Stewart was a mass murderer, this is justified here. Now, I must say that under my circumstances, because of the revenge factor, which is the reason why I did what I did. Now, had I been a white individual, I am not using this as a racial overtone, I am just saying had maybe I been white, then they would have found something saying he had a mental problem and just maybe the death sentence would have been turned into a natural life sentence."

Frankly, playing the race card as reason for not being able to escape the death penalty was a reach in this case. Despite his brief disqualifer that he was not trying to use race as an issue in the case, the fact is he brought it up. It would be naive to suggest there haven't been times when blacks were given harsher punishment because of a racism factor at work. Clearly, there have been many such unfortunate cases. The racial disparities of people sent to death row is the reason the U.S. Supreme Court revoked the death penalty in 1972. While a legitimate argument can be made that those disparities still exist, it is difficult to make a case that racism was a strong force in the decision to execute Ray Lee. If society is going to have a death penalty for the worst of the worst criminals, it is going to be administered when a community is held hostage by a brutal, senseless killing spree, regardless of the criminal's skin color.

The notion that Ray Stewart might have been insane holds some merit. I think with the overwhelming evidence against Stewart at the time of his trial, it would have been better for his attorney to try and make a case for insanity. In the end, even that wouldn't have saved him. It is hard to make a case for insanity when you look at the cooling off periods Ray had inbetween the murders. All the killings were separated by at least twelve hours. Before he went up to Beloit and murdered Boeck and Raines, he had two full days to come to his senses. This was not a spur-of-the-moment lapse of insanity, but rather a long, drawn-out attack. Furthermore, the insanity bid is greatly hurt by the fact that Ray tried to get away with it. Although he could have been more careful (like getting rid of the guns), he did flee all the way to North Carolina in an attempt to elude authorities. This demonstrates he was at least lucid enough to know that staying in the Rockford area would probably mean capture. Prosecutors would have surely pointed out Ray was sane enough to drive across the country, a feat that requires planning and endurance, in a rational attempt to escape justice. The public defender would have had a tough time coming up with a counterargument.

It seemed to me that Ray, like most death row inmates, enjoyed talking about the legal ins and outs of his fifteen year battle to avoid execution. I knew from talking to Jennifer Bishop Jones and others that he was very much up to speed on the legal process taking place at this phase of his case. Despite this, he did not take an active role in his clemency petition. Stewart could have made a statement, either written or recorded, to the board. He chose not to. I asked him why he didn't. I thought it was a rather routine question that wasn't going to generate much of a reaction from Stewart. His answer surprised me.

"I could not ask the clemency board nor the Governor for clemency because I have hurt so many people, and only the inner spirit, I normally use the word inner spirit as basically a godly spirit, if the godly spirit touches those members at the hearing, then they would most likely rule the way they felt or maybe the way they were led," said Stewart.

It was unsettling for me to hear Ray recognizing he had hurt so many people. I had heard he was sorry about the murders from his supporters and family members, but it was rather sur-real to actually hear the man himself talking about the pain he caused. When I asked him the question, he switched into a somber tone. Obviously, this was not comfortable for him. His answer to my question was momentarily delayed while he breathed a deep sigh. Considering that he blew away his innocent victims with multiple gunshots in cold blood, it was hardly a fitting token of regret. However, admitting he had hurt people was a far cry from the lewd behavior he demonstrated during the spree and at his trials. Although he was certainly not a nice guy and his remorse was quite shy of being impressive, this was not the same Ray Stewart who gave me nightmares when I was growing up.

During the clemency process, the Attorney General's office revealed to the Prison Review Board that Stewart was a member of the El Rukn Street Gang, one of the most organized and notorious gangs in the Chicago area and in the Illinois prison system. At the hearing, Stewart's attorney and his supporters expressed outrage at that accusation. Some of them even insisted that not only was Ray Stewart not a gang-banger, but he had worked hard in prison to try and steer fellow inmates away from the gang route. I gave Ray a chance to respond to the Attorney General's accusation.

Stewart responded, "In this case, I am told it was said to them I was an El Rukn Street Gang member. A person may have said I was an El Rukn Street Gang leader, which is totally untrue. This was done for the sole purpose of contaminating the members of that panel. This was done for them to be angry at me. To get revenge at me, because of what the El Rukn gangs are portrayed as. All the time, the officers on this unit know I am not a gang leader. The officers on this unit know that I am not a gang member. This was done to cause anger in the panel."

The Attorney General at the time was Jim Ryan. In a poor attempt to take advantage of a political situation, Stewart said Ryan was "up to his old tricks," and cited the controversial Jeanne Nicarico case where Rolando Cruz and Alejandro Hernandez spent years behind bars and in the courts before both convictions were thrown out. Ryan was State's Attorney in that county at the time. Stewart mispronounced the names of the key players, and it was obvious he didn't exactly have a handle on what happened in that case. I don't know for sure if Stewart was an El Rukn or not. My hunch is that he wasn't. The Attorney General didn't offer any concrete proof in their clemency petition response. I doubt the El Rukns would want someone like Ray, and I doubt he would want to be a part of such an organization. Ray struck me as the kind of guy who would prefer to walk the prison halls alone.

One of the things that stood out at the clemency hearing was the testimony of Capt. Ed Houi about Stewart's disgusting behavior in the Winnebago County Jail. I told Ray I thought this completely sunk whatever minute chances he had at clemency. Several family members of the victims referred to Ray as an 'animal.' By his actions, he seemed to prove them right. It was a damaging image: a man accused of multiple murders, saving his waste in cups and waiting for the guards to check on him and feed him so he could spit at them and throw his urine and feces in their faces. I asked him why in the hell he would do such terrible things?

Ray attempted to explain, "Well, once you heard of my behavior in the earlier years, where I had did certain things to officers. What I did, that was stated there, was the truth. I did do certain things to officers. But, they didn't tell you for ten months, I didn't do a thing to an officer. They didn't tell you, for ten months, everybody that was in the general population of the county jail had access to TV's and radios. Mr. Stewart did not have a TV or a radio for ten months. They didn't tell you that Mr. Stewart had a camera directed inside his cell with the light on 24 hours a day for those ten months before Mr. Stewart did anything to them. They didn't tell you that Mr. Stewart went before Judge Sype and let Judge Sype become aware of the problem I was having within the jail. Now, Ray Stewart took all that abuse for ten months. I tried my best to communicate with the staff, to let them know that I deserved everything that every other resident had or was receiving. But, for ten months, I did not receive that. At that point, I had said enough is enough. If they want to treat me like an animal, I will now act like an animal."

I guess Stewart deserves credit for honesty on this issue, but that is about it. What did he expect jail for murderers to be like? When you are accused of killing six people, they usually don't give you a suite in the Ritz. I doubt too many people, regardless of their position on capital punishment, would be too broken up about the fact that Ray was not allowed to spend his days watching soap operas and listening to Paul Harvey. What a bizarre world Ray lived in. Ray had a totally different way of thinking and a totally different way of looking at the world. It is actually amazing the way he would utilize his imagination to manufacture a perspective he believed could help him. There were two character faults that always did Stewart in. He was selfish and always held a grudge. I could tell he was still angry about the way he was treated in the Winnebago County Jail in 1981 and 1982. I could tell he felt throwing his waste on guards was completely justified. In fact, he was trying to convince me it was justified. Ray didn't understand that there is just no way for people to find compassion for a man's fight to be convenienced behind bars after killing and hurting so many. In comparison to his brutal crimes, the sin of depriving Ray Stewart of a few jail niceties seems quite trivial.

The interview had started to develop a nice rhythm. Ray was getting emotional, and that is what you want in an interview like this. I started to shake off the nerves that come with interviewing the boogieman of your childhood. The interaction of questions and answers was shifting into more of a conversational mode, instead of a rigid turn-taking exchange that rarely produces good results. I think Ray had never come up against somebody like me. In addition to following his case for fifteen years and knowing it backwards and forwards, I knew Rockford; I knew the state's recent history on high-profile cases; I knew the legal intricacies involved in death penalty cases. I quickly corrected Stewart on his facts when he started drawing parallels of his case to the Nicarico case. After that, Ray didn't try to bullshit too much. When I looked back on the interview, it was a rather spooky conversation. Late in the interview, Ray Stewart and I started finishing each others sentences. It is not that we understood each other; I believe that nobody completely understood Ray, including Ray himself. It is eerie to say, but I think Ray enjoyed talking to me. There were several times during the interview when I threw out names he hadn't heard in years. Before he died, Ray wanted to tell his story to a qualified, interested interviewer. I fit the description perfectly.

I knew Ray was bitter about his paintings being removed from the controversial Salvation Army Art Show in 1993. When he brought it up in the interview, it really demonstrated how lasting Raymond Lee Stewart's grudges were. I asked Stewart about feeling remorse towards his victims' families. Ray took the question and led the interview on a strange tangent. His answer ended up opening the Salvation Army wound and gushing out the terrifyingly cold blood that pumped inside his veins.

Stewart said, "One thing for sure, I am not acting in the manner as I have in the past. Meaning this: because of certain things the Kaiser family has done pertaining to me when I had put several paintings in the display of the Salvation Army in Rockford. The Kaiser family asked the Salvation Army to remove my paintings and the Salvation Army removed my paintings. Now, if I was in the frame of mind that I was in before, I could have asked someone to do something to the Kaiser family and let them know even though I am in the penitentiary, I still have access to certain things that could be done out there in society. But, the revenge has to stop with me. I have done everything that I could to stop that revenge. So, I did not do anything against the Kaiser family."

It had been almost four years since the Salvation Army gave into a backlash of protests and pulled Ray's paintings from the

Rockford show. The prison art program was founded by Rock-ford resident Shirley Lindstrom in 1989. Lindstrom knew first-hand what life behind bars was like; she served three years in prison after being convicted of trying to hire someone to kill her husband. Her time in prison had a profound effect on her. When she got out, she started the program through the Salvation Army as a way to instill hope in prisoners. For years, the Prison Art and Craft Show went on with minimal attention. In 1993, when the public found out two Ray Stewart paintings were going be included in the exhibit, Lindstrom found herself in the middle of a big controversy. It was the issue story of the week in Rockford. The radio talk shows took tons of passionate calls on the sub-ject. The newspaper printed a number of editorials. There were a lot of protest phone calls made to the Salvation Army, includ-ing at least one from a family member of one of Ray's victims. Finally, the Salvation Army decided to continue with the show, but without the pair of paintings done by Stewart. The contro-versy was over, the art show had a great turn-out, the local media went on to other topics and everyone pretty much forgot about the whole affair. Everyone, except Raymond Lee Stewart. The show was set-up so the inmates could keep eighty percent of the money from any sales. It is not completely unrealistic to think Stewart's paintings could have sold for surprisingly high amounts. Certainly no art critic would give the actual work a second look. The paintings look like they were done by some-body who learned art from a public television program. How-ever, there are a lot of arguably twisted people out there who are fascinated with serial killers and would have opened their billfolds to own a piece of the perturbing legacy. John Wayne Gacy was able to make quite a bit of money selling his paint-ings.

Stewart claimed he was trying to earn some money so there would be something to leave behind for his daughter after his execution, and firmly believed the family of Kevin Kaiser was the driving force behind the Salvation Army's decision to put the kibosh on his Rockford art debut. The Kaiser family is a large family. Kevin had eight brothers and sisters. That is a lot of hurt people who never forgot their brother and never forgot the man who killed him. Through the years, the Kaiser family had been the most aggressive at making sure the courts and the community never lost sight of the vicious way Stewart murdered young Kevin. I don't know if somebody told Stewart this, or if he just made a guess, but he blamed the Kaisers for not being able to participate in the Rockford show. He was probably right.

It was outright unnerving to listen to Ray talk about the Kaiser family and even insinuate he had considered asking someone outside the prison to inflict harm on them. More than anything, this offered rare insight into the distorted thought processes under which Ray Stewart operated. This guy really held lengthy, vicious grudges. Whenever someone did anything against him, his mind instantly started to orchestrate elaborate plots of retaliation. It is hard to believe that Ray Stewart would really have access to do anything to the Kaisers. However, it would be foolish to completely rule it out. Who would have thought he could have escaped from jail? Who would have thought he would start a killing spree to avenge a ten-year old, measly armed robbery beef? Through the years, his bite was a hell of a lot worse than his bark.

What is even more disturbing than his twisted thought process is the lack of remorse and compassion he had for most of his victims. While he claimed to be sorry for all the people he hurt, his words clearly suggested otherwise. He did go out of his way to make peace with Constance Mitchell, the mother of Albert Pearson; however, that really was an easy task. Constance is an extraordinary woman who was very forthcoming with forgiveness for Ray. She isn't the kind of person who would say or do anything Ray might not like. As far as Ray is concerned, his rhetoric seemed to suggest he was selective with his remorse; it was exclusive to the victims who didn't do anything to piss him off.

While Stewart was talking about the Salvation Army and

about the Kaiser family, his speaking pace quickened, his breathing became noticeably heavier, and he dropped his attempt to tactfully phrase his sentences. It was obvious the angry monster was beginning to surface. I was on the phone and didn't have the luxury of noticing his body language, but I was still getting a rather phantasmic peek at this dangerous man's bad side. After all these years, Raymond Lee Stewart still had a hard time completely understanding and appreciating that this family had forever lost one of their own. Not only did this family have to go on with the weddings and birthday parties without Kevin, they had to cope with the brutal way Ray Stewart gunned him down: shooting him five times, the last bullet to the face after he was already dead. Wasn't that burden far greater than being kicked out of a local art show? Didn't Ray understand what he had done to this family, who originally did nothing to him? When I challenged Ray on this, it fed his fury.

"Ray, they did lose Kevin," I said.

Stewart responded, "They did lose Kevin, no doubt about it."

"Can you understand how they would be upset about what your paintings would represent? You killed Kevin in cold blood and now you get to be a painter?"

"Well, let me say this, I am on death row. Other residents are painters that are on death row. Now, did the Salvation Army take the other paintings down? No. They just took the Stewart paintings down, but then as I said, I am not angry. I did not send anyone out there to do anything to that family. That family says, well, I am a cold-blooded killer. I was a cold-blooded killer. I did kill in cold blood. I was in a frame of mind of revenge, and so now if the Kaiser family is doing this to me, then if I was in a frame of, well, they are doing this to me, why don't I go ahead and have something done to them, before I am executed, then that way I will be satisfied that I have done something to them. In that manner, I could have received gratification, knowing I was going to be executed, well, I did something to them, let them know that they don't mess with me, no. But as I said, all that has to stop," said Stewart.

The Raymond Lee Stewart that the anti-death penalty advocates were describing at the rallies and the hearings was a far cry from the man talking to me on the eve of his execution. This Ray was talking about getting "gratification" from killing and revenge. Despite what he said, he was still very much a "cold-blooded" man. The fact is that without gang ties and with the intense censorship that the Illinois Department of Corrections places on phone calls and letters, he simply didn't have the means to retaliate against the Kaisers. If he had a true opportunity, I suspect he would have taken it. If he wanted so much to stop hurting the Kaiser family, why was he bringing this up? Obviously, he wanted a final message to get back to the Kaiser family. Obviously, Ray wasn't through inflicting terror, even at this late stage in his life. But, it was about to end. When Ray was strapped to the gurney and poisoned to death, it would be over.

I knew the clock was working against my interview. It was already late, and it had to be close to the prison's cut-off time for phone calls. Because of this, I needed to steer the interview towards *the most important issue: Why did he do it?*

The murder of Willie Fredd was tragic; however, there was a clear motive. In 1970, Fredd came forward and told Rockford police investigators that Ray Stewart was bragging about the armed robbery heist of a west side dry cleaners. The tip led to Stewart's arrest, guilty plea and his prison term. So, Stewart was clearly trying to get back at Fredd for what happened in 1970. Also, the motive behind the murder for Albert Pearson is somewhat transparent. Albert was in the store when Ray Lee went to get his revenge on Fredd. It is a tired expression, but Pearson was truly in the wrong place at the wrong time. As difficult as it is to accept the Fredd-Pearson killings, it is not that difficult to figure them out. The other four murders are the real mysteries. There have been a lot of theories, but never a definitive conclusion.

Even today, there are people on the west side who believe

the entire killing spree was the by-product of a drug vendetta. It would be easier to accept that. People don't want to think this could happen to them. In a way, it is mind-easing to write the whole rampage off as a drug thing. The evidence clearly suggests, however, that Kevin Kaiser, Kenny Foust, Richard Boeck and Donald Raines were all random victims. None of them had connections to Ray Lee. Ray Lee had only returned to the Rockford area for a very short time before he started pulling the trigger.

During the spree, the police were very interested in trying to figure why he was doing what he was doing. However, once they had captured him with brain matter on his jacket, blood on his shoes and two .38 caliber guns in his possession, peace of mind was somewhat returned to the citizens of Rockford. It was no longer a priority to figure out why the hell he did it. In recent years, some police officers have suggested this was simply a man who enjoyed killing. The theory is that when he got his revenge on Willie Fredd, it turned on some sort of killing gene that triggered pleasure when Ray killed. But, that is an oversimplification. Criminologists usually marry pleasure killers with sexual overtones. That was completely absent in this case. This was about revenge and hate, not about pleasure. At the trials, the physical evidence was so overwhelming that it was unnecessary to really spell out the motive. The only real task for the State's Attorney was to get a death sentence. They spent most of the trials painting Stewart as a monster, instead of outlining his motive.

I had to get Stewart to open up and just tell his entire story. I wanted my question about why he did it to be general, because I didn't want to pollute his answer. I wanted Ray Lee to try and explain what he did without any help from me. I knew all the guesses that were out there, but I didn't want to bring any of that speculation into the interview mix. I have been thinking about the case from time to time for fifteen years. There were a lot of unanswered questions. Now, I was presented with the challenge of getting the answers from the source himself.

I asked, "Explain to me, this demon called revenge that is a theme through your case. Now, I can understand Willie Fredd. He was involved in the armed robbery case that put you in prison."

This was not a direct question about why he did it, but Raymond knew where I wanted to go with the interview, picked up quickly and started to explain his motive for the murderous spree that put him on death row.

Stewart responded, "Okay, I will go through it. I went to a service station the following day. I wasn't looking at this service station attendant, my mind was getting back at the service station, the building it represented. All right, I pled guilty to two armed robberies of service stations, years ago (Actually it was four service stations, but I didn't want to interrupt him with facts). So, I was getting back at the service station. I wasn't looking at the individuals, the human beings. My mind was focused on the service stations. The day after Mr. Fredd died, a person at a service station was also killed. I believe there wasn't any money at all taken. As I said, I was there to get back at the service station. I am not looking at humanity; the hurt I am causing in all this. So, the following day, another service station attendant was killed. The day Mr. Fredd died, as I stepped over his nephew's body, I believe it was Albert Pearson, my mind went to where President Kennedy had been assassinated and our teachers came into the classroom and said our president had died. At that point, me along with other classmates, we all cried. So, at the point where I am stepping over Albert Pearson's body, my mind goes back to when President Kennedy was shot. Now I want to get back at a white person for killing President Kennedy. That was because at that point, we had, as students, been told how much he was doing for black Americans. I am in the mindset where I want to get revenge.

"Now, you see Ray, I don't understand that because you have killed two black people, first of all. And, you were stepping over Pearson's body, and this triggers the memory of Kennedy, and you decide you want to get back at white people for killing Kennedy, right? But the first murder, Fredd, who was black, was strictly revenge, is that correct?" I asked.

Stewart continued to explain, "That was revenge. You see, when Mr. Fredd was shot, I saw his nephew, Albert Pearson, behind the counter. I had no intention of doing anything to Mr. Pearson. No intentions at all of doing anything to him. Now, Mr. Pearson panicked. He panicked and ran from behind the counter towards the door. When he panicked, I panicked. I had no intentions of doing anything at all to him. Even though he saw me, I had no intentions of doing anything at all to him. He had not done anything to me. So, when he panicked and he ran towards the door, I panicked. I panicked and I pulled the trigger, I think it was three times.

"If Albert wouldn't have run?"

"He would still be alive."

"Would Kaiser still be alive; would Foust still be alive?"

Stewart continued, "Well, if they were in the service station the day that I went there, then they would be dead. You see, my mind was on the service station. Getting back at the service station. I wasn't thinking, well, once you kill a person inside the service station, the insurance is going to pay whatever money there is to pay and that is it. I didn't get back at the service stations at all, because the insurance took care of that. That is the frame of mind that I was in. When I went to Radio Shack, two people died in Beloit, Wisconsin, because of my thoughts regarding President Kennedy. That was the motive for . . ."

"Boeck and Raines at Radio Shack," I said.

"Right, right. The service stations were for the time I had spent behind bars regarding armed robberies."

"Did you take the police scanners? Was that an accurate report?"

"Well, a police scanner was taken. I had two. I wasn't in there to rob."

"Did that dawn on you after the crime had been committed?"

Stewart continued, "Well, I was in Radio Shack. I was in there for the sole purpose of killing a person. It happened that two people were in there. So, I wasn't in there to rob. After I left Radio Shack, I am now headed back to Rockford. I get on Riverside Boulevard and North Second Street. At that point, I am in the mind frame of killing the person that started this whole thing.

"The landlady?" I asked.

"Right. I am now headed to kill her. Around about Riverside and North Second, it was as though a spirit said to me, 'Stop the killing, and stop it now.'"

"You weren't very careful, Ray."

"Greg, I didn't care about living!"

"You didn't care about getting caught?"

"No! You see my life was ruined when the landlady called the cops on me and I heard this on my police scanner. So, my life was over with, then."

"Because you were going back to prison."

"Right. And see, under the Class X law, it was three strikes and you are out. So, I knew that this was my third strike. Although this started out as me trying to help my mother, it winded up being, well, I am executed. That is what occurred," stated Stewart.

During this long explanation by Stewart I noticed some rather odd and revealing speech choices. When he refered to a specific murder he would say, "the day Mr. Fredd died," instead of saying, "the day I killed Willie Fredd." On several occasions, he narrated the events of the murders in the third person, almost as if he didn't have anything to do with them. It doesn't take a professional linguist, or a psychologist, to figure out the meaning behind this unusual speech pattern. Obviously, Ray Lee Stewart had not fully accepted responsibilty for his murderous crimes.

As senseless as it was, there really was no great mystery to the murder of Willie Fredd. Ray Lee Stewart was a two-time convicted felon who had good reason to believe he was going to receive strike number three and be sent to prison for the rest of his life. So, he figured he might as well get revenge on the man whom he felt was responsible for sending him to prison the first time. In the distorted world of a criminal, it does follow a clear logic: Fredd ratted to the cops, so Stewart killed him.

The explanation that Stewart gave for the murder of Albert Pearson is difficult to swallow. I don't buy Ray's story about panicking and killing Pearson on the spur of the moment. It wasn't like a fleeing, skinny nineteen-year-old posed much of a threat to a gun-toting Ray Lee. Clearly, he went into the store to kill Fredd for revenge, but in the Pearson murder, I believe that Stewart was putting to practice a lesson he learned the hard way from his 1970 conviction for robbing Johnny-On-the-Spot Cleaners: you don't leave witnesses. He made that mistake with Willie Fredd; he wasn't about to do it with Albert Pearson.

After the gas station murders of Kenny Foust and Kevin Kaiser, police officials knew they were dealing with a unique murderer. That is when famous criminal profiler John Douglas with the FBI's Behavioral Science Unit was first asked to create a profile to help Rockford Police. That is when my hometown community went into a panic. If Ray Stewart would have stopped with the Fredd Grocery Store murders, the case probably would have been quickly forgotten. But, he didn't stop. Like Paul Logli stated at the clemency hearing, because he did not stop, it is not an understatement to say he terrified an entire generation of Rockford-area residents.

It all started because in his mind he thought he was surely going to be sent back to prison for the rest of his life for threatening his mother's landlady. Figuring he had nothing to lose, he wanted to settle the score. He got his revenge on Fredd. Now, having absolutely nothing to lose, he was going to settle the score with everyone whom he believed ever wronged him. That included the entire gas station industry, whose executives saw to it that he was prosecuted fully for holding up four Rockford gas stations in a 24 hour period, back in 1973.

I buy Stewart's explanation for the murders of Kevin Kaiser and Kenny Foust. I have to believe it, simply because I can't think of any other reason he would have for killing those two men without taking a large sum of money or any valuables from the service stations. Furthermore, I believe it because it fits nicely into the puzzle While I was talking on the phone with Ray, I realized he wasn't as dumb as I thought he might be. Still, he wasn't nearly creative enough to make up such a motive. While talking to Ray, I quickly noticed that when he was exaggerating, he tended to strive for bizarre stories. I don't know if he actually believed he was fooling me, but the stories stood out as inconsistent. Ray's motive for the gas station murders, however, was consistent with his criminal background and the FBI's profile of Ray. Ray was telling the truth about why he went into those service stations and blew away the attendants.

On May 6, 1973, Stewart held up his first gas station. He walked into a Clark Oil Station at 501–15th Avenue in Rockford and forced the attendant to hand over $170. A few hours later, he returned to the same gas station. This time he got $130. He then robbed two west-side stations. All of them were owned by Clark Oil. With the eye-witness accounts of four frightened attendants, and a long criminal record for Stewart, the judge sentenced Stewart to hard time. He spent the rest of 1973, 1974, 1975, 1976 and most of 1977 behind bars. During that time, his anger for the gas service industry built up in his mind. He was a man in his twenties, who was wasting those prime years in a tough prison. Instead of seeing this as motivation to mend his ways, he viewed himself as a victim of corporate America.

Stewart truly believed the gas service industry was making an example out of him. This twisted thought process is almost identical to the thought processes profiler John Douglas described when he profiled Stewart (then, an unknown subject) as an irrational paranoid; a man who felt the whole world was after him. When Stewart was released from prison in November of 1977, I doubt he had designed specific plans to seek revenge, but in the back of his mind, he was angry and bitter and inactively seeking an opportunity to wreak his distorted justice on the entire gas station industry.

The motive Ray Lee gave for the Radio Shack murders stands out as one of those inconsistent, bizarre stories Ray seemed to enjoy manufacturing. Stewart did not begin to champion causes on behalf of his African-American heritage until his final years on death row. The theory about his Radio Shack motive being rooted in some desire to get back at white people debuted in a Beloit Daily News interview with Raymond Lee Stewart. The interview was published the summer before his execution. His lawyer, Joshua Sachs, was not fond of this new direction. Sachs never brought the Kennedy theory up during the clemency phase of his client's case. A mere cursory mental exploration of the reasoning would quickly expose numerous inconsistencies. More than likely, Ray made this theory up years later.

The assassination of John F. Kennedy is believed to be a white-on-white crime. There might be a case to suggest part of the motive was because some people believed Kennedy's political agenda was favorable to African-Americans. However, few theorists and investigators have concluded that was a primary reason. Certainly, the assassination of Martin Luther King might fit better into Stewart's theory. People who knew Ray Stewart at the time just before the murders never described him as a young man with a flair for politics. Furthermore, no one ever described him as a young African-American with a disdain for white people. In fact, Ray didn't take up politics until late into his prison years, when it became advantageous to him. During those years behind bars, Ray Lee came to understand that in the United States, certain leaders are held in such reverence that the mere mention of them instantly triggers emotional responses. That is why he cited the Kennedy assassination as his determinative motive. That is why he blamed the assassination of Martin Luther King for the fight with his father that resulted in his being kicked out of the house and thrown into a garbage can which became a key, downward turning point in his life. That is why he called on Joseph Cardinal Bernardin and Reverend Jesse Jackson. That is why he tried to call on Minster Louis Farrakhan. The Kennedy motive theory is a manipulative, transparent attempt by Stewart to curry favor for his cause by tapping into personal pressure triggers of people who might be vulnerable to taking up his not-so-subtle cause: avoiding execution.

The family members and friends who fought for clemency were correct when they concluded that the horrendous abuse Ray suffered from his African-American father was largely responsible for Stewart's criminal tendencies. I don't think it is unimportant to note that Ray's attorney and his chief advocate, Jennifer Bishop Jones, were both white. Raymond was not truly angry with the white race. Instead, I believe he was more hostile towards blacks than whites.

Why did Ray Lee kill Boeck and Raines? It is a question that can never be answered with certainty. The Raymond Lee Stewart that I came to know, through my interview and by talking to the people close to him, didn't shy away from any opportunity to be the center of attention. His lewd behavior in court, his dramatic attempt at escape and the way he was able to turn his execution into a media frenzy are proof of Ray's tendency to run into the spotlight. After the gas station murders, the Rockford news media went into blow-out coverage mode. I believe Ray was following the reports and was relishing the attention. For the first time in a life filled with dead-end jobs, procedural scolding from judges and humdrum trips to jail, Raymond Lee Stewart was a force to be reckoned with. I knew firsthand how intense the media coverage was during that killing spree. I could only imagine what a strange rush it must have been to be the unknown perpetrator everyone in town was afraid of. Going into the interview, I had a suspicion Ray might have extended the killing spree because of the attention he was getting from the press. When I asked him the question, his reaction confirmed my theory.

"Ray, I was in Rockford at that time. I was a young man. Actually, I was only ten years old. The community was really terrified. It was all over the newspapers. It was all over the radios. It was all over the TV's. Did you know this was a big story at this point? Were you aware of the media reports about this killing spree?"

The man sitting in a prison at the other end of the phone was silent for at least five seconds. Then there was a deep breath, followed by a loud sigh. The reaction was genuine. For the first time in the entire interview, Ray wasn't putting on a show for me. It took him a few seconds to regain his composure, and then he began to orchestrate his answer to my question.

Ray answered, "Well, after the incidents, yes, I was aware of it."

"Were you following it?"

"If you are asking me if was fascinated by this and all that, the answer is no. No. I was in a frame of mind of revenge, so I received no enjoyment, whatsoever, for what has occurred. I have never boasted, whatsoever, about what occurred. I was in the mind frame of revenge."

The deep sigh Ray belted out before answering that question was the most revealing response in the whole interview. It was obvious he didn't want to answer that question. It was obvious it struck a chord. It was obvious to me Ray was lying. I didn't believe Ray when he downplayed the amount of emphasis he placed on the media attention at the time of the killing spree. The outcry in Rockford at the time of this rampage was too complete. Every radio station in town was broadcasting lengthy reports on the spree. The newspaper had blown-up headlines with grisly crime pictures. It would be impossible for the coverage to escape Ray's notice. It would be impossible for that attention to not have an impact on somebody as excitable as Raymond Lee Stewart. It would be foolish to suggest Ray's fascination with the media coverage of his killing spree was the only reason he killed Boeck and Raines. After all, he had already killed four people. However, after listening to the way Stewart reacted to my question, I am convinced there is some merit to my theory. It isn't too far-fetched to suggest that the reason Ray was so angry about being denied a television and radio during his days at the Winnebago County lock-up was because he was missing out on the media coverage of his arrest and trial. Ray Lee didn't strike me as the kind of guy who kept up with the soap operas.

When analyzing the motives behind these murders, it is important to look at the mitigating circumstances in Ray Lee's life prior to the spree. It would be a gross understatement to say Stewart was having a bad week. Stewart had returned to the Rockford area for the birth of his child. In his mind, he thought this was the beginning of a new era in his life. Stewart wanted to create the family environment he was deprived of as a child. It was his intention to live in a new apartment with his girlfriend, new baby and his mother. The key to this new arrangement was getting the security deposit from his mother's apartment to use as the first month's rent on the new apartment. Things didn't work out. First, the mother of his child, Tina Brooks, told Raymond to get lost. She didn't want anything to do with him, and she didn't want him to have anything to do with their new baby daughter. Then, for some reason, the landlady at his mother's apartment refused to fork over the security deposit money. Ray Lee got angry and threatened to kill her. The landlady called the police. In those days, Stewart always kept a police scanner nearby. When he heard the call to pick him up, he panicked because he knew that, under Illinois law, a third felony conviction would mean life in prison. All of these mitigating elements were torturing Stewart, and he just snapped. This was nothing new. Ray Lee had almost snapped several times before. People who knew him before the spree say Stewart was quite famous for making threats and waving his guns around. However, he never pulled the trigger. This time he crossed the hallowed line that separates wanna-be thugs from cold-blooded killers. This time, he pulled the trigger.

The circumstances of the bad week, the lingering revenge and the abusive childhood all contributed to the genesis of this ghastly killing spree. In former FBI profiler John Douglas' book, "Journey Into Darkness" (Scribner), Douglas explains how he got involved in the case after the Radio Shack murders. At the request of local law enforcement, Douglas and his team at the elite Serial Crime Unit produced a psychological profile which, in theory, was supposed to give cops some idea of who they were looking for. Today, Douglas is well-respected and recognized as a pioneer of criminal profiling. He has written several best-selling books. In recent years, he has become a darling of the media, appearing on nationally televised shows to offer insights into high-profile cases like JonBenet Ramsey, O.J. Simpson, and the Unabomber. Back in 1981, criminal profiling was still considered experimental, cutting-edge stuff. Douglas and his team quickly characterized the Rockford-area murders as the work of a paranoid, delusional but functional, assassin-type serial killer. No way were these crimes simple botched robberies as local authorities first suspected. Douglas told police to look for a African-American career criminal in his late twenties, who would undoubtedly hang on to his guns, knew how to use a police scanner and would probably have power dogs (like a Doberman or a pitbull) nearby for protection. Amazingly, the description was right on target. In North Carolina, police arrested 29-year-old Ray Lee Stewart outside a relative's house where two Doberman pinschers were tied up.

I had been talking to Ray for a little less than an hour when he told me our conversation had surpassed the prison curfew, and the guards were on the verge of pulling the plug on our connection. I took the cue as an opportunity to ask him one final question.

"Midnight, the 18th, is when you will probably die. How much thought have you put into that moment?"

"Well, the exact time hasn't played at all on my mind. I

have, awhile back, placed myself lying on the gurney, needles in my arms. I do want to thank St. James Hospital, all the nurses where I have had certain problems, medical problems, where the institution had to take me to an outside hospital for those problems, even where I had almost bled to death, they saved my life. I do want to thank them. I also want to thank the institution, for letting me be in a situation where I could see needles in my arms. I can see tubes going up and all of this, because they prepared me for what is to come. I could take my life tonight if I want, but I have decided to go through this to the end."

When I hung up the phone, I took a deep breath. Then, I ripped the plastic protector off the audio tape so I wouldn't make the bonehead mistake of erasing the interview. Finally, I put on some clothes and drove the tape to the television station. Carol Marin wasn't going to have an exclusive anymore.

CHAPTER 24

*"For it is in giving that we receive, it is in pardoning
that we are pardoned."*

—*St. Francis of Assisi*

2 p.m. September 17, 1996

The audio in the newsroom was at its normal noisy roar. Dispatchers were shouting out information over the police scanners, the phones were constantly ringing, people were talking and the local news radio stations were at full blast. To me, it is music. I was sitting at the assignment desk, and jamming a finger deep into my left ear while pressing the phone hard into the other, so I could hear Ray explain his feelings on the day of his execution. Suddenly, the interview was cut short. Ray told me he had to hang up because Joseph Cardinal Bernardin had just entered his cell. He thanked me for everything I had done for him. I don't know what he meant by that. For one of the few times in my life, I was at a loss for words. What are you suppose to tell a serial killer on the day of his execution? I didn't think it was appropriate to thank him for anything, although for some reason that felt like the natural thing to do. Finally, I simply told him that if he wanted to call the station for one last interview, he could ask for Carleen Mosbach, the nightside assignment editor. Afterwards, I hung up the phone and walked to the front of the building where the live truck was waiting for me. I hopped in the passenger seat, and threw my briefcase and my duffel bag full of clothes in the back by the equipment. The cameraman shifted the van into drive and started to head towards Joliet. I thought about the scene in Joliet as we got on the expressway.

Joseph Cardinal Bernardin was far and away the most beloved man in Chicago during this period. It is hard for people who don't live in or near Chicago to truly comprehend the relationship between Bernardin and the community he served. When Bernardin took over the Chicago Archdiocese in the early 1980's, he faced a number of difficult challenges. His predecessor, John Cardinal Cody, died in the middle of a media flurry over an investigation into misappropriated church funds and embarrassing insinuations about a life-long relationship between Cody and a woman, who was his cousin. When Cody died in 1982, the church was in desperate need of a skillful leader with impeccable moral character. In hindsight, Rome could not have selected a better choice than the Most Reverend Joseph Bernardin from the Cincinnati Archdiocese. It is an understatement to say Bernardin's leadership steered the Chicago Archdiocese in the right direction.

In the biography entitled, "Bernardin: Life to the Full," religious writer Eugene Kennedy detailed the complex ethnic issues facing the Chicago Archdiocese when Bernardin took the helm. Kennedy explained that the traditional Catholic troops of Irish, Polish and German clergy were quickly becoming the minority in the wake of massive immigration by Hispanic, Polish, and Asian Catholics. Bernardin approached this complex scenario with considerable skill. Nowhere is that more apparent than in the story of the St. Francis of Assisi parish. In 1996, the Archdiocese planned to close the church and turn the land over to the University of Illinois. For thousands of Chicago Hispanics, St. Francis was more than just another church; it had served as a religious haven to Mexican immigrants since 1886. When the construction crews showed up to bulldoze it, the Hispanic reaction was incredibly intense. Petitions were drafted. Protests were staged. Some parishioners, including older woman, moved into the unheated church in the middle of a brutal Chicago winter in an effort to stop the demolition and bring attention to their cause. After the outcry, Bernardin realized destroying the church was a mistake. Instead of pushing forward with the demolition plans, Bernardin listened to the concerns of the protesting parishioners and quickly issued a decree to halt the destruction of St. Francis Church. This action made Bernardin a beloved figure in an Hispanic community historically at odds with the Archdiocese.

During his tenure as Chicago's top priest, Bernardin evolved into a fantastic ambassador for the Catholic Church. His humble demeanor, charming personality and noble work ethic often projected his brilliance across religious lines. Many non-Catholics loved and admired him. Although it was never a primary mission of Bernardin, by setting such a remarkable example as a strong moral leader, he made real strides in reaching out to all people, not just Catholics. In 1993, Bernardin was a key participant in a large multi-religious conference in Chicago. Mother Teresa and the Dalai Lama also attended. In his later years, a large amount of Bernardin's writing was dedicated to exploring ways to improve relations between the Catholic Church and the Jewish community. When Bernardin died, the newsroom fax machine was constantly churning out statements from all kinds of churches who wanted to publicly offer their condolences.

Over and above all his other accomplishments, Bernardin achieved the crucial goal of restoring respect to the Chicago Archdiocese. Under Bernardin, there were the occasional protests and the typical critique from both Catholics and non-Catholics, but nothing close to the magnitude of controversy during Cardinal Cody's final years. However, there was one unfortunate situation where Cardinal Bernardin's character was seriously attacked. In 1993, Stephen Cook accused Bernardin of molesting him when Bernardin was the Archbishop of Cincinnati. The news exploded in Chicago. It was a media feeding frenzy. But, the story would quickly fizzle. It didn't take much scratching at the surface to see that this confused accuser was being coerced by powerful enemies and vicious opportunists. Less than four months after the story broke, the case was dropped. Long before that, the allegations were emphatically disproved. In the end, Stephen Cook is just a pathetic footnote. The style Bernardin demonstrated when he was handling the intense scrutiny of those false allegations can only be described as inspirational. Throughout the ordeal, Bernardin never got defensive. He was always forthcoming. He never showed anger towards his accuser. Instead, Bernardin offered him prayers and help. It was truly a testament to Bernardin's awe-inspiring grace. Instead of destroying his career, the incident made Bernardin a legitimate candidate for sainthood. With absolute redemption following his laborious endurance, Bernardin's stature in terms of respect and popularity had skyrocketed. He was now the superstar of the Catholic Church in America.

The legacy of Cardinal Bernardin is more than a mere laundry list of his accomplishments and accolades. There was something about this man that really touched people. On August, 30, 1996, Bernardin called a press conference for two o'clock in the afternoon. Nobody would be sneaking out early on that Friday afternoon. I started calling everyone in town who might know something, trying to get the scoop. As the morning progressed, it became more and more obvious Bernardin was going to announce that the cancer he had fought off with surgery and chemotherapy had returned. In essence, he was going to announce he was dying. My station, WGN, along with all the stations in town, broke into our regular programming and carried the press conference live on the air. It was a moving press conference. Hard-as-nails reporters inside the Archdiocese briefing room were reduced to tears. My desk assistant was crying as she watched it on the monitor. All over Chicago, people were saddened by the day's top story and fearful of what lay ahead for the city's shepherd. It changed everything when it came to covering the Cardinal. Now, every single event he was at was a must-cover event; first and foremost, because our viewers were interested in him, and sec-

ondly, because we didn't know when his last public appearance was going to be.

While it is true that Bernardin was a low-key man, it is a gross error to suggest he ever shied away from controversial issues. The entire country was really introduced to Bernardin when he made the cover of TIME magazine for a pastoral letter questioning the morality of nuclear war. This letter was drafted right at the crest of Ronald Reagan's immense popularity. Reagan ran on a platform rather keen on pro-defense spending. The letter raised a lot of eyebrows. Bernardin continued to chime in on controversial issues throughout his career. In fact, the week he died, he released statements condemning the practice of doctor-assisted suicides. Bernardin believed death should be in God's hands only. He was emphatically against abortion, euthanasia and the death penalty.

In the middle of a massive news planning effort to prepare for Bernardin's death, Ray Lee Stewart's execution came along. Whenever an execution came up in Illinois, Bernardin sent a letter to the Governor asking for clemency. I thought it was quite routine when I listened to an Archdiocese representative read a letter on the Cardinal's behalf at the hearing in Springfield. Now, it was anything but routine. The story of the Cardinal and the killer turned out to be one of the most interesting issue stories of the year.

It is hard to picture the beloved, dying leader of the Chicago Archdiocese, sitting down for a chat with this much-hated and condemned killer. Cardinal Bernardin was truly a prince in the Catholic Church. He had helped countless numbers of people. Ray Lee Stewart was a bona fide serial killer who ranked right up there with Gacy and Speck. He had hurt countless numbers of people. Ray probably knew very little about the Catholic Church that was Bernardin's life. In turn, Bernardin, as intelligent as he was, couldn't possibly fathom the world Ray Stewart came from. They were definitely opposites in many ways. The one thing they did have in common at that point: they were both about to die.

Outside his mansion, earlier in the day, Bernardin had explained to reporters why he was making the trip to Stateville Prison. "I'm going there not to make a statement, though everybody knows where I stand. In a sense, he and I are in the same boat. He knows he is going to die tonight, and I know I am going to die in the near future. He is not a Catholic. But, he is a Christian. He does have faith in Christ, and so, I am willing to do what I can to help spiritually at this critical moment in his life," said Bernardin.

Bernardin wasn't a stupid man when it came to political maneuvering and utilizing the press to one's advantage. It is unlikely that he failed to see the momentum he would be giving to Ray Stewart and his advocates by visiting him on the day of his execution. Because Ray was a non-Catholic, his decision to choose Bernardin as his spiritual adviser is a rather mystifying one. On death row, it is difficult to believe Stewart had a clear grasp of just who Bernardin was. In my interview, Ray suggested he personally might have preferred a black man of God, like Louis Farrakhan or Jesse Jackson, but decided to ask Bernardin because he knew it would bring the most attention to his cause. During this period, it was the dying Bernardin who was getting the big headlines. Bernardin, hardly being the naive pastor, would have instantly recognized the advantages Ray Stewart might have been seeking by inviting him to his cell for counseling and prayer. For Bernardin, that didn't matter. What he cared about was fulfilling the request of this man who, like him, was going to die a "premature death." The media attention, the political ramifications, and the risk of being used weren't paramount to Bernardin. He went to visit Ray simply because Ray asked him to.

Before he visited Ray in prison, Bernardin went out of his way to point out he had sympathy and compassion for the family members of Ray's victims. Bernardin really wanted to make it known that the very last thing he wanted to do was add to the pain of Ray's victims. He went out of his way to repeat this over and over again during his spur-of-the-moment interview with reporters. Bernardin recognized the suffering and loss this man had inflicted on so many people. He wanted to make sure they understood this visit was not designed to dismiss Ray Stewart's crimes. The day before the execution, Bernardin sent a letter, which he had personally written, to all the victims' families. After overnighting the letter to the families, he instructed his press office to fax it to the local media.

> *"You undoubtedly know that I will meet with Raymond Lee Stewart prior to his execution. He requested that I make this pastoral visit, and I will honor his petition. I write to you today to express my condolences to you and your family for the death of your family member at the hands of Mr. Stewart. His murder must continue to cause you grief and suffering, even now, more than 15 years later. I will pray that God's healing touch will ease your pain, and that peace may fill your heart. I want you to know that my visit with Mr. Stewart in no way should be construed to excuse the horrible crimes that he committed. The violence that plagues our nation is a source of deep sadness to me. Society must be protected from perpetrators of such a crime. It is my belief, however, that capital punishment feeds the cycle of violence instead of stopping it. I will be especially mindful of you and your family in these days immediately following Mr. Stewart's execution. You will be in my prayers during this time."*

For Bernardin, this was a tricky affair. It has to be emotionally difficult to do something for a convicted killer when you know it is probably going to be received as an insult by the killer's innocent victims. Bernardin usually studied situations carefully. It is safe to say he probably read the transcript from the clemency hearing. Bernardin probably knew about Alex Fredd, who lost his father and control of his life. I bet he knew the story of Kelly Reeverts who lost her twin brother, and whose children, in turn, never got to met their Uncle Kevin. Bernardin had probably heard of Rosemarie Boeck whose promising son Rick never got the chance to realize his ambitious goals. I am sure he knew these stories; that is why he seemed so distraught as he offered his heartfelt condolences to the families. This is part of the burden of being a priest. Bernardin knew this all too well. He told reporters that although this was his first pre-execution visit, this sort of duty was very much in line with what he had been doing as a priest for the last four decades.

When Bernardin returned from his visit to Stateville Prison, a small camp of reporters were assembled on the yard of his Gold Coast mansion. Back in those days, the sight wasn't all that unusual. Also, as usual, Monsignor Kenneth Velo was driving the car which took the Cardinal on his various missions. The chemotherapy had claimed much of the hair on the Cardinal's head. As he walked up the steps to the front door, he relied heavily on a metal cane to support the right side of his body. The journalists showed compassion and restraint as they approached the Cardinal with their microphones and their questions. Like always, Bernardin handled the reporters with patience and skill.

The Cardinal told reporters he had "mixed emotions" about his visit with Raymond Lee Stewart. At this impromptu press conference, Bernardin stated that, although everyone knew where he stood on the issue, he did not go to the prison to make a political statement. Instead, this was what Bernardin called a "pastoral" visit. Bernardin went to tend to Ray Stewart's spiritual and emotional needs. Obviously, Bernardin knew how terrifying the prospect of eminent death could be, but he told reporters the serial killer seemed to be adopting the correct frame of mind. Bernardin said Ray Lee Stewart seemed prepared to meet his maker.

Bernardin explained, "I found that he was very calm, that he had accepted the inevitable. He said explicitly that he was at peace with his fate. I spoke with him about his need to be sorry. I told him what his focus should be: Are you prepared to meet the Lord?"

It should be pointed out that Joseph Cardinal Bernardin didn't have to see Raymond Lee Stewart. It would have been easy for the Cardinal to side-step the entire affair because of his grave health. Bernardin succumbed to cancer two months after the execution. No one would have criticized him for not ministering to a convicted serial killer at this phase of his life. However, the letter Ray sent to the Archdiocese got into Bernardin's hands, and he decided to honor this dying man's request. He decided this, knowing full well this was going to catapult him into controversy and scrutiny. He did it, knowing this also meant reporters were going to be making camp on his lawn again. Although I know Bernardin would never admit this, by honoring Ray's request he made his own life unpleasant. He endured this, simply because it is what Jesus would have done. It is the right thing for a true man of God to do. This kind of sacrifice was hardly unique for this religious leader. Bernardin spent many of his holidays conducting mass for inmates at the Cook County Jail. Bernardin had prayed with Popes and Presidents, but, more importantly, he never hesitated to pray with and for drug addicts, rapists and even killers like Raymond Lee Stewart. Until the very end, Bernardin was a priest to everyone, good and bad alike.

Bernardin had a rare uneasiness in his voice as he related details of his visit with Ray Lee. At the outset of the meeting, Stewart did most of the talking, basically telling Bernardin the details of his story. Afterwards, the two held hands, prayed and read from the scriptures. Bernardin was surprised and impressed that Stewart had committed many Biblical passages to memory. The Cardinal tried to stress passages that dealt with accepting God. He told the convicted killer that at this point in the game, his focus needed to be geared towards "preparing to meet the Lord." The one passage that stuck out from this one-on-one spiritual session was John 14:6. It reads, "I am the way and the truth and the light."

When it was time to leave the prison, Bernardin had blessed Stewart. There were no last rites given, because Stewart isn't Catholic. The blessing marked the end of a unique meeting of two very different people, both at the end of their lives. I doubt either knew what to expect. While Stewart wasn't Catholic, he did claim to be a Christian. Ultimately, what they did is what Christians always do. They listened to each other, they prayed, and they read the Bible. It was Church on Death Row. In the old movies, you always see the priest walking behind the condemned man reading verses in Latin. On the big screen, the spiritual leader seems placed for scenery and effect. The meeting at Stateville Prison on that afternoon was a lot more meaningful than that. In the end, it wasn't going to change anything, but the visit meant a lot to Ray, and I think it meant even more to Ray's family and his supporters. Even though he was a terrible man who did terrible things, this was still a human being the state was killing, and he had people who loved him and who were going to miss him. Bernardin let them know they weren't the only ones who recognized that.

Despite reaching out to Ray, and in turn to Ray's loved ones, Bernardin wanted to make it very clear this was strictly a "pastoral" visit. Bernardin was against the death penalty, but he also wanted to make it clear to everyone that by his actions, he was not saying society should go easy on these types of violent criminals. He described the week-long murder spree committed by Stewart as "dreadful acts." Although the death penalty would never be an option because of his personal beliefs, Bernardin did firmly believe that killers like Ray Stewart needed to be punished.

Bernardin explained, "Society has to protect itself from the perpetrators of crime. Now, he is going to pay the price. I'm very glad I went. I have always tried to reach out to people in need of help. My visit in no way excuses the horrible crimes this man committed. Society must be protected."

The legacy of pain Raymond Lee Stewart left behind seems

endless at times. He killed six people and ruined hundreds of lives. No matter how changed or how sorry he was at this point, those facts could never be changed. I think Bernardin did struggle a bit with this episode of his pastoral career. It must feel awkward to be beside a man who symbolized so much hate and pain. The last thing Bernardin ever wanted anyone to think was that he was excusing or disregarding this man's crimes. That is why he repeatedly stated to the press he did not want the visit to carry political weight. I doubt Bernardin felt comfortable in the grim prison cell with this serial killer. Although I do believe Stewart had changed a lot since the killing spree, he was still very much a twisted and disturbed individual. I don't think anyone who has ever talked to him in prison, regardless of their political beliefs, came out of the conversation believing this man would be safe on the streets again. Ray Stewart had a distorted value system. Furthermore, although he denied it and so did his supporters, Ray still had a lot of anger. That anger was so much a part of Ray, I doubt he could have disguised it so well that Bernardin wouldn't have detected it. There is something about talking to Ray that makes you feel uneasy. I bet that was the reason the Cardinal had "mixed emotions," and I also believe that is why he was so adamant about making sure everyone knew this was strictly a "pastoral" visit.

On the day of the execution, Jesse Jackson was in the New York area on business. In addition, he made a brief appearance at the afternoon taping of The David Letterman Show. The plan was for the Reverend to join his Operation Push protesters outside Stateville Prison. Some nasty weather hit the East coast, and Jackson couldn't get a flight back to the Chicago area. Reverend Jackson ended up talking to Stewart on the phone for about a half hour. Jackson described Stewart as frightened and remorseful.

The combination of Bernardin and Jackson throwing their names into the mix during Stewart's final days insured the execution was going to receive grandiose treatment from the local media. For Illinois, this execution ended up having the most media interest since the John Wayne Gacy execution. Gacy was the second execution for the state since reinstating capital punishment in 1977. Stewart was number eight. The five executions in between went on with minimal media attention. Because of Stewart's objections, the Illinois Department of Correction changed the rule when it comes to execution night clergy. In the future, inmates will be allowed to choose who they want to be their spiritual adviser. It wouldn't surprise me if the practice of selecting high profile religious leaders becomes routine. Whenever there is an execution the press is interested in, the advocates for and against the death penalty get the exposure they crave. Ray Lee Stewart never would have gotten this exposure if it weren't for Jesse Jackson and especially Joseph Cardinal Bernardin. If it was a ploy for publicity, it worked. If, instead, a doomed Ray Stewart truly wanted to be counseled by a great man of God, he couldn't have made a better selection.

It was two months later when the phone intentionally placed next to my night table rang. It was sometime after one in the morning. Unfortunately, I knew who it was before I even picked it up. It was the overnight assignment editor, John Mirabelli, calling to tell me the Cardinal was dead. I put on a baseball cap, threw on a sweater and drove to work. By five in the morning, my station was completely poised for our wall-to-wall coverage. We had live shots at the mansion, Holy Name Cathedral and St. Francis of Assisi. That morning, we were on the air for seven hours straight. Like all the local stations, we broadcast the entire funeral live. The funeral was attended by a slew of dignitaries including Vice President Al Gore and Governor Jim Edgar. There were over 500 priests, eight Cardinals and a representative attending on behalf of the Pope. The usually bustling State Street had been converted into a quiet parking lot for over one hundred limos and one hearse. Monsignor Velo gave a touching homily. It was a celebration of a man who was, at times, truly grand and magnificent and yet always remained, simply, Brother Joseph.

CHAPTER 25

Father of light, to Thee I call;
My thoughts, my words, my crimes forgive,
And, since I soon must cease to live,
Instruct me how to die.

—Lord Byron

2:00 p.m. Sept 17, 1996, Stateville Prison

There is no discreet way for outside visitors to travel to the Cell Block X building at Stateville Prison. The Most Reverend Joseph Cardinal Bernardin had to maneuver around the overgrown grass, while walking down a cement path that took him through the prison courtyard. Bernardin had to pass the barred windows of about one hundred inmates who would only be residing in this desolate dungeon complex because they were convicted of an atrocious felony crime, like rape or murder. Of course, there were jeers and cat-calls.

"You fucking priest!" one of the many angry inmates had yelled.

Even a man as seasoned and strong as the faithful shepherd Bernardin couldn't possibly escape fear while walking across that prison yard and being stoned with the screams of caged criminals. In less than ten hours, I would have to take a trek down that same frightening path.

5:30 p.m.

The television news truck my station used to cover this execution is the biggest, chunkiest vehicle in our entire fleet. It carries every conceivable piece of equipment needed to do television live shots. This enormous studio-on-wheels is comparable to the size of one of the old ambulances, hence the nickname, "cambulance." It is a pain to drive, but once the vehicle arrives at the scene, you don't have to worry about lacking the technology needed to properly cover a television news story.

The sun was just starting to fade along with the temperature when the cambulance rolled up to the front gate of one of the most famous prisons in the Midwest. The guard assigned to manning the gate automatically fixated his eyes towards the passenger seat where I was sitting. When he realized I wasn't a famous reporter type, he quickly shifted his attention towards the driver. In routine fashion he asked us what station we were from, which I thought was quite bureaucratic of him, seeing as how the letters W-G-N are painted all over the vehicle. The guard needed to see identification, which proved to be quite a chore for me because my lap was occupied with my only meal of the day: a half-eaten Big Mac and vanilla-flavored shake. Finally, we satisfied the checkpoint troll, and he kindly directed us towards the designated media area.

On the heels of what had recently transpired at the O.J. Simpson trial, the mini-media camp congregated in a parking lot on the north side of the prison was hardly shocking. However, it was still impressive. This story had clearly attracted the most media interest in Illinois since the execution of notorious serial killer John Wayne Gacy. The angle most journalists were there to cover was the story of the dying Roman Catholic Cardinal visiting a condemned serial killer in his last hours. Everything Cardinal Bernardin did in the final months of his life was big news. The imagery of Bernardin praying with Stewart instantly drew parallels to the image of Jesus on the cross, promising the kingdom of heaven to the thieves dying along with him. For the most part, the media camp was complete with every Chicago-area and northern Illinois media outlet. In a way, it was nostalgic for me to see people who I work with and compete against in Chicago mixing with Rockford-area journalists, some of whom I hadn't seen in years but grew up reading, listening to, and watching. The story proved to be perfect material for television news writers who have to crank out emotional, attention-catching rhetoric to stop viewers from zapping their remote controls. In the lot, there were ten television news trucks with their 60 foot masts shooting out into the sky and satellite dishes beaming rays into outer space. I had a murky vision of this scene during my sprint to the Springfield prison review hearing. When I saw the reporters and the television trucks, I realized my prophecy had come to fruition. Nobody was second-guessing this story now. Now, it was real and clear. Ray Lee Stewart would perform his swan song in the spotlight he so relished.

6:00 p.m., sharp

The man in charge of public relations for the Illinois Department of Corrections is Nic Howell. Usually, PR folks are liberal arts types who can turn a quick, accommodating sound bite for the demanding media. Nic Howell is more the strong, silent type, which is a better fit for the PR post of the DOC. The guy had been on this job for years; a seasoned veteran who handled everything from the first execution of Charles Walker, after capital punishment was reinstated, to the strange maneuverings and execution of John Wayne Gacy, to the backlash that came with the posthumous broadcast of a home-video showing Richard Speck enjoying a bizarre life of drugs and sex in a prison whose security was clearly too lax. He was the kind of guy who knew what you were going to ask, knew how to answer and knew when not to answer. His press conferences started on time; his information was always accurate. Howell doesn't waste your time, and he doesn't tolerate people wasting his.

The press conference was held inside a large, striped canopy with a podium and an audio system setup for the crews. The bulk of the questions concerned the story everybody was there to cover: Cardinal Bernardin's meeting with Ray Lee Stewart. The questions were being fired at Howell and the spokesperson for the Attorney General's office, Dan Currie, a younger, more traditional public relations type. The questions regarding the execution procedure and what was going on inside the prison were directed to Howell, while questions about Stewart's last minute appeals were handled by Currie. There weren't a whole lot of questions for Currie because this was not a case that included a lot of interesting legal issues. Clearly, Ray Lee was guilty of these serious crimes and even Stewart's attorneys knew there was very little chance for a last-minute stay of execution.

At this press conference, it was revealed that Bernardin had arrived at the prison shortly after two o'clock and met with Ray Lee for a little over half an hour. Jesse Jackson called the prison after five o'clock. The phone call lasted about 25 minutes. Jesse Jackson was not going to be visiting the prison because he couldn't catch a flight out of the New York area due to bad weather.

Stewart was being housed in the Cell Block X building. As per tradition at Stateville, the windows were draped with black sheets. Normally, the building is full of inmates. Illinois prisons are very crowded; however, they make accommodations on the day of an execution so the condemned prisoner has exclusive occupancy.

There is a closed-circuit camera pointing at the waiting inmate in the cell. Howell told reporters that although he hadn't had any personal contact or conversation with Ray Lee, he had been monitoring the camera feed and had come to the conclusion that Ray was agitated and was being difficult with the prison staff.

When we got back to the truck, we called the night assignment editor, Carleen Mosbach, to feed the tape of the press conference for a piece we were going to air on our nine o'clock news. We learned Ray Stewart had called the station for me a couple of times. One of the anchors, Steve Sanders, had conducted an interview with him. It struck me as strange that Ray was now calling so often. For years, he had declined several requests for interviews and now he was almost begging the media to give him an oppurtunity to make his version of his story public knowledge. I had a conversation with Jennifer Bishop Jones where she told me Ray was not the kind of person who wanted to be on television or wanted to make a big production out of his story. The reason for that was because the last thing he wanted to do was cause the families of his victims any more grief. Up until this point, I had believed her. Now, I knew she had misjudged him.

The fact that we talked to Ray Lee just hours before his execution, made for flashier broadcast copy, but it didn't add any additional substance to our coverage. The night before, Ray had told me everything he needed to say. All the phone calls to my desk did was give him something to do on the day of his death. Additionally, I suspect that Ray Lee Stewart had developed an affinity for me because of what Jennifer told him about me and because of our conversation the night before when I asked him questions about things he hadn't been asked about in years. I believe Ray recognized I was the person who was best suited to report his version of the story. There was a sharp chill that went up my spine and I broke out in goosebumps when Carleen told me Ray regretted not being able to talk to me and wanted me to know that he appreciated everything I had done for him. I don't know if Ray really understood how truly terrified I still was of him.

While we fed the tape, I took a short walk away from the truck to collect my thoughts. I started to wonder what it was going to be like to see Ray Lee in person for the first time, minutes before he was going to die. I wasn't that frightened, but I was definitely nervous. I didn't know what to expect. I didn't know how I was going to react. How did I get myself into this mess? This story had fed my curiosity to the point that I manhandled my way into a position where I would have claim to a personal connection. I took a deep breath and conceded that I wasn't going to come to any answers on this night.

The remainder of the evening was dull. There are outsiders who believe the media is always this fast-paced and glamorous profession. The reality is that a lot of the work is hurry-up and wait. I went over the script with the reporter, Jackie Bange, a couple of times, and we called the editor and told him what tape we wanted to put in the piece. After the nine o'clock report, things would pick up quickly with the protestors arriving outside the prison gate and then, of course, the execution. For now, there was nothing to do but sit in the cambulance, watch the Cubs game and wait. This kind of work is nothing that would prompt Walter Cronkite to come out of retirement.

For the most part, the various stations assigned their trench-coat reporters to the story. Those are the journalists who are on the streets reporting breaking news, day in and day out. The one exception to this was the anchorwoman, Carol Marin. Even if you didn't know anything about Chicago television, you would be able to quickly ascertain that Carol was the big celebrity on the scene. Marin had the biggest entourage with the most engineers and assistants to help her. As the night grew older, more and more of the official, big-shot witnesses arrived at the prison: people like States' Attorneys and Assistant Attorney Generals. A few of them went over to the WMAQ truck and paid their respects to Carol.

There are a lot of journalists who would be jealous of this princess treatment; however, I knew better. I knew that Carol had earned this level of respect. Marin had been at this a long time, and while she is not completely immune to the temptation to crank out spicy stories during sweeps periods, for the most part she has consistently been able to break big and complicated stories while maintaing a decorum that is too rare in television reporting today. In a few months, Marin would find herself the subject of a national story when she left the station she had helped to make the top money-maker in the Chicago market because of a dumb decision by management to hire tabloid talk show host Jerry Springer as a news commentator.

Her resignation symbolized the fight against television executives who were resorting to tabloid-like tactics in search of a quick ratings boost. In the end, she signed on to do various work for CBS, including filing stories as a correspondent for a new, prime-time newsmagazine called Public Eye. Jerry Springer didn't even last a week on WMAQ.

9:15 p.m.

On this night, the nine o'clock news followed a Cubs baseball game. We ended up going on the air about fifteen minutes after nine. As I watched Jackie Bange do her live shot with a prison tower in the background, I thought about how complete our coverage was. We had four different shots of Ray being escorted in and out of various courtrooms through the years. We had file tape of all the crime scenes. We had file tape of his escape and capture. We had the interviews with Ray himself. With another crew, we got Bernardin returning to his residence after completing the trip to Stateville. We pretty much had everything there was to get. Later, I was talking to a reporter for another station who was amazed at how we were on top of this story. He confessed his station didn't know anything about it until Bernardin got involved. All he had was a prison mugshot of Ray Lee that Howell had made available at the press conference. It seemed like years ago when I walked into the news director's office and asked if I could enter the media lottery to witness the execution. So much had happened since then. I worked hard on this story that nobody else thought was going to break. The work was paying off in spades. If you work in this business, you have to be motivated by competition. There has to be a desire to scoop your competition, as well as an ever-present and important fear of being scooped by them. This competitive motivation makes you press harder and forces you to work fast. You relish those moments when everyone else in town is trying desperately to catch up to your story. As Jackie stood shivering in the cold, projecting the words of my story into the hand-held microphone, I was standing behind the cameraman and truly treasuring the moment.

10:10 p.m.

When all the newscasts were completed and while the television engineers began breaking down the live shot equipment, a corps of prison guards walked over to the media area to announce they were going to be escorting us to the front of the prison where about 50 protestors had arrived. It was a 100 yard walk, downhill from the media area, to the front gate. There were a half dozen guards walking along with the journalists and camera people. As we got closer to the gate, the audio of the protestors' chants and singing grew louder and more distinct.

"The death penalty is dead wrong!"

"No justice, no peace."

There was a five foot chain fence that separated the prison grounds from the crowd of protestors. I glanced around at the mix of people on the other side of that fence. Most of them were holding signs or candles and chanting while they walked in a circle. I saw a lot of the anti-death rally attendees in the crowd. There was also a good number of Operation Push members who were wearing those billfold-like caps that can be stretched out to fit over a person's head. The name of Jesse Jackson's political army was stitched on one side of the hats. The bright lights of the cameras were turned on, and the engineers began to shoot the protestors.

There was a single protestor who was for the execution. It was a guy in a coat that was too small for him, holding a candle and shouting, "Kill him, kill them all now."

One of the reporters from the trenchcoat patrol asked him why he came to every execution. The guy didn't answer, but smiled and continued to chant.

In the middle of the sea of people, I saw Jennifer Bishop Jones who was holding a candle. It looked as if she were the one who was going to die tonight. It was natural for me to behave like an objective journalist, but I couldn't help but feel sympathy for her. I knew this was going to be one of the worst nights of her life. It was obvious she was exhausted, and even though I had only known her a short time, I could also tell that her energetic heart was being invaded by sadness, and she was on the verge of dire depression. It wasn't even eleven o'clock, but Jennifer was already begining to mourn the death of her friend. It was at that moment when I saw her outside the prison in that condition, that the reality of this event overcame me. I was going to watch a man die. This was a man who had done terrible evil in his day, but he was still a human being on this earth and was going to be missed by people who loved him.

Finally, Jennifer caught me staring and walked over towards the fence to talk to me. I didn't know what to say to her, so I didn't say anything. Instead, I fell back on the thing that I always fall back on, my job. It did hurt me to see a person I had come to know in obvious pain and misery, but at the same time, I knew the terrible pain and suffering Ray Lee had caused so many others. Jennifer had known that brand of pain also. My empathy at that moment was for Jennifer, not for Ray Lee and not for Ray Lee's victims. Those people weren't standing in front me with eyes heavy from soon-to-be-shed tears. I quickly decided to push all of that aside because I was there, first and foremost, to do a job. Instead of offering condolences or encouragement, I interviewed her. When I was done, I turned around and walked up to a prison guard and asked to be escorted back to the media area.

As we walked back towards the prison, we could hear the protestors singing verses of religious songs like "Swing Low, Sweet Chariot" and "Amazing Grace." The prison guard I was walking with was a younger guy. It was close to the end of our walk back to the media area when he turned to me and told me he thought this whole thing was crazy. I asked him to explain what he meant, and he told me he dreaded working these nights because, to him, it was an unneccesary circus. Accord-ing to him, if they did away with the death penalty, they would eliminate all of this nonsense. This kind of crazy event couldn't be doing any good. It was an interesting observation, especially coming from a prison guard.

10:47 p.m.

When I got back to the car, I turned on the cell phone and called the WGN radio newsroom. I was supposed to do an interview with them before I went into the prison. They put me on the air and started asking me about the scene. What were the protestors doing? What did we know about Carindal Bernardin's visit with Ray Lee? How did I feel about witnessing an execution? I was answering the questions when all of a sudden I heard Jackie Bange screaming at me. I cut the interview short, jumped out of the car and broke out in a light jog towards the media canopy. It was almost eleven o'clock and the prison guards were ready to parade the witnesses into the prison. It was time for me to witness the end of the Raymond Lee Stewart story.

CHAPTER 26

*I looked, and behold a pale horse; and his name that
sat on him was death . . .*

Revelations 6:8

11:00 p.m.

While his long, black coat flapped in the wind, Nic Howell
cupped his left hand in a futile attempt to conceal the burning ciga-
rette he was holding. On two minute intervals, the veteran prison
official would quickly move his left arm to his hairy face and let the
smoke in. There were ten other journalists who were standing
around, waiting for Howell and the prison guards to escort us into
Stateville Prison. I was the last media witness to join the herd. When
I arrived, Howell looked around, did a quick head count and decided
it was time to take us inside. Up until this point, the media had only
been allowed in the north parking lot, the grassy area between that
parking lot, and the prison road. The prison road represented an
invisible, forbidden line. Now, I was going to cross that line. I was
walking next to Carol Marin. The photographer for her station
turned on his bright camera light and started to shoot. My photographer followed suit with me, but I suspect it was only to safeguard
my ego while I stood in Marin's shadow. When the group hit the
prison road, the cameras would have to fall back.

It was less than a football-field length from the grassy media area
to the front section of the prison. We were first going to enter into a
rectangular, office-like building that ran parallel to the front of the
real prison. This building, which felt like it was just a big trailer

home, was in strange contrast to the massive, stone edifice that is Stateville Prison. There was a holding room in the trailer-like building where the media witnesses were going to be detained until it was time to travel through the real prison and inside the execution chamber.

When we got into the foyer of the office building, a small corps of prison guards had been assigned to search us. We were told ahead of time we were not going to be allowed to bring in notepads or writing utensils and, of course, no tape recorders or cameras. The two guys from the wire services were both carrying cell phones, and they were both wearing two coats. I thought it was weird. Didn't they listen to the instructions? It took me a minute to figure out what the hell they were doing. They placed the cell phones in their outer coat and left them in the foyer and then proceeded to queue up for the pat-down search. Obviously, for those types of news services, speed is essential. They couldn't afford the time to walk or run back to the designated media area and call their respective desks.

11:10 p.m.

The holding room was the size of an elementary school classroom. On the south end of the room, there was a small buffet of cheap sodas and fruit. There were media kits on our chairs. Inside the folders were facts and information about executions, and the most recent mugshot of Ray Lee Stewart. The folder also had a notepad and two sharp pencils that we would be allowed to take into the death chamber. After dropping us off, Nic Howell disappeared into the hallway.

I didn't waste any time making my way to the food counter. I was experiencing an odd mix of emotional and physical sensations. The night before, I was up late talking to Ray Lee on the telephone, and then I had to drive the tape to the newsroom in time for our morning news broadcast. I worked all day and was only able to grab food at McDonald's in Joliet on the way to the prison. Normally I wouldn't have bothered with this ominous buffet, especially in such an apocalyptic-like setting.

However, I knew that my energy levels were depleted and needed to be replenished. I ate a banana which looked decent enough and drank half a can of soda. The last thing I needed was to have to use the men's room while I was stuck in the execution chamber.

11:15 p.m.

The Attorney General spokesperson, Dan Currie, walked into the waiting room and quietly sat down. This guy was looking haggard and unmotivated. I got the impression that Stateville Prison was the last place he wanted to be. After taking a few moments to get settled in, he announced the U.S. Supreme Court had just turned down an appeal by Ray Lee. The vote was 7 to 2.

11:20 p.m.

I had thrown away my banana peel and was staring at a cockroach dancing along a rivet in one of the floor tiles. Suddenly, I was startled when I felt a finger taping me on the shoulder. I quickly turned around to find a man in a out-of-style suit holding a clipboard. The guy was an assistant warden of the prison. He asked my name and who I worked for. I told him. He then took a few seconds to look at his list, put a checkmark by my name and placed a name tag on my chest. I was media witness number six.

11:24 p.m.

While the check-in guy was working the room and handing out name tags, Nic Howell returned. The video feed of Ray Lee showed a calm inmate who was spending his final moments working on his appeal. After talking to the guards, Howell wanted to amend his earlier statement at the press conference about Stewart being agitated and difficult. Apparently he had misjudged Stewart's non-verbal signals. The guards told him that Stewart was actually quite cordial and wasn't giving them any trouble at all. They brought this to Howell's attention after watching his comments on the evening news. While Howell was talking, Dan Currie left the room.

The television reporter from a Rockford station, Mike Wagner, asked Howell if the families of the victims and the family of Ray Lee were at the prison. There were thirteen family members of victims representing four out of the six victims. They were going to be able to watch the execution on a closed circuit television feed from a camera inside the death chamber. The feed was going to be turned on when the execution started and turned off when all the drugs were adminstered to Ray Lee. They were not going to be able to watch his final words. There were a few members of Stewart's family inside the prison. They arrived at 6 p.m. They were not going to be able to watch any of the execution.

11:32 p.m.

I asked Howell to go over the exection from begining to end. We were going to enter a small room where we could see the execution chamber through a viewing glass. The glass was to be covered by a curtain until the warden was ready to begin the execution procedure. The first couple of rows in the viewing room will be occupied by official witnesses. When the curtain opens, the warden of the prison will be standing on the left side of the chamber. Stewart will already be hooked up to a gurney. There will be a one-way mirror behind Stewart where the single executioner will be ready to plunge the poison concoction through the tubes and into Ray Lee. The warden will ask Stewart if he has any final words. After a couple of minutes, he will order the execution to begin and walk off the stage. The executioner will first inject sodium pentothal, which makes the inmate unconcious. Inbetween each drug there is a saline flush. Following the sodium pentothal comes pancream bromide, which stops the breathing. Finally, the executioner injects potassium chloride, which shuts down the heart. Howell went on to explain the one thing he has learned about executions is they are all different. There have been gruesome ones, and there have been quiet ones. Howell told us he didn't want to spook us; however, we should walk into that execution chamber knowing we could be in store for some haunting imagery.

The executioner is known only to the prison staff who need to know. It used to be that Illinois employed a machine to adminster the drugs. They had some problems during a couple of executions and a few years ago decided to adopt this single, anoymous executioner policy known as "The Texas Method." When all the drugs have been injected into the inmate, the warden will shut the curtain, and that will be the end of the execution. At that point, the county medical examiner will take custody of the body and move it to their lab so they can perform an autopsy. The family of Ray Lee won't get to view the corpse until the autopsy is complete. If they wish, the family can take custody of the body for burial. The autopsy is automatic and the cause of death is always homicide.

11:44 p.m.

Dan Currie walked back into the room. There was nothing to report in terms of last-minute appeals. One of the reporters asked Howell what he thought of the media attention for this execution. For Illinois, it was the most publicized execution since John Wayne Gacy. For the last couple of executions before this one, the media attention was small; in fact, a lot of stations had sent what Howell called its' "second-stringers." Nic said he knew this wasn't going to be a routine execution night when Cardinal Bernardin got involved. There was also a lot of media interest from Wisconsin because of the two murders in Beloit.

12:01 a.m. September 18, 1996.

I looked at my watch and was surprised we were still in the waiting room at what was supposed to be the scheduled execution time. Nic Howell was no longer talking about the execution, instead he was blabbing about prison costs and the possibility of the state building a new prison facility. The conversation would normally have put me to sleep, but I was antsy in light of what was about to happen. I was tired, but my mind didn't know it. At this late hour, the adrenaline had taken over. I was wide-awake and focused. My heart-rate was off the charts. The minutes were now going by slowly. Very slowly.

12:04 a.m.

Someone finally asked why the execution wasn't happening yet. The 12:01 time is actually when the prison staff goes to the cell and gets the inmate. They take him out of the cell and strap him into a waiting gurney and carefully place the needle into a vein in his left arm. I thought about what was going on at the other side of the prison. Would Ray voluntarily lay down on the gurney? What was he thinking as they wheeled him from his cell to the death chamber?

12:07 a.m.

The assistant warden popped his head into the room and nodded at Nic to come out into the hallway. When he returned, he told us Ray Lee had refused to take the sedation of valium offered to him. Ray was going to face his death sober.

12:10 a.m.

"Don't pet the skunks." That is what Howell uttered as he got up and gave a nod to let us know it was time. We followed him as he led us up a stairway that connected the office building with the actual prison. The group walked quickly down a large, grey hallway until Nic stopped halfway down at a section where an opening gave us access to the prison courtyard. The wind was blowing into the hallway, and we all shivered as we waited for the prison staff to give us clearance to walk through the courtyard to the death chamber.

12:14 a.m.

While I waited, I spotted three skunks running wild in the courtyard. Nic smiled, turning to the group as if to say I told you so. The prison was on lock-down and had been for months. The residents knew who we were and knew what was going on. They began to let us know that they knew.

"God bless Raymond Lee Stewart!"

"God bless Jesse!"

"God bless the Stewart family."

"I am going to fuck you all in the ass."

"Fuck you, fuck you, you fucking murderers."

The screams and chants were coupled with the eerie, echoing sound of banging. The inmates were banging on the walls and the bars. It was an angry audience.

12:18 a.m.

We could see the first group of official witnesses walk into the prison yard from a different entrance. When they entered the yard, the chants and the banging grew louder.

12:21 a.m.

"Okay, bring in the second group."

That was the cue that came across via the hand-held radio Howell was carrying. We stepped down from the opening and started to walk across the prison yard while the inmates, who could see from their concrete-encased windows, screamed profanities at us.

12:23 a.m.

The group made its way through the door into the viewing room of the execution chamber. The first two rows were taken by official witnesses. The witness from the Attorney General's office looked back at Carol Marin and waved her over to an empty seat in the front row. He had saved her a seat. I sat in the fourth row, next to Jim Wagner and behind Rockford Police

Sgt. Tom Nimmo and Winnebago County State's Attorney Paul Logli.

"How are you doing tonight, Jim?" asked Nimmo.

"Fine," replied Wagner quickly, as he fumbled with his notepad and pencil.

12:25 a.m.

Suddenly, the curtain opened. The warden wasn't wasting any time. Before the curtain even had an opportunity to settle down from being pulled open in such dramatic fashion, the warden asked Raymond Lee Stewart if he had any last words.

It was a grotesque scene. The room was lit by a red, ultraviolet-like light. Stewart was held down on the gurney by two large, brown leather straps. You could barely see the straps under the white sheet that covered him. His right hand was facing the audience and was restrained by a silver handcuff attached to a metal bar on the bed. Ray Lee had grown his hair into a huge afro style that shot out almost two whole feet from his scalp. His face was covered with a patchy and wild beard. The only good reference I had to compare his appearance to was from the dramatic video of his escape and capture from 1982. Clearly, he had gained a considerable amount of weight in prison. It was very easy to make out the heaving of his large belly because of his awkward position on the gurney. It was obvious to me that he was breathing heavily. While he may have put on some pounds behind bars, he didn't look good at all. Ray looked like a man who was in his 60's, instead of 44.

Almost as quickly as the warden had opened the curtain, Raymond turned his head and faced the people who had come to watch him die. To me, his eyes were the size of silver dollars. I was momentarily hypnotized by the wide-open pupils which seemed to glow in the blood-colored chamber.

Ray Lee was taking a second to glare at the crowd. I felt like he was trying to focus on the people in the room. He was trying to see who was there to witness his execution. I had seen those eyes before. This was the monster of my childhood, and now I was staring him straight in the eye. These were the same eyes that stared at me from the front page of the Rockford Register Star when I was in charge of hand-delivering the news to my neighbors that it was safe to go out again. They were the same eyes that I saw when I was watching the local television news and saw the dramatic footage of a bleeding fugitive being dragged back into custody. When I saw those eyes, I was terrified again. It instantly brought all the fear back. I was trying to write down notes about the scene, but I couldn't because my hand was shaking so much. The image of him held so much evil symbolism for me, that I was stunned when he began to talk and fire wasn't coming out of his mouth.

"Hello to everyone."

His voice was clear and soft.

"May you all have peace because of this. May my victims' families have peace."

Ray Lee slowly turned his head away from the audience, and was now staring at the ceiling of the execution chamber.

"Thank you, Jennifer, for playing the song for me."

Raymond Lee Stewart closed his eyes. The warden nodded at the executioner behind the two-way mirror, and then quickly walked out of sight.

12:27 a.m.

For 45 seconds, nothing happened. I knew he was alive because I could see the white sheet covering his stomach going up and down. Then, he made a terribly weak attempt at coughing, which turned into an eerie hacking fit that lasted about five seconds. It was a sound I have never heard before. It was obvious he was losing his ability to breathe.

12:28 a.m.

It was 15 seconds later when I saw Stewart die in front of me. It was as if someone had hit him in the chest with a Louisville Slugger. He let out a sharp grunt and then his body began to convulse wildly. This all happened in less than two seconds. His movements were greatly reduced by the hand-cuffs and the restraints. After the convulsions passed, I couldn't see the large belly moving at all. It was over. Raymond Lee Stewart had been executed.

12:30 a.m.

For two mintues, the body of Ray Lee lay on the gurney, motionless, before the warden finally reappeared and closed the curtain. While I was waiting for the door to the courtyard to open, I could see the shadowy figures of four people behind the curtain, walking around in the execution chamber. Everybody in the viewing room was silent.

12:32 a.m.

The door to the prison yard was pushed open, and it made a loud slamming sound when it hit the outside wall. I was the third person to exit the viewing room. As I walked through the prison yard, I blocked out the noise that was coming from the unruly inmates. I was talking with Greg Tejeda from United Press International. This guy had witnessed a lot of executions. I told him I was amazed at how quickly this went. Tejeda said it did go quickly, and, for the most part, it was uneventful. Our conversation was interrupted when the Associated Press guy ran past us, and Tejeda broke out in a jog to catch up with him. They were racing to get the news on the wires first. Now that I was alone, I was listening to the screams again.

"I am going to kill all you sons of bitches."

I quickly made my way through the prison yard. When I got to the front gate, I passed the two wire service guys. They were screaming information into their cell phones. When I finally made it back to the media area, I felt a comforting sense of relief. For the first time in my life, I felt I had truly visited a place on Earth that had been forsaken by God and handed over to Satan.

12:41 a.m.

I made my way to the cambulance and placed a cell phone call to WGN radio. They put me on the air, and I did my first post-execution interview.

While I was doing the WGN interview, the rest of the media was busy at work in the media tent.

First, Jim Wagner from the Rockford television station offered his account of the execution and told his colleagues about Ray's last words.

Then, Nic Howell came and introduced his boss, Odie Washington, the Director of the Illinois Department of Corrections. Washington told reporters the execution occured without incident. Everything went as planned.

Following the prison officials, the law enforcement types came down to the podium to talk to the media. Tom Nimmo and Paul Logli gave the standard line: the execution was a cakewalk in comparison to the brutal way the victims were killed. It was true. The image, still fresh in my mind, of Ray dying on the gurney was tame when weighed against the crime scene pictures of Kevin Kaiser, who was shot first through the hand while he was on his knees begging for his life; then, shot multiple times at point blank range, the last bullet fired after his heart had already stopped beating. Add to all this the fact that Kevin was just a 17-year-old kid who had done nothing to deserve his disturbing death. Clearly, the manner in which Ray Lee Stewart was killed was much more humane.

The last person to talk to reporters was Ray's sister, Faith Crocker. I am not quite sure how she found her way to the media tent, because I doubt prison officials wanted her to talk to the press from their podium. It was an emotional night for Crocker, and she was having a difficult time keeping her composure. Crocker was talking about her brother going to heaven and how brave he was on his final day. Finally, her speech broke down into an incoherent babble, and the reporters in the audience collectively decided to stop asking her questions.

The WGN interview was the first of many post-execution

interviews for me. The next day, I even got a call from WROK'S Fred Speer. They all asked the same questions: What happened inside the execution chamber? How did I feel about seeing a man put to death? Would I do it again? For all the interviews, I described the execution as vividly as I could and tried to answer the questions. The truth was that it was going to be a long time before I could sort out all my thought about what I had seen.

It didn't take a lot of processing for WTVO's Jim Wagner to conclude that he didn't want in on this sort of story again. "We got in there; it was a damp, cold room. If they asked me to do it again, I would probably tell them to find someone else," said Wagner from the podium inside the media tent.

For Carol Marin, it had also been an emotional night. In an interview on Chicago's top-rated Bob Collins radio show on WGN the next morning, she talked about the execution. "I don't think there was anyone who wasn't mindful that they had just seen someone die. There were people with positions and people who don't take a position, like myself. Ray Lee Stewart committed six horrible crimes in a frightening rampage that is scorched in the memory of Rockford and Beloit. It terrorized children at the time, because they didn't know who was killing people and someone was dying almost every day. I talked to him. I don't think he was always rational. I think he was ruined as a child and he remained a ruined adult. You still watch someone die. I am still processing this. As we walked out, reporters, who talk all the time, were sort of looking for their own vocabulary. We live in a different world than Ray Lee Stewart. It is one of those things that I will think about for a long time. My friends worry I am going to have nightmares. I really don't think that. I can't say that this is something everybody ought to go see. I can't tell you that I would ever do it again." said Marin.

I would later have the opportunity to enter media lotteries for other executions. I chose not to. If I was ever outright given the assignment by an employer, I wouldn't decline. I am a journalist. I am supposed to find out what is going on and pass that information on to the public. There have been executions where things didn't go the way they should have gone. According to witnesses, inmates suffered on the gurney. If we are going to have a death penalty, there have to be objective witnesses, not connected with the state or law enforcement, to report on what happens when society commits this serious act. Witnessing executions is a good example of the basic watchdog function of the media. Furthermore, there are times when journalists have to witness unpleasant things, whether that is in Bosnia or at Stateville Prison. It comes with the job. I love being in the media, but that doesn't mean I enjoy everything I do. There are a lot of terrible chores: like calling up the family of a murder victim, or putting an obvious hate monger on the air to balance an issue story, or witnessing an execution. This execution was truly a terrible thing to watch.

The subject of death is never easy to deal with. When you see video tape of victims from an earthquake or a war zone, it is difficult to really put those images into tangible terms. It is impossible to grasp the full magnitude of what happened. It is an obvious tragedy. While the tragic element is arguably absent due to the crimes, executions are exactly the opposite when it comes to tangibilty. Before it happens, you know when it is going to happen, you know what is going to happen, and you know why it is going to happen. I was able to talk to Ray Lee beforehand and asked him how he felt about it. Even though he is just one person, and an appalling person at that, it is still outright troubling to sit down in a folding chair, like you were at a concert or a sports event, and just watch as that person gets poisoned to death.

The image of Ray Lee Stewart strapped on the gurney inside the execution chamber does haunt me from time to time. When I think about it or explain it to people, the picture is still vivid in my mind: the red glowing room, Ray's eyes staring out at me, the gentle tone to his final words, the grotesque noises coming from his body while he died in front of me. Before the execution, I was outside the prison talking to reporters, some of whom had witnessed previous executions. I had heard that this was a very clincal way to kill a prisoner, and that more than likely the execution was going to be uneventful. They were wrong. While it wasn't an action-packed three minutes like you usually see in the motion pictures, it was hardly uneventful. We quietly watched as Ray Lee Stewart died. Although it only lasted a couple of minutes, my own heart almost exploded when he started hacking and later when his body began to convulse. It was nothing like the movies, not because it wasn't as breathtaking, but because it was so real.

CHAPTER 27

Out through the fields and the woods
And over the walls I have wended;
I have climbed the hills of view
And looked at the world, and descended
I have come by the highway home,
And, lo, it is ended.

—Robert Frost

I thought about calling Jennifer and asking her if I could attend the funeral, but decided against it. Finally, I had come to a point where I had had enough of the Ray Lee Stewart story.

For me, it wasn't just the end of a terrible killer; it was the end of something else. I chose to follow this tragic case from beginning to end. This horrendous crime spree happened in my hometown when I was ten years old. At the time, it consumed Rockford. The emotions of shock and fear spread through that city like a flu. I never shook the bug. At age 25, I chose to follow this case to the end, regardless of personal expense. I went out of my way to make sure I got on the list to witness the execution. I called in sick to drive to Springfield and attend Stewart's clemency hearing. Without getting paid, I volunteered to go to Rockford on a Sunday to put together a Ray Lee story for my station. To make sure I wouldn't miss his call, I gave Ray Lee Stewart my home phone number. In hindsight, I recognize I was right on the edge of being an obsessed maniac instead of an aggressive journalist. There are critics and colleagues who would argue that I was on the darker side of that edge.

288

I became borderline obsessed with this ugly story because it was real for me. It was real for me because it all unfolded on my stomping grounds. When something big happens around the corner from you, it is always more interesting than things happening halfway around the world. From age ten, I felt like I wasn't just a spectator. I really felt like I was a part of it. It was hard for me to be afraid of the Ayatollah Khomeini. It was natural for me to be afraid of Raymond Lee Stewart. While I was growing up, my father would take me on hunting trips to Sugar River, just west of Rockford. We would always drive past Fredd's Grocery Store, and I would know that this terrible double homicide had happened there. When I went downtown to the Rockford MetroCentre to see a show or a game, I knew that the alley just off Main Street is where they captured Ray Lee. The cop who captured him was the same guy that came to my classroom and told me to keep my nose clean. Like the assassination of President Kennedy, the escape incident is able to trigger vivid flashback memories for people who were in Rockford at the time. Those people, like me, know exactly where they were when they heard the news about Stewart's escape. Whenever you mention Ray Stewart, you get all kinds of stories about where people were and what they saw while he was running loose in downtown Rockford.

From beginning to end, from age 10 to age 25, this was real to me. When the fax announcing the execution came out of my machine, it instantly brought back all my childhood memories and fears. How strange that I was in a unique position to watch and participate as the scheduled ending unfolded. Of course, I was going to have to take full advantage of this position. I have a proactive curiosity that is as much a curse as it is a blessing. It is why I went into journalism.

When it was all over, I did not feel bad that Ray Lee was dead. I know that he got what he deserved. However, I couldn't help but feel sad for Ray's friends and family. This was an awful ordeal, and I watched them all go through it. I felt especially bad for Jennifer Bishop Jones, who was such a good friend to him. However, I knew that the pain his family and friends were suffering after his execution wasn't even close to the terrible torment that the families of Ray's victims had endured for years and years. The family of Ray Stewart got to say goodbye. In addition, whether you agree with capital punishment or not, there was logic behind his execution: Raymond Lee Stewart had inflicted terrible suffering on people who had done nothing wrong.

The crimes this man commited were unnerving. Willie Fredd, Albert Pearson, Kevin Kaiser, Kenny Foust, Richard Boeck and Donald Rains. It is unbearable to think of the hideous way they were all were killed: shot multiple times at close range, most forced to lay down or get on their knees. From all appearances, they did nothing to provoke Ray Stewart. When he walked in the door, they never had a chance. None of them deserved to die. The man who killed these six innocent people spent part of his time behind bars throwing his human waste on guards and lobbying to get cash for his lousy artwork.

At the very end, Ray Lee did make an effort towards redemption. In interviews he told reporters, including myself, he was sorry for the murders. When he talked to Constance Mitchell, he was always cordial and respectful. On several occasions, he expressed regret for taking Albert away from this world. While I suspect he didn't mind the attention he got as his execution grew closer, I have no reason to believe his apologies were void of sincerity. In his final words, he did say he hoped his execution brought peace to the victims' families. Ray Lee didn't have to say that. The needle was already in his arm and the executioner had his hand on the poison plunger. The statement wasn't going to do him any good. I don't think Ray was a genuis, but I believe he was smart enough to know nothing he did was going to save his life. His terribly evil sins would undoubtedly outweigh any last-minute apologies. Most of the victims would say it was too little, too late.

When I first started approaching this story as a journalist, I didn't anticipate I would become so interested in the ethical debate surrounding the death penalty. I crave good issue stories that make people think, but I didn't believe for a second I was going to find that in the Raymond Lee Stewart story. I quickly learned that the death penalty debate is not going to go away anytime soon. It turned out that I really came to like people on both sides of the capital punishment issue in this case. I can't help it; I am a sucker for good people. Jennifer Bishop Jones, Ed Houi, Constance Mitchell, Alex Fredd; they are all decent people who endured anguish and came to different viewpoints. Capital punishment is one of those tough issues a lot of people go back and forth on, myself included.

While I see no practical reason to have capital punishment and while I believe that it does more harm than good, I could never aggressively seek its abolishment. It seems to me there is a basic balancing error in the capital punishment equation: killing is wrong, so we are going to demonstrate that by killing anyone that kills. To me, it is a clear case of stooping to the killer's level. But with murder, it is impossible to find a just punishment because there is no way to correct what the criminal has done. While I don't think convicted killers should be afforded the luxury of being allowed to paint in prison and sell their artwork, I don't see the benefit of executing them. There is nothing that can bring the victims back. The real danger with the death penalty is that it can delay the grieving process for family members of victims. I saw family members who were relying on the execution event to provide the closure they desperately needed for them to get on with their lives. In reality, it does not solve anything for them. The next morning, their loved ones are still gone, forever. This is sadly epitomized by Alex Fredd, who since the execution has had serious setbacks in his struggle to remain sober. While I am against the death penalty in theory, I am not about to take up the fight on behalf of people like Ray Lee Stewart.

What could very well be the best argument against the death penalty is the circus atomsphere it attracts. It is possible that

the guard who walked me from the prison gate where the protestors were, back to the media area, was right on when he said
they should just do away with the death penalty, and in turn, do
away with all the nonsense. In a way, we did Raymond Lee
Stewart a huge favor by executing him. It gave him one final
chance to get in the limelight. He took full advantage of the
opportunity. For Ray Lee, obscurity would have been a much
crueler punishment.

If I learned anything, I have learned that with death comes
consequences. It was truly an eye-opening experience to sit in
that hearing room at the state capital and listen to family after
family talk about the far-reaching and not-so-evident impact of
the murders. The weddings that seemed incomplete because
Uncle Kevin wasn't there, the son who went way off track
because dad wasn't there to give his advice, the couples who
are afraid to have childern because they don't want to risk losing them to violence. When I talked to Ray on the phone, even
he was amazed at how much damage he had done. It is an
astonishing legacy of anguish. Ray Stewart's own death had
consequences. Even though he was an incorrigible criminal,
his family and his friends fought a seemingly impossible battle, only to lose. Now, they mourn and look for ways to carry
on with their lives. I also know that some family members of
his victims are still struggling to sort out the bittersweet feelings that come with this kind of justice.

The Raymond Lee Stewart story is a true American tragedy.
It is impossible to find any upside to this case. It is all down-
side. There is no silver lining to be found. There aren't any
winners. Everyone who had the misfortune of being involved
or attached to this case lost in the end. The tragic story has
come full circle, but it hasn't ended. When Ray Lee went on
his spree, Rockford and Beloit instantly took a giant step
towards losing its innocence. It is not a stretch to suggest that
ever since then, people in the area look over their shoulders
more. I am one of those people. Even today, I always think of
Ray Lee when I go into a gas station and have to slide my fuel

money under bullet-proof glass. I know there are a number of people who, for some reason, were inspired by Ray Lee and the attention he attracted and have now dedicated much of their lives to fighting against the death penalty. I know there are still brothers and sisters and sons and mothers who wake up every morning and have to find a way to face this world without a person they deeply love because of Raymond Lee Stewart.

Unfortunately, this legacy of loss will never be over. At least now, there won't be any more killing.